Ford/Southampton studies in North/South Security Relations

Managing editor: Dr JOHN SIMPSON

Executive editor: Dr PHIL WILLIAMS

Conflict and consensus in South/North security

Ford Foundation Research Project 'North/South Security Relations', University of Southampton

Principal Researchers:
Professor P. A. R. CALVERT
   Dr J. SIMPSON
   Dr C. A. THOMAS
   Dr P. WILLIAMS
   Dr R. ALLISON

While the Ford Foundation has supported this study financially, it does not necessarily endorse the findings. Opinions expressed are the responsibility of the authors.

Titles in this series

Nuclear non-proliferation: an agenda for the 1990s
edited by JOHN SIMPSON

The Central American security system: North-South or East-West?
edited by PETER CALVERT

The Soviet Union and the strategy of non-alignment in the Third World
ROY ALLISON

Conflict and consensus in South-North security
edited by CAROLINE THOMAS and PAIKAISOTHY SARAVANAMUTTU

Superpower competition and crisis prevention in the Third World
edited by ROY ALLISON and PHIL WILLIAMS

Conflict and consensus in South/North security

Edited by
CAROLINE THOMAS and
PAIKIASOTHY SARAVANAMUTTU

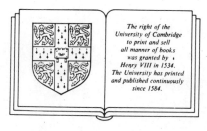

The right of the
University of Cambridge
to print and sell
all manner of books
was granted by
Henry VIII in 1534.
The University has printed
and published continuously
since 1584.

CAMBRIDGE UNIVERSITY PRESS

CAMBRIDGE
NEW YORK   PORT CHESTER   MELBOURNE   SYDNEY

Published by the Press Syndicate of the University of Cambridge
The Pitt Building, Trumpington Street, Cambridge CB2 1RP
40 West 20th Street, New York, NY 10011, USA
10 Stamford Road, Oakleigh, Melbourne 3166, Australia

First published 1989

Printed in Great Britain at the University Press, Cambridge

British Library cataloguing in publication data

Conflict and consensus in South/North
security
International security. Implications of
economic conditions in developing countries
I. Thomas, Caroline, *1959–*
II. Saravanamuttu, Paikiasothy
327.1'16

Library of Congress cataloguing in publication data

Conflict and consensus in South/North security / edited by Caroline
Thomas and Paikiasothy Saravanamuttu.
   p. cm. – (Ford/Southampton studies in North/South security relations)
Includes index.
ISBN 0–521–37268–2
1. National security. 2. Developing countries – National security.
3. World politics – 1985–1995.   I. Thomas, Caroline.
II. Saravanamuttu, Paikiasothy, 1958–   III. Series.
UA10.5.C665   1989
355'.033'0048 –dc20   89–7210

ISBN 0 521 37268-2

Contents

Contents

Notes on contributors

Graham Bird is a Professor of Economics in the University of Surrey.

Christopher Coker is a Lecturer in International Relations at London School of Economics and Political Science.

Stephany Griffith-Jones is an economist at the Institute of Development Studies in Sussex.

George Joffé is a journalist and broadcaster specialising in North African and Middle Eastern affairs.

Aswini Ray is a Professor of Politics at Jawaharlal Nehru University, India.

Paikiasothy Saravanamuttu is a Lecturer in Politics at Southampton University.

John Simpson is a Reader in Politics at Southampton University.

Caroline Thomas is a Lecturer in Politics at Southampton University.

Stephen Thomas is a Lecturer in Economics at Southampton University.

Paul Wilkinson is a Professor of International Relations at Aberdeen University.

Marc Williams is a Lecturer in International Relations at the University of Sussex.

Phil Williams is Senior Lecturer in Politics at Southampton University.

Matin Zuberi is a Professor of International Relations at Jawaharlal Nehru University, India.

Acknowledgements

The conference which formed the basis of this volume was made possible by financial aid from the Ford Foundation for the Southampton Project on North/ South Security Relations. The editors would like to thank the participants at the conference as well as the paper givers, and colleagues on the Project. Special thanks go to Darryl Howlett and Liz Schlamm for organising the conference, and to Liz and Jo for the preparation of the typescript and their patience.

Introduction

Images of famine, debt, economic stagnation and decay in the Southern hemisphere, coupled with an uneasy acknowledgement of the interdependence of military and economic security, have made a revaluation of the security relations between North and South urgent. In March 1987, an international conference took place in Guernsey, in the UK Channels Islands, under the auspices of the Ford Foundation funded project on North/South security relations conducted by members of the Politics Department of Southampton University. The objective was to bring together academics with differing perceptions of security, in order to explore the areas of convergence and divergence between what can broadly be described as 'Southern' and 'Northern' views. Contrasting perceptions of justice, order, norms of international behaviour, events and priorities are core problems facing the international security analyst and national policy makers intent on decreasing the gap between their assessment of security requirements and their perception of the international environment. An examination of different perspectives with regard to the security equation – especially the relative importance of economic, social, political and military elements – thus forms a vital backdrop to an understanding of international security issues in general.

The purpose of the Southampton project has been to explore the sources, past and present, of security and insecurity in the South, and to assess alternative forms of crisis prevention regimes and crisis management techniques for the Southern areas of the world. Projections were to be made about a likely international security agenda for the 1990s, based on assessments of possible future sources of security and insecurity in the South and appropriate Northern responses. In order to tackle these questions with any degree of balance, legitimacy and credibility, it was imperative that the obvious Northern bias of the group undertaking the research had to be tempered by the involvement of scholars from and in the Southern states. From the outset several Indian academics became closely involved with the work, and this has resulted in a fruitful and enduring series of exchanges. Apart from these strong links with the sub-continent, several individuals from a wide range of Latin American, African, Asian, Arab and Far Eastern states have participated in the project on an *ad hoc* basis, attending conferences and study groups and so forth.

It was largely as a result of the early involvement of these Southern scholars that the pressing need for a study of the very nature of security became evident to all concerned. For not only were there widely divergent attitudes towards the security process – that is, the mechanisms outlined in the initial project for the attainment and maintenance of security – but at an even more fundamental level there was profound disagreement about the actual structure of security which was being aimed at. What constituted security, and for what political unit? Without a consensus on this, then it would be impossible to agree on legitimate and appropriate techniques for the attainment and management of security.

The initial project outline was based on Northern perceptions of what constituted a threat to security. Thus most of the causes for concern over the South involved the activities of the two superpowers or perceived repercussions of these activities on each other: the possibility of symmetrical superpower intervention; the problem of reverse influence as a few Southern states acquired leverage *vis-à-vis* a superpower; strategic and resource rivalry by the super-powers; the effects of nuclear weapon acquisition by Southern states and their access to the most modern conventional weaponry; the activities of proxy states and so forth.

The involvement of Southern scholars quickly showed that the hierarchy of concerns from their point of view was different. While superpower rivalry and direct or indirect military intervention was a constant threat, exogenous economic factors were equally threatening and in some ways more of a constant problem. Moreover, indigenous factors contributed crucially to the generally insecure environment in the South. The lack of domestic consensus evident in the very slow progress of state and nation building was a major security problem. The arbitrary nature of territorial boundaries continues to pose intrastate and interstate difficulties. The formidable challenge of modernisation places massive strains on these young polities and repercusses on the security of the international system. The current transfer of capital from South to North via debt and interest repayments, coupled with the fact that many of the least developed states are actively regressing in terms of GNP per capita, adds to the tensions within and between societies. The challenge of fulfilling basic needs and keeping pace with population growth seems insurmountable in the contemporary international economic environment. On top of all these socio-economic problems, and to some extent interwoven with them, are the military ones of regional arms races and the dilemma of guns or butter. Moreover, many of the problems with indigenous roots in the South are exacerbated by superpower insensitivity, ignorance or even intention. Many of the Northern actions perceived as most insidious and detrimental to Southern security by Southern leaders, being of an economic nature, barely feature in the Northern security equation and the consequent calculation of priorities. Above all, the burden of certain of these economic features, such as floating interest rates, is something which Southern leaders often feel to be within the power and responsibility of the North to change, and not the product of the operation of an autonomous market.

Given these differing perceptions, what criteria can be used to assess remedial measures for the problems of insecurity in the South outlined in the original project? Moreover, are competition-free zones, self-regulating 'no go' zones, free competition but crisis controlled zones, arms limitation techniques, third party mediation, superpower codes of conduct and so forth, adequate or even appropriate given the lack of consensus on the fundamental structure of security being aimed at? A whole new avenue of concerns was opened up for investigation and debate by questioning the basic assumption that there could exist a common perception of security. While the establishment of free competition but crisis controlled zones might seem pragmatic and even legitimate in the eyes of Northern statesmen, to their Southern counterparts they might appear illegitimate, illegal, imprudent and counterproductive; increasing insecurity rather than reinforcing security.

A great gulf exists over the basic issue of what constitutes security, and therefore over what constitute the most legitimate, desirable and appropriate methods of pursuing the goal of creating a more secure international environment and more security for each individual and state within it. Indeed controversy exists even at the level of determining what the appropriate targets are for security policies (the system, the region, the state, the individual or some combination of these) and how, if at all, they can be rank ordered.

In the case of the Guernsey Conference, it became apparent that there were, very broadly, two reflections of these concerns and sets of answers to them. First, there were those who saw security mainly in terms of stability. For them the elaboration of a reliable regulatory order to govern the existing international system of theoretically sovereign states, underpinned primarily by military sanctions, was the foremost concern. Secondly, in contrast, there were those who adopted a holistic approach, seeing social and economic change not as a threat to, but as an integral part of, security, and for whom the security of the individual was a prerequisite for the security of states and indeed of the international system. Again at a broad level, the basic tension was in the relative importance given to military and socio-economic factors, and the necessity for change. This seemed to stem directly from competing notions of justice and order and the relationship between the two, and this in turn was in part the product of different historical experiences of state-building and development in which the changing character of the international environment has played a critical role. In a nutshell, one conception of security was basically top down, while the other was bottom up.

The conference was convened under the title 'Conflict and Consensus in the *South/North* Security Debate'. The order here is important, for almost invariably in security debates it is the positions of the Western states or the superpowers (all these developed states being categorised for our purposes as Northern), which are given prominence and priority, while the concerns of states in the developing world are regarded as secondary or derivative. It is usual for security to be assessed in an East/West framework, and for scant regard to be given to the indigenous developments, concerns and priorities of the developing states. The conference was consciously structured in such a way as to redress this imbalance. This concern is reflected in the organisation and content of the current volume, which highlights the fact that another important dimension exists in the security debate. For analyses which stress the East/West context and fail to adequately address the South/North dimension will fall short of the academic goal of the pursuit of objectivity and relevance, and will fail to serve the policy-maker in the developed and the developing worlds well.

The topics chosen for debate at the conference reflected the mutual and the competing concerns which became evident in discussions during the earlier stages of the project. Thus, the economic dimension of security, which is prominent in the perspectives of many Southerners but rarely enters the formulation of Northern security analysts, had a prominent role, as did the traditional concerns of the North grounded in physical territoriality, violations thereof and military relationships. Terrorism, a mutual concern, also featured.

The aim of the conference was to cover the main areas of agreement and disagreement in the current security debate, either in the papers or in the discussions; the current volume attempts to offer a flavour of these proceedings. The papers are organised into six pairs. Each pair addresses a major element of the security problem from the point of view of a Southern and a Northern perspective, thereby highlighting similarities and differences in approach and identifying areas where constructive engagement may take place and areas where it is unlikely. Just as it is possible to identify a multiplicity of 'Western' and 'Northern' perspectives on particular elements of the security debate, it is also possible to identify numerous approaches emanating from the developing countries. There may be differences both within and between states, resulting from the varying perceptions of interest groups within the state and of national

4

interest between states on particular issues. However, this volume is based on the premise that, while there may be differences in detail, in broad terms it is possible to distinguish common concerns and priorities both between the 'Southern' states and between the 'Western' states and also to a certain extent between the 'superpowers'. Hence a thematic approach is adopted here, with broad general issues being discussed, rather than a particularist approach which would highlight divergences within these groups of states. There is no intention to suggest that any such grouping is a homogeneous unit; indeed, it is vital, especially in the case of developing states which are all too often collectively labelled 'Third World' within Northern literature, to recognise the heterogeneity of their individual strengths and weaknesses. Yet states have discernible common positions in the security debate which are borne of common challenges, vulnerabilities and perceptions of justice. It is at this most basic, yet in many respects most difficult level, of the highest common denominator that the editors feel the contested concept of security can be addressed most usefully.

The first pair of essays addresses the question of the position and role of the Third World in the international political system. Aswini Ray, noticeably subtitling his paper 'A View from the *Periphery*', presents a picture of a structurally hierarchical international political system which is morally unjust and ultimately unstable. He argues that stability has been bought for the Northern hemisphere in the post-World War Two period at the expense of instability in the so-called 'Third World', and indeed, the 'Third World' itself is the product of rivalry between East and West. The hegemony of the East–West Cold War, with its clearly Eurocentric concerns, has created a hierarchy of beneficiaries of the international political system in both economic and geopolitical terms. 'Third World' countries find themselves at the base of a pyramidal structure, while the Northern states occupy varying positions towards the apex. There is little chance of upward mobility within this rigid structure. Ray warns that the continuity of the international political system should not be taken as evidence of its stability.

The Northern view on the position and role of the 'Third World' in the international political system offered by John Simpson stresses the difference between what exists 'out there' and is observable in that system, and what is part of a non-observable cognitive structure which assists us as we try to understand what is going on in the world. Simpson explains how developing states of the South have been faced with the choice of accepting an interpretation of the international system based on either realism or idealism, both of which pre-dated the existence of the 'Third World', or of formulating an entirely new approach. He maintains that the majority of Third World elites have been coopted into the realist tradition. Thus, while they call for changes in the international economic order and so forth based on egalitarianism and ideas of a community of mankind, they realise that these will not be attained unless the North wills it so. The Western tradition of realism, accepted by Southern elites for whom Western intellectual dominance exists in the mind, has played a crucial role in preventing attempts at revolutionary change in the international system as much as has the existence of a power hierarchy 'out there'. Yet Simpson argues that the lack of an alternative vision of the nature of the international system makes possible a dialogue on North/South security, for a consensus exists on how the system functions, even if there is no uniform acceptance of the consequences of that functioning. As far as he is concerned, the evolution of the international system over the past three decades has been 'dominated by the cooption of the Southern political and security elites into an international consensus on the nature of that system'. They have accepted the agenda on security issues set by the North, rather than taking radical initiatives. Many of the positions taken by these elites are the result of a desire to increase their relative power position rather than a desire to attain other specific objectives per se. They suffer from a lack of indigenous alternatives and priorities.

The second group of papers considers how far the international economic order has addressed the developmental needs of the South. Marc Williams, presenting a Southern perspective, argues that this must be assessed in terms of the development of post-war capitalism. The hegemony of the United States at the close of World War Two allowed that state to create a liberal international economic order which advanced US business and security interests, but which also resulted in growth within developing countries. However, growth and development in the latter has been very uneven. Instability in the international monetary system, higher oil prices, falling commodity prices, global recession and fluctuating interest rates have increased uncertainty and added to the imperfections already existing in the operation of the liberal economic order because of differential political power, bargaining strength and unequal access to information.

In proscribing interventionist policies to correct this bias, the economic order contributes to the continuation of inequality. Williams examines the performance of the major international economic organisations – the International Monetary Fund (IMF), the General Agreement on Tariffs and Trade (GATT) and the International Bank for Reconstruction and Development (IBRD) – through the criteria of efficiency, stability and economic justice. He concludes that, although a Southern coalition favouring reform of the international economic order has been created and maintained because of a general feeling of powerlessness in the shaping of economic decisions, below this global level a variety of postures are evident deriving from local elites' calculation of interest.

Graham Bird's Northern view of the international economic order and the developmental interests of Third World states concentrates specifically on the international monetary arrangements, and this emphasis is itself important because it reveals a hierarchy of priorities. Bird stresses that the 'South' is not a homogeneous grouping in financial terms and should not be treated as such, and hence the North/South division is far too simplistic a categorisation to be useful for policy-makers; indeed it may be very misleading. Bird outlines alternative reform plans and concludes that in the present circumstances only piecemeal reform is viable, for example in areas where developing countries can identify shared concerns with the developed countries such as over debt. He concludes that, while international arrangements may be important, it is essential not to lose sight of the fact that domestic arrangements can have a profound impact on the economic health of developing states too. Thus persistently over-valued exchange rates will impinge on development, irrespective of the international economic environment.

The third set of essays deals with the question of alliances and bases in the South. Paikiasothy Saravanamuttu maintains that this question cannot be separated from the wider one of intervention in the South and the Northern belief that the primary demand of international order legitimises it. Bases attest that, decolonisation notwithstanding, the modes of thought characterising great power behaviour are little different from those prominent in the days of empires. Saravanamuttu outlines how basing policy is changing to meet contemporary technological and political conditions. Bases are called technical facilities, and they come under the sovereignty of the host country which may in theory restrict access, though this happens infrequently. He argues that, far from enhancing international security, bases compound the problem, since they are in direct conflict with core elements of the Southern perspective of security: non-alignment; the desire of host governments not to be 'short-changed' in their security relations with the superpowers; and their desire not to have social and political change overseen or directed by an outside power.

In his Northern perspective on bases and alliances, Christopher Coker concentrates on the role of the US since it has a far more extensive network of bases and communications facilities in the Third World than the USSR. He argues that many of the issues raised by the South are common property to all who regard association with the US as a threat to regional security, and he is thinking here particularly of the West Europeans. Coker maintains that the strategic recoupling of the Third World and the West represents less a threat to the security of any particular region and more a threat to the self-image of the Non-Aligned Movement. The US has found its freedom of action severely constrained in three areas: its ability to intervene in the domestic affairs of the host nation; its right to use bases for military operations against other Third World states; and its right to compromise the essential non-aligned status of those countries which have been willing to provide base facilities. With the massive diversity existing within the Third World, Coker suggests that, while the base issue may be relevant to the image the Third World has of itself, it is entirely irrelevant to its future. He stresses that, apart from Diego Garcia, the only overseas base outside Europe which is vital to US security interests is Subic Bay.

The fourth section addresses the problem of the debt crisis. Stephany Griffiths-Jones reiterates that one of the effects of the debt crises in the 1980s has been to reduce the amount of new private capital flows to the South; yet solutions to the debt crisis are hindered by the lack of such flows. She argues, however, that the present 'vicious circle' type of situation could potentially be transformed into a 'virtuous circle'. This would require several conditions to be met, and Jones advocates a clear technical and bargaining strategy by several major debtor governments, a willingness by them to use 'bargaining strength' which negative net transfers give them, and a sympathetic response from industrial governments and private financial institutions. The paper examines the main elements which give bargaining strength to major debtors, outlines how the debt crisis has been managed until now, and concludes with suggestions about how to move from short-term crisis-management techniques to a system of international financial mediation more in tune with the developmental needs of the developing countries and of world economic growth.

The Northern view offered by Stephen Thomas stresses that the international debt crisis, which in common usage refers to the difficulties faced by developing states in repaying loans to international banks, forms but one aspect of a larger – indeed global – debt crisis being played out in the North as well. The North is affected not only because its banks are over-exposed to the South, but because of domestic strains within the Northern financial system. He cites the enormous proliferation of household debt in the US due partly to the massive proliferation in credit cards. Thomas suggests that financial deregulation and lender of last resort facilities have led to a *global* debt explosion; this is a problem both for the South and for the North. He maintains that case-by-case rescheduling of Southern debt has done nothing to tackle the fundamental problems in the international monetary system. He criticises as untenable the implicit Northern position that neither banks nor governments must lose and praises the recent Citicorp decision to increase its loan loss provisions massively and take an operating loss as a step in the right direction. Moreover this has been repeated by other banks, including some concerned with domestic US debt such as First Interstate.

The fifth pair of essays tackles the issue of intervention. Matin Zuberi offers a

8

Southern view. He maintains that the novelty of the present international situation with respect to intervention lies in the fact that, unlike the old imperial systems which were territorially confined and constrained by technology, there are now two overlapping global military powers which are pursuing conflicting global policies in the dynamic setting of change and turmoil in the peripheries. The era of risk-free intervention is over. He argues that the premium placed on pre-emption leads to spiralling interventions, and that this is made worse by the invitations given by certain fragile polities suffering from the disorientations of the development process. The consequences could be catastrophic for both North and South.

Phil Williams offers a Northern view which is territorially and militarily based, and which sees great power intervention in weaker states as a result of the anarchy and hierarchy within the international system that has a respectable history in the Hobbesian view of the relations of states. There is an inherent tension between the norms of international society and the reality of international politics, and the attempts of superpowers to offer justifications for their transgressions of the non-intervention rule suggest that these norms are not unimportant. Williams examines why superpowers intervene militarily in other states, and points particularly to the bipolar structure of the international system, the self-images of the two superpowers which give their competition a Manichean quality, and the geopolitical mind-sets. He draws attention to certain characteristics of the Third World state and of interstate relations which encourage superpower intervention. Williams highlights also the justifications offered for intervention; national security is frequently used, and he argues that it is the only one necessary in an anarchic international system. Given the ideological dimension of superpower rivalry, justifications also often take on an ideological dimension. Thus the US points to the need to uphold freedom and democracy, while the USSR stresses the importance of national liberation. The superpowers do not see their own interventions as violations of established norms but rather as specific responses to problems and challenges in particular geographic areas. Reducing incentives for intervention will depend on the state of superpower relations, and Third World states have little control over this. However, they may be able to reduce the opportunities for such intervention if they can strengthen the institutions of their states and establish effective regional mechanisms for crisis management and conflict resolution in the Third World. The superpowers cannot be relied upon to stop acting as such.

The final set of essays addresses the question of terrorism. A Southern view, offered by George Joffé, uses the Middle East as an illustrative case study. Joffé stresses that neither terrorism nor fundamentalism sprang *ex nihilo*, and that there are objective circumstances which explain their existence and suggest more appropriate solutions than the use of the armed force of the state currently in vogue. Attitudes in the West, dismissive of attempts to understand causality, lead to a hardening of attitudes in the Middle East among the very groups on which future hopes of cooperation, peace and stability must be based. If this continues, violent confrontation between the Islamic Middle East and the secular West will be accepted by both as the norm for dialogue. Joffé argues that the profound changes taking place in Middle Eastern societies are being misrepresented in the West, to the detriment of Western relations with that area of the world. If a reduction in terrorism is to be achieved, then the West must address the issue of the Palestinian people in a more constructive manner than it has done to date, and it must learn to live with Islamic revival and accept notions of cultural diversity and equality. Greater understanding of the problems and changes besetting Middle Eastern societies could help release some of the tensions in the area that stimulate a terrorist response. A massive policy shift in Washington is vital.

In his Northern perspective on terrorism Paul Wilkinson begins by discussing problems of definition and he suggests a basic typology of international terror perpetrators: nationalist terrorists, ideological terrorists, religious fanatics, single issue fanatics and state-sponsored international terrorism. Next, Wilkinson offers an outline of Northern perceptions of the underlying causes of the growth in terrorism since the late 1960s. He highlights the general strategic situation which favours unconventional war, weaknesses in the response to terrorism of the international community and particular states, the military defeat of the Arab states in the June 1967 war with Israel and the resurgence of the neo-Marxist and Trotskyist left among the student populations of the advanced industrial states of the West. He outlines also specific reasons in Southern states, such as regime terror by military dictatorships, ethnic and religious divisions within the states, economic weakness and urbanisation. Special attention is given to state-sponsored terrorism, with reference to Iran under Khomeini. Finally Wilkinson addresses the issue of countering state-sponsored terrorism in the South.

The concluding chapter by Paikiasothy Saravanamuttu highlights the areas of convergence and divergence that became evident from the conference papers and discussions, and thus indicates likely areas where progress in the security debate may be made and others where it is less hopeful. The conclusion provides a statement of where the debate has reached and possible future scenarios.

Part I: The international political system and the developing world

I A view from the periphery

Aswini K. Ray

Any system of autonomous units in mutual interaction tends to produce a hierarchy among those units. The interaction of the various units does not have the same impact on the equilibrium of the system. This criterion distinguishes the core-area of any system from its peripheral areas. It would not be surprising therefore, to underscore the existence of a structural hierarchy within the present international system.

Analysing contemporary international relations from the standpoint of systems theory, this paper addresses the more important question of the legitimacy of the structural hierarchy, both in moral terms and in terms of its ability to provide a relatively durable basis for stability in the system.

Any analysis of the legitimacy of a social order involving human beings unavoidably involves a moral question based on certain transcendental human values. A similar moral question is implicit in any analysis of the international system. Impervious to the social and human costs involved in the process, a positivist approach could find evidence of the stability of the system simply from its continuity. However, when the inequitable burden of such costs corresponds with the built-in structural hierarchy of the system, such a system becomes morally questionable.

The stability of any system of social order also involves an assessment of its ability to promote and accommodate progressive changes within it, and conversely, to resist retrogressive distortions. Such progressive changes must be reflected in the quality of life in the societies constituting the system, and also in the ability of the system to restructure its core and peripheral areas to correspond with such progressive changes. Any view of contemporary international relations that ignores this would remain flawed. The continuity of any system is a necessary, but not sufficient, condition of its stability, and much less of its moral legitimacy.

The present analysis will, in underscoring the built-in structural limitations of the system in its historical context, avoid the pitfalls of the positivist approach, particularly its patent moral inadequacies. It will emphasise the impact of the post-war international system on what has come to be euphemistically described as the countries of the 'South'. Inhabited by the overwhelming majority of human beings and consisting of a majority of the member states of the global system, they are often referred to by the conceptual monstrosity of the 'Third World' – the latter being neither scientifically conceptualised nor clearly delimited.[1] Explanations from the standpoint of the 'Third World' will be offered for the abiding continuity of the system's structural limitations. It is in this sense a view of the system from its periphery.

HISTORICAL ROOTS OF THE SYSTEM

The post-war international system emerged relatively quickly from the debris of two world wars. These conflicts were characterised by the power rivalries among the European states and Japan, the only erstwhile Asian colonial power, and extended into their colonies. Consequently, colonies as objects of colonial masters became subjects in their wars of mutual aggrandisement. They provided men, material, and territory for wars in which they had little at stake. Even after this, the ex-colonies were for historical reasons inadequately equipped to play any effective role in the process of institution-building of the post-war international system. The main point is while the initial structural hierarchy of the system emerged out of the historical circumstances of its origin, the built-in hierarchy has continued to be reinforced by the system itself.

The post-war era created the most significant break from all previous international systems. The European colonial powers, after their historical role of integrating the far-flung areas of the world within the capitalist international division of labour, had collapsed in their war of mutual attrition. The boundaries of the post-war system were more truly global than ever before. With the decline of the European powers, the United States of America emerged as the undisputed leader of the capitalist world. For the first time within the international system one dominant economic and military power had emerged. According to one calculation, three-fourths of the world's invested capital and two-thirds of its industrial capacity was concentrated within the United States – 'One nation had acquired a near monopoly on all the important factors of sustaining life'.[2] In the military sphere the United States had total monopoly over nuclear technology and weapons, and by 1949 there were 400 US military bases around the world.[3]

In sharp contrast, the Soviet Union lay virtually in ruins, with twenty million people killed and its economy devastated by the war fought within its territory.

This happened soon after the disruption caused by the revolution, the *cordon sanitaire*, and the prolonged civil war. Born in the midst of the earlier world war with long experience of military aggression and external intervention, the Soviet Union in the immediate aftermath of the war was obsessed with the question of its national security. This obsessive concern was also shared in different degrees by many other European powers with a similar history of conflict.

The immediate Soviet response to countervail its post-war economic and military weakness was to indulge in the *realpolitik* of creating a buffer zone along the entire stretch of its Western frontiers. From historical experience, this posed the most potent security threat to its territorial integrity. In the process, this Soviet *realpolitik* managed to further stoke the European states' elemental fear for national security which, given their past of internecine rivalries, had been an integral historical component of European political culture.

The consequent division of Europe for the first time along the ideological lines of capitalism and socialism, coupled with the critical new global power configuration, also had its impact on post-war international relations. Beyond Europe, the global power balance within the ideological divide tended in some sense to be tilted against the capitalist world by a conjuncture of events, some of which were precipitated by the world war. These included the communist victories in the civil and anti-colonial wars of China and Indo-china, the resurgence of national liberation movements in Asia and Africa, the weakness in the economic and military strength of the European powers, and the diminished ideological appeal of capitalism for certain liberals produced by some of its perverse manifestations namely colonialism, racialism and fascism. The tilt against the capitalist world in the global power balance was largely in terms of the ideological and political components of power, rather than its economic and military content. In the latter respects the United States, as the dominant power and undisputed leader of the capitalist world, provided more than an effective counterweight in the global power balance within the ideological divide. For the first time Washington was willing to play the global role by formally jettisonning its historical policy of 'isolationism' and adopting a post-war crusade of global 'containment' of communism and 'Soviet expansionism'. These economic and military components of power have provided the basis for the more enduring aspects of rivalry within the post-war global system.

For the purposes of our present analysis, it is significant that the origins of the East-West cold war, like the preceding world war, were essentially European in their concerns. Furthermore, in the cold war, the critical role was played by a non-European power – the United States – with little known history of either external threats to its territorial integrity or internal threats of disruption posed by repressive regimes. Therefore absent from the social base of US public policies has been the historical experience of modern war fought within its territory and widespread hunger or malnutrition – not to mention even a long enough continuous civilisation to instill a sense of importance of history.[4] These historical asymmetries in the social base of US public policies from the rest of the world had an abiding influence in the capitalist world's policy planning for global containment during the most bizarre phase of the cold war. Within the emerging global system of the era, the impact of these policies was more sharply manifested in the countries of the 'South', particularly the erstwhile colonies which had inherited deep-rooted, multi-tiered, structural nexi with the capitalist world. These historical nexi shaped much of the post-war global system by constraining the policy options of the bulk of the 'Third World' from its inception.

THE 'SOUTH' ON THE EVE OF THE EAST–WEST COLD WAR

When the East–West cold war was already raging in Europe, the bulk of the countries of the 'South' were still under European colonial rule. India and Indonesia were on the verge of national liberation whilst most other Asian and African colonies were liberated in the fifties and sixties during the most intense phase of the cold war.

In these countries colonial rule, geared primarily to the needs of the mother country, had created or exacerbated a series of distortions which in their cumulative impact constituted a vicious circle of enduring structural impediments to progressive development. The main problem was not so much under-development, as is often believed, as distorted development. Many of these distortions were reinforced and new ones created by wars amongst the colonial powers. 'Development' often led to sectoral maladjustments and structural imbalances; agriculture, particularly of food crops, was neglected in favour of plantation cash crops and/or mining and extraction of non-renewable raw materials, both for export to the mother country. While indigenous village industries and local handicrafts were destroyed in many ingenious ways, 'industrialisation' was allowed in some of the colonies. It took place largely in the secondary and service sectors in support of the imported primary products of the mother country, a form of industrialisation which made their dependence on the metropolitan centres of production less reversible even in the long run. Infrastructural developments, insofar as they were necessary to make the colonial economies profitable, or war worthy, were largely geared to reinforce such built-in structural distortions. Consequently, enclaves of 'modernisation' grew up either around the colonial production centres, or port towns along the route of transfer of the colonial 'surplus' to the mother country, and in artificially created cantonments, hill stations or beach resorts of such hostage economies, surrounded by vast hinterlands of primitive traditional economy.

The dependent colonial economy spawned its corresponding social distortions by engendering a parasitical local elite enterprising enough to take advantage of the available opportunities, including the windfalls of the two world wars. The relatively affluent sections of the colonial elite created in the process, imitating the life styles of their colonial masters in the midst of the widespread poverty, tended to exacerbate regional disparities and social tensions. The social and political instability endemic in such forms of distorted development was managed within a tolerable level of equilibrium by a brutalised state-machinery. This included a section of the local elite as 'hewers of wood and drawers of water' of the colonial process of exploitation. Such a colonial political economy, forcibly superimposed on the traditional social structures, created tiers of long-range distortions in these societies and divisions among the peoples which have posed serious long-term problems.

The most important task of development was to undo these distortions. It involved meticulous planning to create new institutions for nation-building and economic development. The principal problem for most of the 'South' during the most intense phase of the East–West cold war brinkmanship in Europe was essentially socio-economic in content and created or exacerbated by European colonial rule. This concern was also central to the national security of these countries in the early phase of their entry as sovereign states into the global system.

The prevailing cold war version of the Western institutions of national security sharply contradicted with the objective priorities of post-colonial development. This was the most significant aspect of the prevailing asymmetry between the political economy of the Western world and most of the post-colonial societies in the early phase of their nation-building. In the former case, thanks to the preceding war, provisions for the military dimensions of national security were often inputs into economic development.

The colonial political elite of the liberation movements had little experience of dealing with external threats outside the framework of their respective anti-colonial struggles and little patience with the complexities involved in dealing with such perceptions. Due to their experience of political struggle, they tended to be cautious of their colonial rulers and allies. In these respects, the political elite of the liberation struggle often proved to be liabilities in the pursuit of global 'containment'.

By sharp contrast, the colonial military and civilian bureaucracy inherited much of the sensitivities and prejudices of their colonial masters as part of their process of training and socialisation. This group provided a powerful social base for the dissemination of the Western version of national security within the political culture of post-colonial nationalism. The Western countries involved in the struggle for global 'containment' nursed these ready-made, powerful, allies in many ingenious ways. They were hailed by some crusaders of 'containment' in the West – including some social scientists – as the only vehicle of 'modernisation' in what came to be called in the cold war historiography the 'Third World', consisting of humanity outside Europe and the United States. This generic residual category, the 'Third World', not only reflected the structural hierarchy of the global system which created it, but also in many ways came to reflect the hierarchy of human concerns institutionalised within the global system.

THE STRUCTURE OF THE SYSTEM

There was an obvious historically determined asymmetry in the problems, perceptions, and priorities of the member states of the global system. The 'Third World' was particularly asymmetrical, both from the 'First' and the 'Second', as well as within itself. While the principal common problem of distorted development emanated from the shared experience of colonial rule, the nature of each distortion was historically specific, depending on the traditional society, political economy and the nature of colonial exploitation. Consequently each of the countries' specific post-colonial developmental priorities could only be identified and resolved at the local level within a structure of indigenous and/or locally innovated institutions and by a political leadership accountable and sensitive to local aspirations. Therefore political democracy was particularly relevant to resolve the immediate and most critical problems of the post-colonial world during the initial period of the present international system.

The historically inherited infrastructural asymmetry of the post-war world also called for the creation of a global system that was loose enough to permit the widest range of unit-level autonomy in the sphere of local policy planning of problems and priorities. In other words, democracy, both at the micro-level of the units as well as the macro-level of the global system was particularly important for the progressive development of the 'Third World'.

The United Nations Organisation, based on the principle of collective security, was essentially predicated on this realistic principle of unit-level autonomy. It was created as 'a centre for harmonising the actions of nations', 'to promote social progress and better standards of life in larger freedom', and to 'employ international machinery for the promotion of the economic and social advancement of all people'. As the principal institutional structure of the post-war system of global security, 'to save succeeding generations from the scourge of war', it paid due attention to the important problems of respecting national sovereignty and the principle of sovereign equality of its member states. Its charter also underscored the priority of creating the socio-economic, cultural, and humanitarian underpinnings of any durable structure of global security.

Though created in the chastened milieu of the immediate aftermath of the global war, this institutional fulcrum of the post-war global system was never given a chance to prove itself due to the over-riding politics of the East–West cold war unleashed in Europe even while the fledgling institution was still taking shape in San Francisco. The cynicism with which the dominant power of the post-war world viewed the new institution could be gauged from the statement of its erstwhile Commerce Secretary, Henry Wallace – 'I cannot but feel that these actions must make it look to the rest of the world as if we were paying lip-service to peace at the conference (San Francisco) table.'[5] He was forced to resign immediately after he made this *faux-pas*. The contribution of the leader of the communist world to the subsequent cold war brinkmanship has also been indicated.

The important point is that while the emerging global system, consisting of the cold war institutions, continued from the outset to undermine the UN-system which was more in conformity with the needs of the post-war world, the globalisation of the East–West cold war, particularly its critical component of military 'containment', enabled the principal architects of the cold war to cut their losses at the cost of those who were weak. The global system, based on the principle of military 'containment', was *ab-initio* weighted against the weak.

While the cold war was raging in Europe, with its principle of military 'containment' first leading to the creation of the NATO, followed, predictably, by the creation of the Warsaw Pact, there was little scope for laying the social, economic, cultural and humanitarian underpinnings of peace and security, as envisaged by the UN-system, on a global scale. On the contrary, the cold war in Europe influenced the infant UN-system itself and established its hegemony over the 'minds of men'. This began with the military alliances encompassing Europe and North America and subsequently, in the rest of the world through the Western-sponsored global chain incorporating for example CENTO and the SEATO. Consequently a concern for national security in a form and content that was essentially European in its origin and concerns was globalised. In fact, the 'Third World' as the conglomerate of the state systems outside the 'First' and the 'Second' worlds was an off-shoot of this hierarchy of concerns built into the over-arching global system.

But the global rivalry between communism and capitalism, the two ideologies – both again of Western origin – was concerned with two principal questions of relevance to the subsequent problems of the 'Third World': 1) the battle for the 'minds of men' in the ideological and institutional vacuum created by the imminent collapse of the colonial systems; 2) the actual induction of allies within the institutions of military 'containment' to provide the global infrastructure in the struggle.

In both these facets of the global struggle, the role of the capitalist world was of critical importance to the non-communist parts of the post-colonial world, with their historically inherited structural linkages. At any rate, when, by the mid fifties, the Soviet leadership also extended its *realpolitik* to the 'Third World' beyond its communist allies in the region, parallelling the Western version, the hegemony of the cold war global system, with all its economic, military, social, cultural and ideological corollaries, was firmly established across the globe. The cumulative consequences of this hegemony were inequitably harsher within the 'Third World' because the problems and priorities of this part of the world were more sharply divergent with the institutions of the cold war global system which originated from the rivalry among the other two parts of the world. In fact the 'Third World' itself was a product of the rivalry within the Western hemisphere.

The hegemony of the East–West cold war immediately created a hierarchy of beneficiaries of the international system. The pyramidal structure of the system, heavily skewed at the apex, inducted the bulk of the countries of the 'Third World' at its base within a rigid bipolar structure. This provided little choice for lateral entry or for upward mobility.

THE IMMEDIATE IMPACT: 'NORTH'–'SOUTH' ASYMMETRY

Based on the military and political realities of the immediate post-war era, there was an element of historical logic within the ideological divide of Europe. Nevertheless there was little historical inevitability, much less any logic, in the divisions within the 'Third World', particularly the most important contemporary conflict within this world, between those militarily aligned with the West and those opting to remain non-aligned. This important source of conflict and division within the 'Third World' – the problems of which demanded cooperation among them – was the direct consequence of the extension of the European cold war into this part of the world.[6]

At any rate, in two significant senses Europe immediately benefited out of the East–West cold war, in sharp contrast to the 'Third World'. First, the relative 'Balance of Terror'[7] among the ideological divides of Europe, and the chastening experience of the horrors of the earlier war, helped in avoiding another European war. In spite of the tensions created by the cold war, in fact because of it, the stakes of their respective patrons to rebuild both parts of Europe spared the continent another war of the type that had characterised much of its earlier history. The 'proxy-wars' among the two ideological divides immediately shifted from the terrain of Europe to the 'Third World'.

According to one study of armed conflicts since 1945,[8] no war has been fought inside Europe or North America, and the majority of them have taken place in Asia and Africa. In all these wars, according to the same study, troops alien to the theatres of operation participated. Apart from indirect interventions, in the first thirty-two years after 1945, direct external military interventions occurred in eighty-seven conflicts; the developed countries of the 'North' intervened in 80 per cent of the cases, 73.6 per cent being from the Western bloc and 6.4 per cent from the communist countries. Among all the countries, the United States intervened in a majority of cases – 42.2 per cent of all the wars between 1945 and 1976. In the last ten years covering the period of the study, between 1966 and 1976, US intervention alone amounted to 58 per cent of all the wars. Since then, the Soviet military intervention in Afghanistan, the American bombing of Tripoli, the creation of the Rapid Deployment Force, and the recent revelations of the grisly details of US interventions on both sides of the Iran–Iraq war as well as in the civil wars in South America, tend generally to reinforce the basic conclusions of the empirical study already cited.

Europe, in contrast to the 'Third World', also benefited directly from the cold war in economic terms via the Marshall Plan. This brought in a massive transfer of capital and technology from the United States to rebuild infrastructure. In fact, the post-war political economy that spawned the global cold war had already created a high degree of complementarity within the Atlantic community, enabling both sides of the Atlantic to enjoy an economic bonanza.[9] Admittedly, Western Europe, later Japan, benefited relatively more out of this bonanza, largely because their cold war patron had more such aid to spare. This also in its turn provided the necessary challenge to the communist states involved in the cold war to rebuild their part of Europe and integrate them within a structure of economic complementarity. Within the structure of its ideological divide, and reinforced by it, the cold war provided the political momentum towards the process of greater integration within the Western hemisphere, thus reversing its earlier process of history. However, the cold war divided the 'Third World' states from the early phase of their history as independent nation-states.

At any rate, the developmental institutions of both parts of Europe already existed in different degrees since at least two centuries of development had occurred since the beginning of the Industrial Revolution. In most of Western Europe, considerable technological progress had already been sustained within the institutional structures of economic development and liberal democracy. Even in most parts of communist Europe, the motivations for economic development already engineered before World War Two were reinforced by the ideological challenges of the cold war. The temporary set-back to European institutions of economic development caused by this war was more than off-set by the zealous pursuit of reconstruction sparked off by the cold war. This included its military component – for which the infrastructure was already created during the earlier war – and the easy availability of liberal foreign aid. Yet even in Europe the process of reconstruction under such circumstances created its own disparities. The 'First' and the 'Second' worlds, both located in the 'North', capitalised on the momentum for political stability and economic development within the framework of their ideological rivalry. Comparable policies extended to the region of the 'Third World' created a qualitatively different range of distortions. This was largely because the historical options available to Europe and the United States in this period did not exist in the 'Third World', for reasons already indicated. In fact, the political economy of the cold war global system created many new distortions within the 'Third World', more so, within its non-communist parts which were more closely integrated within the international capitalist division of labour. The divisions within the 'Third World' did not follow the ideological pattern, as in the Western hemisphere, and the split between the aligned and the non-aligned was largely confined to its non-communist part. In these distortions, the role of the capitalist world was most critical, simply because of its historical advantage of multi-tiered access to parts of the 'Third World', whether aligned or not. At any rate, the communist superpower, initially with little to lose and much to gain from these divisions, soon reoriented its policies towards these parts of the world in a way that reinforced the distortions of the cold war within the 'Third World'. Some of the more significant aspects of such distortions will be briefly mentioned.

First, the overarching global ideological rivalry with its euphemistically posed choice between 'liberty' and 'equality' – however relevant to Europe – was somewhat incongruous within the developmental options of these parts of the world suffering from human degradation and mass poverty under long colonial rule. Such artificially contrived contrasts based on the European empirical realities of the cold war, and couched in Western ideological trappings, were forced upon the Western-educated elite of the colonies as the only available alternatives of their post-colonial developmental strategies. These conceptual and ideological traps of the two Western paradigms, both developed without adequate empirical experience of their relevance to societies with colonial distortions, presented the post-colonial elite with the choice between two competing and integrated sets of options. This stifled indigenous intellectual creativity regarding developmental alternatives relevant to specific local needs at the uniquely propitious time of nationalist resurgence in the aftermath of national liberation. This historic tide is largely irretrievable in the bulk of the post-colonial world.

Secondly, the induction of allies of 'containment' within the 'Third World' often also involved the destabilisation of their weak democratic institutions, and/ or, the creation of regional tensions among many new neighbours. Very often, this resulted in the total collapse of democracy, and the emergence of repressive 'military-bureaucratic cliques', or other local variants which by their very nature were more receptive to the doctrine and institutions of 'containment' and also less capable of providing any durable form of political stability to these plural societies of the 'Third World'.[10] Such regimes created a vicious circle of instability and repression in these parts.

Thirdly, alliance with 'containment' invariably involved heavy defence outlays financed by foreign aid. This was at sharp variance with their objective developmental imperatives and also tended to reinforce their dependence nexus inherited from the colonial era.

Even for such countries as India which struggled to remain non-aligned against heavy odds, the options were relatively limited. Since most such countries found themselves in a situation of adversary relationship with a militarily aligned neighbour that continued to beef its military muscles through external aid, regional arms races were fuelled. This resulted in the replication of the overarching global arms race at the local level, but with more severe consequences. In the period of the cold war the available options distinguishing the aligned and the non-aligned were not so much between dependence and independence, as between relative degrees of dependence, with the non-aligned having only a relatively wider margin of policy options emerging from a structure of diversified dependence within the cold war divide.[11] For many of the countries of the 'Third World' at the height of the cold war, the exercise of the choice even between this limited range of options was not available within the jurisdiction of their state-sovereignty. For those considered strategically critical for the global struggle, even this decision was often made by one or the other superpowers. Since geo-strategic criticality was determined largely by the stage of superpower technology, there were no permanent 'key-dominoes'. The entire 'Third World' has been haunted by the spectre of instability spilling into the sovereign jurisdiction of the individual states from the pressures of rivalry within the global system. Many of them simply did not have a stable institutional base in critical areas of national decision-making, and this constrained their exercise of national sovereignty when confronted by the superpowers.

The most critical structural constraint in the exercise of national sovereignty by 'Third World' countries has been the rigidity of the bipolar structure. Challenges to this rigid bipolarity, first from the non-aligned movement, and subsequently, from Sino–Soviet rivalry, the OPEC countries, and in recent times, by the 'North'–'South' confrontations have till now failed to make any significant dent in the basic content of this power structure. In fact, the optimum potentials of all such a series of challenges have been stymied by the continuous shadow-boxing of the East–West cold war. While the ebb and flow of the cold war has enabled readjustments in the Western hemisphere across the ideological divide, most 'Third World' states remained ossified at the base of the global structure. The mid seventies detente in the cold war simply did not encompass the 'Third World'.

LONG-TERM DISTORTIONS

The cold war not only distorted the problems, perceptions and priorities of the 'Third World' countries from the initial stage of their nation-building process, but also reinforced some of the historically inherited distortions of the colonial era. The 'Third World' became even more disparate and divided; it created, or exacerbated, regional tensions based on primordial loyalties, some of which were stoked in the colonial era. The cold war global system created a hierarchy of importance within the new nation states largely determined by the Great Powers' shifting geo-strategic considerations and often by some historically inherited sociological prejudices. While the rigid global system has inhibited the national sovereignty of almost all the member states in different ways, in this sphere too it has inequitably affected all the militarily, economically and institutionally weak, 'Third World' states. At the height of the cold war, the global hierarchy of national sovereignty broadly corresponded with the military-economic power structure, against which the political assertion of national sovereignty has often proved to be a weak counterweight. In the long run, the political culture of post-colonial nationalism, with all its creative potentials, has tended to fade within the 'Third World'. This historic tide of popular resurgence, as a possible substitute for the institutional weaknesses of the 'Third World' in providing the political momentum for the process of post-colonial reconstruction in the take-off stage, has been irretrievably lost.

Consequently the bulk of the 'Third World' – especially its non-communist part – continues to 'develop' as a distorted version of the 'First World', lacking the widespread social base of either democratic institutions or economic growth. This was caused initially by the absence of the historical options in these parts of the world that were available within the Western hemisphere and, subsequently, by the options denied to it by the structural constraints of the global system.

The parasitical elite, inducted during the cold war and sustained largely by external aid, has created a vicious circle of domestic repression and external dependence. In the contrived battle for 'human rights', devalued in the cold war rhetoric by concern for the problem of racial integration in the 'First World' and the rights of the 'dissidents' in the 'Second', the repressive regimes of the 'Third

World' have violated the most elementary forms of human rights and constitute a structural precondition for the relative stability of the global order.

The 'Third World' regimes continue to depend increasingly on repression, largely as the only available soft option within a rigid global hierarchy. These regimes, using local political euphemisms to soft pedal their essentially dependent character, constitute the major vested interest against the long-delayed process of social transformation and political modernisation. Their utility to the principal beneficiaries of the existing global system lies in their role of perpetuating regional tensions, and as obstacles to regional cooperation in a way that could pose greater challenges in the emerging 'North'–'South' confrontation. Till now, these regimes have provided the necessary local repressive agencies to meet any potentially viable political challenge to the continuity of a global order that ensures that an increasingly smaller number of people enjoy an increasingly larger share of global resources.

The strength of many of these repressive regimes is derived from the global system which created them and which in some cases sustains them. Their linkages with the global system make them asymmetrical to their Western counterparts in the early stage of modernisation when democratic movements within Europe restructured relatively autonomous and decadent political systems which collapsed when confronted by mass upsurge. Yet the post-war global system is more integrated, rigid, and sharply bipolarised at its apex, which makes each of these repressive regimes at the base so much more critical to system maintenance. The difficulties facing the indigenous development of democratic mass movements in most of these countries are exacerbated. There is a dialectical relationship between the struggle for democratisation of the present global order and the struggle for democracy within the 'Third World'. The present global system ensures for the two worlds of the 'North' relative stability, security, freedom, access to resources and quality of life at the expense of the 'South', the countries permanently condemned to the periphery of the rigid structure of power.

HAZARDS OF THE SYSTEM

Despite – even because of – all its inequitable structural constraints, the post-war global system has survived long enough to produce a sense of optimism among its principal beneficiaries of the 'North', who remain insensitive to its creeping distortions. It is also possible to explain such insensitivities in ethnocentric terms.

Yet the global system is already manifesting many signs of its atrophy. It is producing considerable internal challenges in many crucial areas of global interactions, particularly in the potentially most dangerous sphere of nuclear proliferation, and the 'North'–'South' confrontations on the questions of the new international economic, information, and technological orders and on the political demand for the democratisation of the global power structure.

Many of the hazards of the system transferred to the 'South' in the process of its globalisation are now spilling over within the core area of concern for the system. For example, regional conflicts and arms races have already produced a dangerous level of armaments production and transfer. Vertical nuclear proliferation, till recent times confined within the core area of the global system, now threatens to lead to a dangerous level of horizontal proliferation encompassing unstable and insecure fingers on the nuclear trigger. Terrorism, often fuelled by the repression of unrepresentative regimes sustained by foreign aid, has been internationalised to a point that poses a threat to the quality of life across the world. The continued distortions in the developmental process of the 'South', its narrow social base of economic growth, political freedom, and human dignity, has already engendered a level of increase in immigration from these countries to the 'North' thereby creating new sources of tensions within the Western hemisphere. Even in the countries of the 'North', maintenance of acceptable living standards has increasingly involved a general reversal of the process of democratisation of the pre-war era. In the Western democracies, the visible trend is towards greater de-democratisation manifested, in the economic sphere, in greater technocratism and the shrinking of their social security systems, and, in the political field, by the conservative backlash. This is likely to be a major constraint against the structural compulsions of liberalisation within the communist countries of the 'North'. Therefore, on almost all counts, the global system's stability, predicated on the unequal distribution of benefits between the 'North' and the 'South' within an integrated system, and the advantages of the privileged, are threatened. This is the sense in which the global system is showing signs of dysfunction; systemic equilibrium within the inequitable structural hierarchy is proving difficult to manage.

Significantly, such manifestations of the creeping atrophy within the global system, instead of producing the structural compulsions towards reform, has produced the opposite reaction from the principal beneficiaries of the system. The UN-sponsored Development Decades have made little dent on the aid and trade policies of the 'North' towards the 'South' or any visible progress on the first few steps towards the creation of a new international economic order. The emaciated UN-system continues to be undermined with recurrent threats of withdrawal unless it shows greater respect to the interests of the global hierarchy of power and national sovereignty in voting patterns on various issues. There have already been withdrawals from UNESCO, the specialised UN-institution geared to the social, economic, cultural and humanitarian underpinnings of any durable structure of global security. There are even talks of limited nuclear wars that could be won, and attempts to prove it by carrying the nuclear arsenal to the realms of space. The logic emerging from the pattern of responses of the principal beneficiaries of the post-war global system helps to underscore the key point of the present analysis, viz: to survive, the system needs to be continually skewed at the apex, and at multiple tiers of its interrelated spheres of interaction. The system provides little scope for any flexibility within the structural hierarchy determining the relationship between the core area at the apex and its periphery at the base. The stability of such an ossified structural hierarchy that is so inequitable needs more careful management.

Historically, the global system has also followed this pattern, initially covering the sphere of national security in its military dimensions, spreading to the realm of economic development, to the sphere of cultural values, technology, information and to other spheres of intellectual and creative endeavours. In the process, the corresponding global hierarchies have been created. The management of the global system has progressively involved control over the 'minds of men' in spheres of human concerns that increasingly encompass the 'Holy Cow' of national security across the globe. In the process, the world is less secure, less stable, less free, and the quality of life, almost across the board, shows an increasingly retrogressive trend by any standard. The global system has created a world order in which a minority of the people of the world are, at best, less unhappy than the majority from a historical situation in which the minority was happier than the majority. The continuity of such a global system could not provide adequate evidence of its stability, and much less its moral legitimacy.

NOTES

1 Aswini K. Ray, 'Third World perspectives on security and nuclear proliferation', in John Simpson (ed.), *Nuclear non-proliferation: An Agenda for the 1990s* (Cambridge University Press, 1987).
2 Howard K. Smith, *The State of Europe* (New York, 1949), p. 232.
3 David Horowitz, *From Yalta to Vietnam* (Middlesex: Penguin, 1971), p. 28.
4 This, according to our view, makes it often difficult for the American to appreciate why it is near impossible for countries with ancient civilisations to replicate the undoubted achievements of the US.
5 Horowitz, *From Yalta*.
6 For a case study of the extension of the cold war in South Asia, and its impact on Indo–Pakistan relations, see Aswini K. Ray, *Domestic Compulsions and Foreign Policy* (New Delhi, 1975); and 'Myths in American and Pakistani foreign policies: their contemporary relevance', *Foreign Affairs Recorder* (New Delhi, September–October 1980).
7 Not in any strict quantitative sense. But the Red Army, based in Europe, could still inflict an unacceptable level of damage in Western Europe and which, given the level of contemporary technology, the US could countervail only by the use of nuclear weapons that, obviously, could not be used in the crucible of Western civilisation. At any rate, European public opinion was too exhausted to welcome the prospect of another test of military strength.

8 Istvan Kende, 'Wars of ten years (1967–76)', *Journal of Peace and Research*, Vol. XV, No. 3 (1978); and 'New features of armed conflicts and armaments in developing countries', *Development and Peace*, Spring 1983.

9 See Note 6.

10 In Pakistan, military alignment almost directly led to military rule, and the latter accelerated the process of the country's division, and the creation of Bangladesh. See note 6.

11 India provides a classic case of this diversified dependence in its 'Socialist' development strategy of the Nehru-era. See Note 6.

2   A view from the North

John Simpson

John Simpson

INTRODUCTION

The international political system is a term frequently used in both the media and the international relations literature but its conceptual and empirical implications remain obscure. In part, this may be a result of its wide range of usages. On the one hand, it includes the formal rules that underpin both diplomatic protocol and relations and the everyday functioning of international organisations such as the United Nations. These rules rest on the sovereign equality of all states. On the other hand, it encompasses invisible and intangible 'hidden-hand' processes and structures, which some analysts argue determine the outcomes of international interactions. These structures include hierarchies of states based upon differences in their power.

The idea of a system carries with it considerable intellectual baggage. It implies the existence of something more than random connections, but something less than a community or society. Systems consist of interacting elements which exist in a functional relationship, and some minimal common goal is often imputed into them, even if it is only survival or maintenance. As a consequence, the claim that a system exists must be linked to implicit or explicit choices over what is believed to be encompassed by it and what is outside of it. In the case of the international political system, this means delimiting the boundary between that system and other systems and specifying possible relationships of subordination between them. Systems analysis can either take place at an abstract level or at a more tangible and empirical one. It may involve an exploration of the boundaries between the international system and specific state systems. Further, it implies that distinctions can be made between the economic, military, cultural and ecological systems and the political one, and that the relationship of all these functional systems can be specified in detail.

The issues raised above merit a book length study, and several distinguished scholars have already produced such volumes. It is sufficient here to note that the term international political system has many meanings and implications, no one of which can be demonstrated to be 'correct' in any absolute fashion. The discussion which follows is predicated upon this relativist assertion. If it is accepted, then a better understanding of what is taking place in our world can arise only from relating the usage of terms and the assumptions that underpin them to specific contexts, rather than by attempting to attach absolute meanings to them.

Another basic methodological issue relevant to this investigation is whether the words international political system refer to a phenomenon which exists in a substantive and potentially observable form in the world (i.e. it is out there) or whether they refer to a non-observable, cognitive structure which assists individuals and groups to organise and understand what is going on in the world (i.e. it is all in the mind).[1] In practice the two usages of the term are often employed indiscriminately. In what follows an attempt will be made to distinguish clearly between them.

The term international political system thus appears to describe a minimal collection of relationships, mechanisms, behaviours and rules that bind states together. Such a system has no obvious inherent objective and no state or group of states appears to totally dominate it. It is the product of the independent actions of many states, and appears to possess no inherent values that it is designed to pursue. Yet the existence of its minimalist rules and structures make it something other than a total wasteland.

The nature of the international political system has fascinated Northern political thinkers for many centuries, starting with the Greeks and moving through Machiavelli to Morgenthau. The nature and mechanisms of the system have been central to this inquiry, and in recent decades it has taken the form of a dialogue between two schools of international political thought, the political realist and the idealist. Both pre-date the existence of a developing world, which has been faced with the choice of either accepting one of these two approaches or developing its own. To explore further the term international political system it is necessary to embark on a detailed examination of these contrasting schools of thought.

REALISM, POLITICS, AND POWER

The most famous contemporary spokesman for the political realism school is Hans J. Morgenthau Jr., author of *Politics among Nations: The Struggle for Power and Peace*.[2] Morgenthau's basic assumption is that human nature is both unchanging and unchangeable. At the same time he regards man as a rational

30

being, and views decisions of statesmen as acts of rational choice between all available alternatives. Rationality in this context implies acting on the basis of 'interest defined in terms of [or as] power',[3] thus freeing the approach from a concern with human causation. Interest is the essence of all politics, but the substance of both interest and power may change with time and circumstances.

Morgenthau offers both a descriptive and prescriptive theory as 'Political realism contains not only a theoretical but also a normative element . . . [It] presents the theoretical construct of a rational foreign policy which experience can never completely achieve'.[4] For reality 'must be understood and evaluated as an approximation to an ideal system'[5] and any attempt to investigate it has to involve an examination of the 'essence' of the phenomenon under investigation. The use of this 'ideal system' method has links to Hobbes and other Western writers who base their arguments upon the existence of a 'state of nature', to Weber and his sociological methodology and to the techniques used by Clausewitz in *On War*. Its weakness lies in the inherent ambiguity between an 'ideal system' which describes mechanisms in a fifth dimension 'out there' and this system being no more than a heuristic cognitive device 'in the mind' intended to assist understanding.

Morgenthau implies that an 'ideal system' does exist 'out there', for he argues that change can be engineered in the world 'only through the workmanlike manipulation of the perennial forces that have shaped the past as they have shaped the future'. It cannot result from 'confronting a political reality that has its own laws with an abstract ideal that refuses to take those laws into account'.[6] Morgenthau thus offers 'a theory which tries to understand international politics as it actually is and ought to be in view of its intrinsic nature, rather than as people would like to see it'.[7]

This view of the world contrasts sharply with one which regards ethical precepts as the supreme guide to action; to the idea that men and states should act in certain ways because they are right and just. For Morgenthau, 'Ethics in the abstract judges action by its conformity with the moral law; political ethics judges action by its political consequences'. This leads him to the conclusion that 'prudence – the weighing of the consequences of alternative political actions – . . . [is] the supreme virtue in politics'.[8] It also results in him asserting that the prime objective in the search for peace is 'the mitigation and minimization of those political conflicts which . . . pit the two superpowers against each other and evoke the spector of a cataclysmic war'.[9] This he terms 'peace through accommodation. Its instrument is diplomacy'.[10] Conflict resolution and crisis prevention are the means to prevent nuclear war, not nuclear disarmament.

The writings of Morgenthau and his fellow political realists are very persuasive. Their ability to associate theories of political *realism* with political *reality*, in a manner beloved by advertising executives, reinforces their claim to describe a phenomenon which actually exists 'out there'. Yet Morgenthau's claim to prescribe the manner in which policy should be conducted suggests a reality which exists, at least in part, in the mind. Other weaknesses of this school of writing lie in its treatment of politics; in the way the state is regarded as a unitary actor; in the lack of precision attached to the key concepts of interest and power: and in the lack of any *a priori* distinction between the intrinsic nature of politics within the state and between states.

For Morgenthau, normal political activity functions in much the same way as 'frictions' do for Clausewitz: it is a force which corrupts the ideal international system. Viewed in this light, the bureaucratic politics perspectives upon foreign policy and the related politics/logic dichotomy can be assimilated into the realist literature on the international political system. If political bargaining, not rational assessments of state interest, determine both state policies and international outcomes then ideas of bureaucratic politics undermine political realism. On the other hand, if outputs from the international system are determined by immutable mechanisms 'out there', this literature merely explains why irrational or sub-optimal policies are pursued in specific instances. Yet actual foreign policy outcomes must be a product of the *interaction* between inputs into the international system and whatever mechanisms exist within it. This appears to necessitate a theory which specifies detailed interaction between categories of input, mechanisms and types of output, something which is lacking in Morgenthau's work.

The essence of politics for Morgenthau is not bargaining; it is the use of power. He does not distinguish between power and coercion as his focus is upon outcomes, not the detailed processes through which inputs and outcomes are related. In particular, he appears to exclude from his range of relevant outcomes ones in which voluntary bargaining results in states agreeing an outcome which is contrary to their 'interest defined in terms of power'. For Morgenthau the state must act according to certain imperatives; if it fails to do so it will not survive for very long. Yet one cannot help feeling that this conclusion rests on belief rather than observation. For how are the existence of power mechanisms to be proven, rather than just hypothesised.

Political realism also leads to a vision of the international political system in which all states are depicted as mechanistic hard-shelled billiard balls which collide (i.e. conflict) with each other to a greater or lesser degree. Emphasis is placed on their qualities of sovereignty, willingness to defend their boundaries against external intervention and ability to respond to the interests and needs of their populations. Survival of the state is the supreme good, and the only justification for accommodation with other states and the acceptance of rules of behaviour is interest and prudence. This has led to the international political system being characterised as an 'anarchical society'. Cooperation and common norms are transient, rather than intrinsic, features of this 'society' while the actors are non-human entities termed states. This leads to the separation of international political theory from domestic political theory, as states being non-human cannot act in a moral manner. It also leads to distinctions being made between international politics and international relations, with the former being characterised by interactions involving power.

Political power is a very elusive phenomenon, with a 'you will know it when you see it' character. Discussions of power often have a *post-hoc* quality about them, with its existence being proven by changes in state policies. Morgenthau argues that power may include 'anything that establishes and maintains the control of man over man',[11] even though this appears both to be a truism and to negate any possibility of a precise, operational definition. Power is what power does. Politics and bargaining appear to be part of power, rather than an arena in which power is one means of achieving a desired outcome. Power is much more than politics, it is the determinant of outcomes, and includes all the manifold qualities that enable a state to impose its will on others.

Morgenthau differs from some other realist writers in regarding the international and domestic political context as similar to each other, with both being arenas within which US style pluralist interest politics can operate. Thus he contends that power is essentially a human phenomenon, covering a range of interpersonal and group relationships ranging from 'physical violence to the most subtle psychological ties by which one mind controls another'.[12] Others writers, however, exclude violence from its ambit. At the same time, Morgenthau believes that there can exist structures or mechanisms of power, in particular the balance of power, within this pluralist interest context.

Frequent attempts have been made to elucidate the several usages of the phrase 'balance of power'. There have also been numerous attempts to expand on the concept, including elaboration of different types of two-actor balance and more complex multipolar structures. This in turn has produced attempts to describe the essence of these mechanistic structures by reference to terms derived from Newtonian physics such as stability and equilibrium. There is also a hint of the existence of something akin to an economic market mechanism in this situation. Outcomes may be naturally determined by an unchangeable 'hidden hand'. These abstract mechanisms and essences are assumed to exist in an unseen dimension, even though they can only be described by analogy to more tangible structures and processes. By positing their existence, the world of international politics can be likened to the natural sciences, where the development of knowledge is apparently a process of uncovering information about static phenomena. This reinforces the argument that there are laws, structures and processes in the international political system which cannot be changed by any single state, however powerful. All states must work within these limitations if they are to achieve their foreign policy goals. The art of foreign policy-making therefore involves identifying those elements within the international system that can be altered, while making no effort to change the rest.

These international political structures are invested with a certain benign quality. If they are allowed to operate as an 'ideal system' then the result will be a stable international environment. The suggestion is, however, that such a mechanistic international system demands certain actions from states if its stability is to be sustained. These actions may include the use of violence by a state to ensure the survival or maintain the stability of the international political system. This enables the good of the state, especially the dominant state or states, and the good of the system to be equated. All action in the state interest becomes synonymous with action in the international or global interest. Thus the concept of interest, even if defined as power, is open to a very wide range of interpretations. In the absence of an unambiguous way of operationalising some equivalent of a 'global will' it will tend to become equated in a conservative manner with the interests of the dominant state or groups.

Morgenthau makes no attempt to differentiate between the nature of power within states and between states. Other writers, however, have seen it as a situational concept with power and politics differing radically in these two contexts. They point to the monopoly of violence held by the government within a state in contrast to the absence of such a monopoly in the international system. They highlight the lack of both coercive governmental structures within the international system and common norms and values to underpin them. Finally, they emphasise the discontinuity between the substance and pursuit of individual values within the state and the acceptance of organisational survival as the highest value of the state. This appears to some of them to be the supreme good in the international system.

In parallel, other writers argue that existing alongside this 'billiard-ball' political realist international system is a 'cobweb' system. In this latter system, the boundaries of states are seen as insignificant. The most significant action occurs through cross national exchanges either between sub-units of states or between units not directly controlled by the state. However, these contradictions can be reconciled if the 'cobweb' system is seen as largely relevant to economic and other functional exchanges, while the 'billiard-ball' model applies to more political relationships, particularly those involving physical coercion. In this situation, the political system has the capability to dominate the other functional systems.

A political realist vision of the international system thus possesses a number of qualities that make it appealing to the North. It legitimises their dominant position in the existing international political system by equating it with a natural state of affairs. It allows them to act in the name of the global system in a manner which may protect their position and it allows them to equate their actions with the global interest. Above all it suggests that there is no alternative to the existing nature of relationships within the international system as any attempt to change them would just not succeed; the 'hidden hand' would defeat it. And, if such a mechanism cannot be proven to exist in an absolute way, neither can its existence be convincingly disproved. While some may argue it exists only in the mind, it is difficult to provide convincing evidence that it does not exist 'out there'. As a result, the debate over the methodology to be used in analysis of the international political system is imbued with wide-ranging political symbolism and significance.

IDEALISM, MARXISM AND THE INTERNATIONAL POLITICAL SYSTEM

The Third World has been argued elsewhere to be a term only comprehensible as a residual of the First and Second Worlds. Similarly, the idealist view of the international system can be seen as a residual of the realist perspective. Yet the situation has many more dimensions than this dichotomous perspective implies, for idealism pre-dates the post World War Two revival of political realism. Idealism comes in a number of versions and is more a Wittgensteinian family of ideas than a thesis resting on a search for necessary conditions or attributes. Its core belief is that human nature is not unchanging or unchangeable. This has generated two basic strands of thought, one reformist and the other revolutionary. The first, whose expression is found in Locke, Kant and Burke, sees politics as concerned with providing conditions under which man can realise his full potential. It also sees man as capable of living in harmony with his fellow men. The second approach, found in writers such as Marx, holds a similar basic view of man, but believes that his potential can only be realised through revolutionary structural change. The difference between the two perspectives is instrumental: *how* to achieve human perfection, rather than *whether* it can be achieved.

An essential part of any debate between realists and their critics lies in the labels used to characterise the differing schools of thought. The realist label has inherent in it the idea of describing the world as it is. The idealist (or utopian) label implies an ideal world, and possibly one that can never exist. While there is little to choose between the basic methodology of realism and idealism, the meanings inherent in their names suggest otherwise. In particular, Morgenthau's realist 'ideal system' is seen to be of a different nature from methodologically similar devices used by idealist writers. It has inherent in it an element of attainability, while the idealist vision lacks this.

Realists and idealists also differ over the role of the state in international political analysis. For the idealist, the state is not the key actor in the international political system, rather the focus is on ideas ranging from economic relationships to the existence of a community of mankind. From a realist perspective, economic relationships are either subsidiary to, or divorced from political ones. Indeed in classic liberal theory and modern Western neo-conservatism it should not be a sphere for political and state intervention at all, but be a separate arena involving the behaviour of economic man and the domination of the market. The role of the state is limited to ensuring the conditions under which the market can operate with maximum effectiveness. This leads to the greatest efficiency of production and thus a larger overall economic product. How this larger product should be distributed tends to be discussed in terms of investment and consumption. Yet by default the market appears also to operate as a mechanism for distributing the product among potential consumers. The person or group which controls investment and the means of production also controls this distribution.

Who produces the additional product and how it should be distributed has been the subject of various Western theories of surplus product, starting with Hobson and Lenin and moving to various marxist and neo-marxist theories of dependency and imperialism. The latter characterise the market thesis as capitalist, in contrast to the redistributory theories they offer. In addition, they see political systems, both domestic and international, as a dependent superstructure placed upon the basic sub-structure of economic relationships. Marxism in its original form incorporates a determinist theory of history; no man is held capable of standing against the underlying economic forces. It is thus similar in its methodology to the 'out there' school of political realists, though its determinism explicitly embraces human values as well as political mechanisms. Political leaders are not in control of the key international and domestic economic systems, it is the non-elected and politically illegitimate financiers and multinational enterprises of capitalism. Further, the structure of investment and production discriminates against economic activities in certain states, making their economic development impossible. The centre-periphery thesis of writers such as Galtung arises from these propositions. They argue for the existence of a conspiracy between economic and political elites in the developed and developing countries to sustain the existing trading structures in their narrow sectional interests.

The idea of 'a community of mankind' is buried deep in Western political thought, and has religious origins in the Judeo-Christian tradition of 'love thy neighbour as thyself '. It holds that certain human values override loyalty to the state, and provides the basis for war crimes accusations and the belief that all men possess basic human rights. In this perspective the community of states and the community of mankind coexist uneasily together, with man often having conflicting commitments to the state and his fellow men. This conflict finds its practical expression in questions of intervention on behalf of the oppressed citizens of other states, be they in Amin's Uganda or the Soviet Union. Its international institutional focus is organisations such as Amnesty International. It directly relates man to the international political system, and regards international politics as something other than a crude exercise of power in an arena lacking almost all rules.

Intimately linked to the 'community of mankind' school of thought is the idea that, if individual man could express himself fully, this would ensure peace and harmony with his fellow men. Some have argued that such expression can only be achieved if all states have democratic institutions and allow group self-determination. Democracy thus becomes equated with peace and harmony, and it is the detailed arrangements within states, rather than the existence of states themselves, which are seen as the cause of disharmony and war in the international political system. Precisely what is meant by democracy, in particular whether it is concerned with equality of opportunity or equality of outcome, suggests that this instrumental thesis is not as persuasive as it might otherwise be. But the idea persists and democracy continues to be advocated as the most appropriate form of international political system. This debate also shades into the East–West arguments over human rights and individual versus collective economic and political freedoms.

The idea that the international political system can be both of a similar type and integrated into the domestic one, with similar operative mechanisms, is found not only in idealist writings but also in Morgenthau. It reflects an innate inability of those who have thought and written about the international political system to escape from the domestic analogy which leads them to regard both international politics and its mechanisms and institutions as domestic ones writ large. In an idealist context this has led to notions of a world state as a solution to the problem of war. In a realist context the international system is viewed as a larger version of the US political system.

The idealist writings of both East and West thus have in common an emphasis upon the improvement and basic harmony of human relationships. They differ on the instrumental question of how this is to be achieved. The East, in common with the political realists, sees it as something arising from basic forces 'out there', whereas Western idealists concentrate on changes in the minds of men. This produces a curious dichotomy. Western realists and Eastern idealists both emphasise 'scientific' methodology and the existence of natural and unchanging forces 'out there'. In contrast, the Western idealists assume the total malleability of the social domain and the voluntarist nature of change. Both types of idealists offer eschatological and optimistic theories of change through which both the future and the present may be understood. In contrast, the political realists possess a very pessimistic vision of the future.

The nature of the international political system remains rather unexplored territory in all these writings. It is side-stepped by the idealists. They argue it is either a by-product of the internal organisation and decision-making of states, and thus a totally dependent entity, or that it is irrelevant or anachronistic. Some realists see the international political system as identical to the domestic one. Others regard it as one in which the only form of political activity is the exercise of power. Power then becomes synonymous with politics and interest. From this latter perspective, the international system is a barren area in which politics, understood as the rational pursuit of human values, does not operate.

Whatever the rhetoric of international politics, the reality of the international political system is seen by many in the North as the Hobbesian one of a brutish and nasty context in which states interact with each other in terms of power. Despite the lip service paid to the sovereign equality in the protocol of international diplomacy, in practice there exists a distinct hierarchy of states. This is headed by those which can impose their will on others, by armed force or economic leverage if necessary. It leads some Northern diplomats to regard the United Nations as a 'non-serious' institution because it fails to reflect the realities of power. They see bi-lateral diplomacy as much more important than participation in large multinational conferences. Yet this political realist vision of the world is in methodological terms inherently no more valid than the various varieties of idealism. It just instinctively and empirically appears to be so to people in the North, in part because human experiences and recent history reinforce it. For, if a person's own world is full of hierarchical power relations, why should he or she accept that the international political world operates any differently?

THEORY AND PRACTICE: SECURITY AND EQUITY IN THE MODERN WORLD

It should now be apparent that the context for any discussion of North–South security issues and the place of the developing world in the international political system is a dense thicket of complex methodological and philosophical questions. The problem posed by North–South security relations is not only one of different Northern and Southern interests and power capabilities. It also includes definitions of the North–South boundary and basic conceptions of the nature of the international political system.

The claim that political realism reflects the 'true' nature of the international political system is reinforced by the observable fact that representatives of the major industrialised states appear to act on this basis. The leading Western states regard the economic sphere as a separable area of activity from the political one. They may even contemplate relations of considerable conflict over trading issues, such as import tariffs, while yet retaining harmonious relations on security matters. Linkage is not an issue here unless frictions, in the shape of the United States Congress, should intervene and complicate matters.

Similarly, nuclear weapons are regarded by Northern states as an unchangeable fact of international political life. The focus of their security activities is the enhancement of national and alliance nuclear capabilities. In addition, these states pursue pragmatic arrangements to both limit those capabilities and reduce, if not eliminate, the risks of nuclear war. But for the political realist, the dangers of war arise out of political conflicts, not weapons. It is only through negotiation and diplomacy that this danger can be reduced, and not through unworkable attempts to achieve nuclear disarmament (which in itself would require a change in human nature). Thus to the political realist arrangements to reduce the risks of political conflict leading to war are seen as a global necessity. Any attempt to condemn such activities on the grounds that they are discriminatory or designed to further sectional interests can be argued to be against the global interest of preventing nuclear catastrophe.

This mode of argument, and the methodological and substantive assumptions underlying it, is persuasive to many in the North. It is challenged by the needs of the South, however, and the frustration arising from their non-fulfilment. If Third World states passively accept that the existing international political system is natural and unchanging, they accept also the corporate equivalent of imminent death. Elites in these states may continue to thrive despite lack of improvement in the economic and security situation within their state. Yet the real human problems of starvation and armed conflict will continue. If the international economic system operates through an unchangeable market mechanism, the future development of many states will rest on a random lottery over which they have no control. Yet what is the role of the state but to try to maximise that development in the interests of all its citizens?

For such states either a revolutionary change in the international political system, or acceptance by the North of a new vision of the reality of that system, appears to be a necessity. Hence the failed attempt to negotiate a New International Economic Order and their pressure for total nuclear disarmament. This latter originates from concern that the South will be physically destroyed as a result of events in which they had no role and over which they had no control, and from desires to divert resources released from disarmament into development. It also relates to questions of the power hierarchy in the international political system and the role of nuclear weapons in sustaining it. Yet ultimately the South knows that it cannot force the North into total nuclear disarmament by direct methods. It is within the domestic political environment of Northern states that such a change must originate. Only by creating strong domestic lobbies in the North akin to the Israeli lobby in the United States, lobbies which favour reform of the international political system in favour of the South, can such changes be achieved.

Northern perspectives of the international political system are thus dominated by political realist ideas, and because Southern diplomats and political leaders tacitly, if not overtly, accept this vision they tend to be self-deterred from acting in ways which ignore this framework. After all what is the point of implementing policies you do not believe will achieve their objective? This Western tradition of political thought has thus played a crucial role in preventing attempts to change the current international political system in a revolutionary manner. Western intellectual dominance over the Third World and the lack of any viable alternative mind set, even in Iran, are as much responsible for the relatively passive acceptance of the present situation as the existence of power mechanisms 'out there' or theories of an economic conspiracy between First and Third World elites. At the same time, this lack of acceptable alternative visions of the nature of the international political system makes possible a North/South dialogue on security issues. A basic consensus exists on how the international system functions, even if there is no acceptance of the consequences of that functioning.

The evolution of the international political system over the last three decades has thus been dominated by the cooption of Southern political and security elites into an international consensus on the nature of that system. In addition, they have accepted that Northern security issues, such as those concerning nuclear weapons, are key concerns on the international agenda and have been self-deterred from contemplating revolutionary action in respect of the international economic system. Above all, they have lacked any indigenous Southern intellectual alternatives to a political realist view of that system. Moreover, the leading non-aligned states such as Argentina, Brazil, India, Nigeria, Senegal and Mexico are seeking to attain increased power within this political realist international system, rather than attempting to change or overthrow it. Their vision of the future is one of 'we are the masters of your system now', rather than one of a new system which will be inherently more just or equitable than the old. Hence the concern among the elites in these states with issues such as technology transfers, nuclear power, aircraft production and space launchers. At the same time these concerns mean that such countries can be assimilated into any North/ South security arrangements, on an informal if not a formal basis, so long as tangible industrial benefits are offered to them. For their political arguments in the UN and elsewhere about discrimination and equity are as much designed to improve their international power position as to attain these objectives per se.

What does the future hold in this situation for Northern idealist ideas of a community of mankind and the proposition that the international political system is something other than a barren wasteland possessing little if no societal features? At first glance, not a lot, particularly if the state remains the dominant actor in the international system. But if attention is focussed upon the intangibles of the international system, rather than the tangibles, it is clear that, while the state as an institution has been strengthening itself over the last half century, at the same time the ability of ideas and information to penetrate its borders has been increasing. Our understanding of the consequences of the move to the modern information-based state upon both individual human values and the institution of the state is limited, not least because very few scholars or writers have attempted the difficult and speculative task of analysing what is taking place. But even the changes currently discernable within the USSR appear partially to be a response to the evolution in the nature of technology. Yet, if the state and the individual are affected by such changes, what will be its impact on the international political system? Are we moving to a global village linked by information technology, in which the international political system will reside in these communications channels? The current attempts to set up an alternative information order under UN auspices suggests that Southern leaders are aware of some of the consequences of this and are attempting to limit them. In future therefore will international security be more a function of the control and structuring of communications technology than possession of physical resources? What will be the North/South equivalent of the current East/West concern with Command, Control, Communications and Intelligence issues?

One implication of these developments and questions may be that the scope for developing ideas and activities appropriate to a community of mankind, rather than a minimalist international political system of states, may become enhanced. Yet the irony seems to be that it is the weak states of the Third World which may be more open to this marginalisation of the state through communications technology than the strong states of the North and their Southern clones. For a divide is already discernable between the industrially strong and potentially economically viable states of the South and the rest of the developing world.

At the same time, the ability of Northern states to actively shape what is taking place in the South may be diminishing. The case of Lebanon illustrates this process at work. As weak states crumble internal factions will be supported by competing developed states, their local proxies, other local states, proxy non-state groups and international non-state movements. For given the economic prospects for many Third World states, this type of governmental collapse seems likely to occur on an increasing scale. In such a complex environment of competing influences the role of individual states, however powerful, may be limited unless they choose to contemplate the uncertain prospects of direct military intervention.

If weak developing states collapse, how is the international political system to respond? Will the superpowers intervene or will they agree to leave them as barren territory; will other advanced states or developing and regional ones join in this self-denying ordnance; will it be possible to mobilise the United Nations or some other type of multinational force to restore cohesion and law and order to future Lebanons; or will they suck in the superpower's proxies and ultimately the superpowers themselves and pose the risk of initiating a thermonuclear confrontation? The options are many. The substance of the international system is changing fast. Yet whether states and the ideas which infuse the action of statesmen will permit a more egalitarian international society must at this stage be very doubtful. For, in the last resort, ideas about the nature of man, the state and the international political system seem to be more unchanging than the phenomena they attempt to describe and explain.

NOTES

1 This issue has been central to the evolution of the methodology of social science in general and the study of politics in particular. For a concise discussion see Cornelia Navari, 'Knowledge, the state and the state of nature', in M. Donelan (ed.), *The Reason of States* (London: Allen & Unwin, 1978), pp. 108–21.
2 Hans J. Morgenthau, *Politics among Nations* (Knopf, numerous editions). All succeeding references are to the 3rd edition, 1962.
3 Ibid., pp. 4–5.
4 Ibid., p. 8.
5 Ibid., p. 8.
6 Ibid., p. 10.
7 Ibid., p. 15.
8 Ibid., p. 10.
9 Ibid., p. 539.
10 Ibid., p. 539.
11 Ibid., p. 9.
12 Ibid., p. 9.

Part II: The developing countries and the international economic order

3   A view from the South

Marc A. Williams

The relationship between domestic economic performance and external economic conditions has occasioned much debate in the broad field of development studies. The perspective taken on the extent to which the global economy constrains or provides conditions conducive to economic development seems to rest on certain prior assumptions. The first concerns the relative importance to be attached to domestic and international factors. Insofar as the analyst stresses the salience of internal factors in generating growth then the impact of the external environment will be suitably minimised. Similarly, if one sees external conditions as determining, then the role of the international economic order will be magnified. The second assumption concerns the nature and consequences of capitalist development. On the one hand are those who stress the positive impact of capitalism in raising living standards, and on the other those who emphasise the development of underdevelopment. It follows then that we can delineate a number of positions dependent on the intensity with which a particular view is held and the internal coherence established between the different sets of propositions.

These questions underlie the major issues probed in this paper and it is imperative at the outset that we clarify our own position. Concrete analyses of the international political economy require a method of analysis which engages both theoretically and substantively with the totality of social relations. Such a method is available within the discourse of political economy. The historically specific issues of growth and development are located within a holist perspective which argues that causal explanation must rest at the level of the system and is not reducible to the behaviour of individual actors. State behaviour, then, is not solely the result of unit level attributes but is rather conditioned by the structure of the global system. In other words no separation is made between the internal and external in real terms. The domestic and international are not abstract categories which can be applied regardless of content. A variety of linkages exist between the two levels and the importance of one level cannot be known in advance but must be located historically. The dominant mode of production in the world today is capitalism. The international economic order thus reflects the dynamics, needs and interests of a world system shaped by capitalism. The experience of the post-war world shows both the robust nature of capitalism and its ability to bring material progress to most of the world's peoples and the uneven nature of growth and development.

This paper further presupposes that the economic and political differentiation of the developing countries should be a starting point for analysis. It is obvious that the developing countries are not homogeneous and their specific location within the global system significantly affects the effect of the international economic order on development prospects. Nevertheless, it is possible to look at their combined position and so view them as a single unit. This arises partly from a structural disjuncture in the global economy and partly from the existence of a Third World coalition which bargains for global economic reform. Moreover, we must guard against the fallacy of composition, e.g. expanded manufactures exports from Southeast Asia does not mean that the same possibilities exist for all developing countries. This is because they would be competing for the same market and secondly, would soon face Northern protectionism if their combined market share was held to be threatening. Hence, whilst disaggregation of country and product is necessary, aggregation can also be helpful in assessing broad trends.

Order in the context of the international political economy can have two meanings. First, order can be defined as the norms and rules which are prerequisite for the creation and maintenance of stable international economic relations.[1] Secondly, order can be used to denote the total sum of the complex web of arrangements which make up the world economy. In this sense the concept of order subsumes and includes the first concept of order. In other words order refers both to the rules and norms and the resulting matrix of relations which are derived for functionally specific but interrelated areas of economic transactions. Order is both a systemic requirement and a necessity for individual actors. All social orders face a problem of legitimation and a necessity to demonstrate a continuing relevance of the rules for the majority of those governed by the particular order.

This paper is a tentative and partial analysis of certain aspects of the relationship between the developing countries and the post-war liberal international economic order (LIEO). It will present an overview of the construction of the LIEO, its historical development and the economic performance of the developing countries, offer some observations on the role of the Bretton Woods organisations and discuss the issue of global reform.

THE LIBERAL INTERNATIONAL ECONOMIC ORDER AND THE DEVELOPING COUNTRIES

The rules of the game

It is often asserted that when the LIEO was created the developing countries were excluded because most of them were still colonies. It is further argued that this lack of representation resulted in the creation of a set of rules that were fundamentally biased against their interests.[2]

This lack of representation thesis is unconvincing when set against the historical fact that of the forty-four nations gathered at Bretton Woods twenty-seven are classifiable as developing countries.[3] The developing countries lacked not numerical superiority but the economic and political power to decisively alter the outcome of the negotiations. Planning for a world economic order was essentially an Anglo-American exercise which in the final phase reflected the preponderance of American economic and political power. American hegemony at the close of World War Two enabled the United States to create a multilateral system of trade and payments which protected and advanced American business and security interests. It does not follow, however, that because the order was an American creation that it was necessarily inimical to the interests of all other countries.

Two principles stood at the base of the new order – non-discrimination and multilateralism. States were enjoined to create the conditions whereby capital would move freely and trade would be unrestricted. It should be noted that this was a qualified rather than a simple liberalism.[4] In the first place it noted and accepted the importance of state actors in creating the framework of economic activity. Secondly, given the immense problems of reconstruction, practices which clearly breached these principles were allowed as temporary measures as long as participants were working towards a longer-term goal of liberalisation. Thirdly, it was never meant to be a *laissez-faire* system insofar as the necessity for some controls of a non-temporary nature was admitted. In practice certain mechanisms were created and others outlawed under the new regime. In the trade field this meant the gradual dismantling of tariff barriers, the binding of tariff rates once reduced, the elimination of quantitative restrictions, and the use of consultation and conciliation to settle disputes. In monetary matters the new order ushered in a regime of adjustable peg exchange rates, market convertibility and the provision of finance for countries in balance of payments difficulties. Three international organisations were created to both monitor and promote adherence to these principles and to work towards their adherence. The relationship between the developing countries and these organisations will be discussed below.

It is fashionable to assert that the Bretton Woods Order collapsed either in 1971 (American suspension of dollar-gold convertibility) or 1973 (the move to generalised floating by the world's major currencies). Nevertheless, there has been no sweeping set of changes to replace the Bretton Woods institutions and indeed the central pillars still exist. Some of the mechanisms have been adapted over time, e.g. the creation of Special Drawing Rights as a reserve asset; others have been circumvented e.g. the rise in non-tariff barriers countering the impact of reduced tariffs; but the underlying liberal philosophy still remains intact and it would be more accurate to speak of a post-Bretton Woods Order. In other words this view accepts the continuing centrality of Bretton Woods ideas and ideals in the prevailing order, i.e. a liberal market oriented approach.

The norms and rules and changes therein must be viewed in the context of changes in the patterns of global production and reproduction. Salient features of the world economy since 1945 include growing interdependence, the rise of transnational corporations, massive locational shifts of production, the relative decline of the United States and Great Britain, the rise of Japan and the Federal Republic of Germany, increased differentiation in the Third World with the rise of the newly industrialising countries (nics) and the newly found wealth of the oil exporters, and changing patterns in the gender division of labour.[5] The international economy can be characterised as experiencing two broad phases since World War Two: the long boom of rapid growth and expansion which lasted until about 1973 and the years of crisis from the early 1970s to the present.

Performance

Assessment of the economic performance of the developing countries under the LIEO reveals some interesting statistics but does not point in the direction of inescapable conclusions. There is little doubt that the developing countries experienced growth rates not only in advance of the industrial countries but in excess of what those countries achieved at a similar 'stage' in their development.[6] Between 1950 and 1975 the developing countries achieved average annual growth rates of 5.6 per cent and the industrial countries 4.7 per cent.[7] The onset of global recession reduced these rates to 2.2 per cent for the industrial countries and to 3.3 per cent for the developing countries in the period 1980 to 1985.[8] These aggregates, however, conceal wide regional and country variations. Many developing countries have experienced growth rates significantly below the trend.

In the trade field the experience has been mixed. John Spraos calculated that between 1950 and 1977 the relative price of developing countries' primary commodity exports had done well by the standards of the pre-war decades.[9] He concluded that there was no strong negative terms of trade trend. However, the 1980s have witnessed unfavourable conditions in world commodity markets. The average annual rate of decline 1981–5 for the export prices of non-oil primary commodities was 7.5 per cent.[10] For a number of commodities prices have fallen to their lowest levels in the post-war period. Another salient feature of the 1980s has been the increase in Third World debt. The debt crisis is both economic and financial and has provided constraints for all the indebted nations, not only the most heavily indebted. The magnitude of the debt problem is apparent at a glance at three of the most important indicators between 1980 and 1985. The ratio of debt to GNP increased from 21.1 per cent to 33.0 per cent, the ratio of debt to exports increased from 90 per cent to 136 per cent.[11] The debt crisis is the result of a number of factors including the expansionary policies of middle-income countries during the 1974–6 recession, the recycling of OPEC surpluses, the rise in interest rates, the increasing amount of loans denominated in floating interest rates and the growth in private credit in preference to official credit. Direct foreign investment has increasingly shifted away from raw material extraction towards manufacturing. What appears to be occurring is the relocation of certain types of industrial activity away from the advanced economies to certain Third World countries. Fröbel, Heinrichs and Kreye[12] argue that a new international division of labour is being created in which through the establishment of free production zones and world market factories industrialisation is taking place in some developing countries but that this is a limited form of economic growth which intensifies the tendency towards uneven and dependent development. On the other hand, a more optimistic assessment of the development prospects of the nics in Asia relying on this form of industrialisation is given by Edward Chen.[13]

The record of the post-war LIEO is one of uneven growth and development. The impact of the LIEO is mediated by particular local factors in specific cases but as a group the developing countries have had to adjust to adverse changes in the global environment since the early 1970s. Instability in the international monetary system, higher oil prices, falling commodity prices, global recession and fluctuating interest rates have all contributed to a climate of uncertainty. The Bretton Woods institutions have made some attempts to adapt to the changing environment but increasingly the major states have conducted important negotiations outside the institutional structure agreed at the end of the war. The central organisations have attempted to preserve the liberal system but the relevance of these principles in a changed environment is debatable. Moreover, the extent to which the LIEO, even before the onset of increased turbulence, adequately fulfilled the needs of the developing countries is open to question. The market is a social product which does not correspond to textbook stipulations. Political power, differential bargaining strength and unequal access to information contribute to the creation of various market imperfections. The LIEO is a particular market order and the extent to which it promotes efficiency and equity is a theoretical and empirical question which cannot be investigated here. Evidence exists, however, which suggests that the overall impact of the LIEO on developing countries may be negative. Helleiner has argued that there are major imperfections in the markets of most crucial concern to the developing countries and therefore the distribution of gains under the LIEO is inequitable.[14] Spraos argues that the traditional pattern of specialisation by developing countries on income inelastic primary commodities leads to incremental inequalisation.[15] Insofar as the LIEO proscribes interventionist solutions to correct this bias it contributes to the continuation of inequality.

INTERNATIONAL ECONOMIC ORGANISATIONS AND THE DEVELOPING COUNTRIES

This section presents a brief sketch of the performance of the major international economic organisations (IEOs), with an emphasis on differing interpretations of their rates of success. We can apply three criteria to assess the performance of IEOs. These are efficiency (the extent to which they promote an efficient allocation of global resources), stability (the extent to which they contribute to the smooth functioning of the international economy and promote orderly change), and economic justice (the extent to which they reduce disparities in income and allocate increased wealth so that those members starting from a position of advantage do not increase their gains merely as a result of the original inequality). The Bretton Woods organisations were established with the first two criteria in mind but this does not preclude the application of the third. The record of the International Monetary Fund (IMF), World Bank Group and the General Agreement on Tariffs and Trade (GATT) in fulfilling the objectives of efficiency, stability and economic justice is a mixed one. IEOs exist within a changing global environment and their ability to achieve states' objectives is conditioned by the impact of environmental variables. Therefore in assessing the performance of the three IEOs some consideration will be taken of the changing environment.

In some respects the IMF has responded creatively to the challenges posed and the needs of the developing countries. It has extended the range of financial services it provides to take account of the special requirements of the developing countries. The Compensatory Financing Facility and the Buffer Stock Financing Facility were created in respect of commodity problems. The Extended Fund Facility and the Supplementary Fund Facility were designed to meet the serious balance of payments problems attendant on the oil price rise. The IMF has also been at the forefront of adjustment efforts in the management of the debt crisis. The IMF's greatest impact arises from its role as a lender to countries experiencing balance of payments disequilibrium. Fierce controversy rages over the Fund's stabilisation programmes. Critics argue that the IMF employs a rigid monetarist approach which fails to differentiate among countries and between endogenous and exogenous causes of balance of payments problems. Policy prescriptions are usually deflationary and often hit the poorest members of the borrowing country.[16] IMF supporters retort by stressing the flexibility and variability of the Fund's approach.[17] Critics maintain that IMF conditionality far from alleviating the problem only makes it worse. The IMF counters by arguing that it has a medium-to long-term strategy which does succeed and that difficulties arise from the failure of governments to act sooner. A comprehensive survey of IMF stabilisation policies concluded that 'there was not a stereotyped IMF package which was applied to all cases but that there were fairly severe limits to the degree of flexibility which the Fund achieved in its programme during the 1970s'[18] and argued that IMF programmes have limited effectiveness.[19]

Wider questions pertain to the role of the IMF in the international monetary system. The IMF has been a reactive rather than an initiatory organisation and decision making in international monetary matters is often taken by the major industrialised countries outside the institutional framework of the Fund. The IMF has failed to provide conditions of stability but has been instrumental in maintaining some semblance of order and discipline in the international financial system, especially since the move to generalised floating in 1973. The commitment to liberalisation underlying IMF interventionist policies has had a questionable effect on efficiency. Moreover, the asymmetrical adjustment mechanism which penalises deficit countries has not contributed to an enhancement of economic justice.

Like its twinned institution the World Bank has shown a degree of adaptability to the needs of the developing countries. The International Finance Corporation (IFC) was established in 1956 to promote private sector growth in developing countries by mobilising domestic and foreign capital. The International Development Association (IDA) was created in 1960 to provide soft loans for the poorest countries. The Bank also changed its development philosophy in the 1970s with the rejection of the trickle down theory and placed a new emphasis on basic needs and a focus on rural development. For example agriculture and rural development increased its share of Bank lending from 8.6 per cent in 1963 to 29.3 per cent in 1986.[20] The World Bank is often accused of taking a conservative stance, e.g. only financing the foreign exchange costs of projects and being obsessed with growth. It is also criticised for the intrusion of political criteria into its lending policy.[21] There are a variety of constraints which prohibit the World Bank from becoming a development agency. It is a bank and as such has to ensure that countries repay their loans and it also has to operate in private capital markets which are dominated by multinational banks and large insurance companies. Furthermore it is dependent on the financial contributions of its members especially in respect of the IDA. Nevertheless, the World Bank has provided considerable finance for development on favourable terms. The extent to which one thinks that this has improved efficiency, stability and justice depends on the view one takes of foreign aid and an analysis of the World Bank's lending activities.[22] Despite various policy changes especially during Robert McNamara's tenure as President of the Bank it has retained a strong liberal philosophy.

Unlike the other two organisations the GATT is more of a forum than a service organisation. It is only accidentally a part of the Bretton Woods framework since it was meant to be a temporary device until a fully fledged International Trade Organisation was created. GATT's main contribution to the achievement of LIEO objectives is through the series of tariff cutting rounds which are held periodically. To date seven of these rounds have been completed, the most significant being the Kennedy Round (1964–7) and the Tokyo Round (1973–9). The GATT has been very successful in reducing barriers to trade, e.g. both Kennedy and Tokyo rounds achieved tariff cuts in excess of 30 per cent. However increasing protectionism in the 1970s and 1980s suggests that trade liberalisation is easier to achieve in times of prosperity. Nevertheless, the influence of liberal norms in restraining further protectionist action should not be discounted.

Assessment of GATT's contribution is dependent on the view taken of the beneficial effects of a free trade regime. The developing countries have adopted a contradictory position in respect of the GATT arguing for increased protection for their home markets, but freer entry to world markets for their exports. The attempt to amend GATT's rules has been partially successful but in so doing it has undermined efforts to preserve an open system which might be more beneficial for the developing countries. The erosion of the principle of non-discrimination was first recognised by the addition of Part IV to the GATT and strengthened by the waiver which sanctioned the creation of a Generalised System of Preferences (GSP). The resulting confusion over non-uniformity of treatment has not worked to the advantage of the developing countries since it has aided protectionist elements in the industrialised world. Moreover, the gains from the GSP have been very limited. Although GATT has been successful in reducing barriers to trade in manufactures it has failed to do so for agricultural products, thus the results have been biased against the traditional exports of the developing countries. Furthermore GATT has been unable to stem the tide of protectionism aimed specifically at Third World countries, e.g. the Multi-Fibre Arrangement. The resort to non-tariff barriers has also hurt Third World exporters. Finally, negotiations are conducted on the basis of principal supplier and buyer thus marginalising developing countries. GATT contributed to system stability and efficiency particularly during the years of expansion and growth, since when it has been fighting an uphill struggle against protectionist tendencies. The tendency of free trade regimes to work in favour of the strongest countries coupled with a failure to liberalise agriculture and inhibit protection against competitive Southern manufactures exports points to limited success in securing greater economic justice.

Developing countries are concerned with the distribution of influence in IEOs. They question the extent to which the liberal economic philosophy espoused by the Bretton Woods organisations adequately serves their interests. Attempts to change the LIEO include attempts to restructure the orientations of these organisations and to imprové the South's influence in decision making. The international economic order is a material and an intellectual construct. The perceptions of actors are important in ascribing political legitimacy to the order. The next section examines the perceptions of the developing countries of the LIEO and their demands for global reform. '

REFORMING THE INTERNATIONAL ECONOMIC ORDER

Analysis of the South's attempt to reform the existing international economic order which began with the New International Economic Order (NIEO) proposals in 1974 tends to view this as a political challenge based on new found commodity power. An historical analysis, however, reveals the NIEO to be the culmination of a series of reform attempts which began with the push for a Special United Nations Fund for Economic Development in the 1950s. Indeed, a definite Southern interest is identifiable at the creation of the Bretton Woods Order. It was Latin American pressure which added the development role to the proposed international bank for reconstruction and in negotiations for the Havana Charter developing countries expressed a distinct view on the organisation of commodity markets. The non-ratification of the Havana Charter created an institutional lacuna in world trade which the developing countries persistently attempted to fill and the creation of the United Nations Conference on Trade and Development (UNCTAD) in 1964 was the culmination of efforts to fill this institutional vacuum. The founding of the Group of 77 (G77) at UNCTAD I in 1964 provided Southern countries with a pressure group to campaign for global economic reform.

Examination of the demands made for reform by the developing countries since 1964 reveals a constancy and a continuity which suggests that the NIEO is neither new nor a radical break from past practice.[23] Reform proposals relate both to world market organisation and the distribution of influence in IEOs. The major demands of the G77 can be summarised as follows: (i) the creation of orderly and stable commodity markets which provide for equitable remuneration to the producers of primary products; (ii) increased access to Northern markets for their manufactured and semi-manufactured exports; (iii) increased aid flows on improved terms; (iv) greater accountability of transnational corporations; (v) permanent sovereignty over natural resources; (vi) increased effective participation in the international decision-making. Some moderate success had been attained prior to the onset of NIEO negotiations. For example, the developed countries had agreed to provide economic aid equivalent to 0.7 per cent of GNP, reciprocity was no longer a universal rule in trade negotiations, and the Committee of Twenty established to address reform of the international monetary system included nine developing countries.

Grudging piecemeal reform with no guarantee that the acceptance of a new principle transformed real relations, coupled with the success of OPEC in quadrupling oil prices between 1973 and 1974 ushered in an era of optimism and concentrated pressure by the developing countries. The gains from the GSP are limited because of limited product coverage, safeguard measures and the increased importance of non-tariff barriers. As a percentage of GNP real flows of development assistance declined from 0.52 per cent at the beginning of the 1960s to 0.34 per cent at the beginning of the 1970s. Futhermore, many economists argue that developing nations in pushing for non-reciprocal concessions gave away the main instrument governments have for lowering their own trade barriers, namely, the ability to tell the protected home industry that protection must be lowered as part of a reciprocal bargaining process. Many developing countries are faced with over-protected domestic industries hence increasing domestic inefficiency.

OPEC action heralded the false dawn of an increase in the 'power of the powerless'. North–South negotiations were conducted in an international economic environment clouded with uncertainty and lacking effective leadership since the decline of American hegemony. Growing interdependence did not result in a similarity of perception concerning common interest. Once the threat of effective commodity power had passed, the leading Northern states were disinclined to engage in meaningful negotiations. Moreover, the Third World coalition found it more difficult to maintain effective unity in the face of an external economic environment which accentuated the apparent disparities in income and resources among its members. North–South global negotiations have been in stalemate since 1980 and there are no visible signs of life being injected into the dialogue. Two primary questions can be asked with respect to the present situation and the immediate future. First, is reform desirable, i.e. does the international economic order need changing? Secondly, is reform feasible, i.e. what is the realistic probability that change can be negotiated? A set of secondary questions follow from these two and include consideration of the type of reform, the negotiating venue and the organisation of the negotiations. Answers to these questions depend on the perspective taken by the analyst. I suspect that, in the light of the debt crisis, continuing monetary instability and rising protectionism, there are few who would argue that change is unnecessary. But the ability of the current system to survive various crises without a major collapse leads many to accept the soundness of the basic framework and to argue in favour of limited amendments and/or a return to the rules agreed at Bretton Woods. This perspective gives little comfort to the developing countries since their interests with the exception of debt are treated as marginal to system maintenance. An opposed perspective rejects reformism and exhorts the developing countries to delink from the prevailing order. Somewhere between these two opposed views are those who stress the interdependence of North and South and see the possibility of mutual benefit flowing from a series of reforms.

Perspectives on the feasibility of change depend on prior assumptions concerning the configurations of power in the global system and the creation and maintenance of regimes.[24] If the South is held to have some power either because its assent is needed to legitimise the order by the hegemony or through threat of debt default or commodity power then the possibility of change is held to be reasonably good. The perspective which stresses Northern dominance in the international political economy negates the possibility of change. Similarly, if one argues that a hegemony is necessary for the creation of an international order then the current polycentric international system with the absence of a sufficiently dominant economic power fails to satisfy the conditions under which such an order would emerge.

Prospects for all-embracing negotiations similar to the NIEO appear non-existent. The most feasible scenario is one in which particular regimes are negotiated. In other words a return to the piecemeal attempts which characterised the reform effort prior to 1974. We should, however, concentrate not solely on the desirability or feasibility of change but on the direction of change. Discussion should focus on the interests served by particular proposals. We need to ask to what extent do increased aid flows or improved commodity prices benefit the poorest people in poor countries. Global negotiations take place between governments and redistributionist efforts take the state as the basic unit. It does not follow however that North–South redistribution will ameliorate the condition of the rural and urban poor. Northern spokesmen are of course frequently willing to point this out but this is often done with the cynical intent of blocking any proposed change to the status quo. Southern negotiators resist any attempt to link international redistributional measures with internal ones. And yet, the domestic order cannot be completely divorced from the international order. Global reform should not be viewed as solely encompassing international rules and regulations but must also include national policy. This is by no means an easy task but the first stage lies in the conceptualisation of the international economic order so that it encompasses both levels.

The intimate connection between the two levels can be seen in a consideration of the role of the state. Throughout the South the state is crucial mediator between foreign economic forces and local resources. From the right to the left of the political spectrum the state is instrumental in setting the conditions under which economic development takes place. For example, the capital-labour relationship is mediated by the state which sets the terms and conditions under which capital and labour interact, e.g. laws in respect of trade unions. Local rules influence the decisions of transnational corporations to invest and the demands of foreign capital influences state policy in respect of the organisation of its domestic economy. The differential success of developing countries in attracting foreign capital is partly a consequence of the domestic climate with respect to the welcome given to foreign investors. The foreign trade regime adopted by a particular state affects its ability to benefit from the international economic order. Liberal or illiberal domestic trade regimes are rewarded or punished by the wider international economic order. The ability of developing countries to benefit from the international economic order is differentiated by the role and location in the global processes of production, surplus extraction and capital accumulation.

CONCLUSION

It has been argued above that the effects of the LIEO must be assessed in the context of the development of post-war capitalism. The world capitalist system has produced economic progress and a rise in living standards in the developing world. This growth has been uneven and patchy and the experience of individual countries depends on the particular linkages which exist between the domestic social formation and the global capitalist system. The expansion and contraction of domestic forces of production occurs within an evolving global framework. The general features of global accumulation and the international division of labour in conjunction with local policy choices determine the outcome for specific social formations. In this paper we have been expressly concerned with the institutional features of world trade and payments and have tried to show that the application and relevance of rules and norms and the behaviour of IEOs are to be understood in the context of a dynamic international economic environment.

To date Third World elites have campaigned for reform which assigns neutrality to the domestic variable. They have questioned the legitimacy of the prevailing order but this dissatisfaction is based (for the most part) not on a rejection of the mode of production which sustains the order but rather on the liberal principles which enshrine a particular form of capitalist organisation. They demanded redistributionist measures which ameliorate some of the negative tendencies of the unrestricted play of market forces. However, it must be recognised that many contemporary practices in both developed and developing countries are far from liberal and it is debatable to what extent the current order is a liberal one. Nevertheless, the organisational ideologies of the central international economic organisations are liberal and their command over material and intellectual resources and ability to influence other actors and to set the conditions under which certain types of transactions take place contributes to the continuing relevance of the market oriented philosophy.

Concerted campaigns to reform the LIEO have been mounted in international fora but state policies have reflected local elites' calculation of interest. Hence a wide variety of postures is discernible at levels below that of global bargaining. The contradictions inherent in the position of the developing countries fosters an approach which favours both adaptation to and rejection of the LIEO. Third World pressure has succeeded in implementing marginal and incremental changes in international economic regimes but it has been unable to secure radical structural change. Lack of effective influence in the shaping of international economic divisions and a feeling of powerlessness in the face of external shocks help to maintain the Southern coalition. The LIEO is also a political order and as such will be subject to political challenge.

In the context of global security considerations, an order which is unjust and inefficient will promote both economic and political instability. A climate of increased economic insecurity hinders the development of peaceful, democratic politics. The failure of Third World elites to meet the economic demands of their populace will lead either to mounting repression or to violent struggles from below. At the global level North/South conflict over the allocation of resources will continue and will be shaped by changing production patterns and technology and actors' perceptions of gains and losses.

NOTES

1 For a similar definition see Lars Anell, *Recession, the Western Economies and the Changing World Order* (London: Frances Pinter, 1981), p. 12
2 See for example Orlando Letelier and Michael Moffat, *The International Economic Order (Part 1)* (Washington DC: Transnational Institute, 1977), p. 12.

3 Bahram Nowzad, *The IMF and its critics* (Princeton Essays in International Finance, No. 146, 1981), p. 3 makes a similar point but he asserts that superiority of numbers meant an important role in the shaping of the institutions.

4 See J. G. Ruggie, 'International regimes, transactions and change: embedded liberalism in the postwar economic order', *International Organization* 36 (1982), pp. 379–415.

5 See Swasti Mitter, *Common Fate, Common Bond* (London: Pluto Press, 1986).

6 S. Kuznets, 'Aspects of post-World War Two growth in LDCs', in A. M. Targ, E. M. Westfield and J. E. Worley (eds.), *Evolution, Welfare and Time in Economics* (Lexington, Mass.: Lexington Books, 1976), p. 42.

7 S. D. Krasner, *Structural Conflict: The Third World Against Global Liberalism* (Berkeley: University of California Press, 1985), p. 97.

8 World Bank, *World Development Report 1986* (Washington DC: World Bank, 1986).

9 John Spraos, *Inequalising Trade?* (Oxford: Clarendon Press, 1983), pp. 63–8.

10 UNCTAD, *Commodity Outlook 1986* (Geneva: UNCTAD, 1986), p. 1.

11 World Bank, 1986.

12 F. Fröbel, J. Heinrichs and O. Kreye, *The News International Division of Labour* (Cambridge University Press, 1980).

13 Edward K. Y. Chen, 'The newly industrializing countries in Asia: growth experience and prospects', in R. A. Scalapino *et. al.* (eds.), *Asian Economic Development–Present and Future* (Berkeley: Institute of East Asian Studies, University of California Press, 1985), pp. 131–60.

14 G. K. Helleiner, 'World market imperfections and the developing countries', in G. K. Helleiner, *International Economic Disorder* (London and Basingstoke: Macmillan, 1980), pp. 22–61.

15 Spraos, *Inequalising Trade?* p. 3.

16 See e.g. E. A. Brett, *The World Economy Since the War* (London and Basingstoke: Macmillan, 1985), pp. 219–26.

17 Nowzad, *The IMF and its Critics*, pp. 11–22.

18 T. Killick (ed.), *The Quest for Economic Stabilisation: The IMF and the Third World* (London: Heinemann and ODI, 1984), p. 221.

19 Killick, *The Quest for Economic Stabilisation*, pp. 227–69.

20 World Bank, *Annual Reports 1963 and 1986* (Washington DC: World Bank, 1963 and 1986).

21 See e.g. Cheryl Payer, *The World Bank: A Critical Analysis* (New York: Monthly Review Press, 1982).

22 For a critical but sympathetic analysis of the World Bank see A. L. Ayres, *Banking on the Poor* (Cambridge, Mass.: MIT Press, 1983).

23 See K. P. Sauvant (ed.), *The Collected Documents of the Group of 77* (New York: Oceana Publications, 1982), 6 vols.

24 See J. A. Hart, *The New International Economic Order* (London and Basingstoke: Macmillan, 1983), pp. 62–85 for a discussion of negotiating regime change.

4   A view from the north

Graham Bird

Recent years have witnessed considerable debate about the position of developing countries in the world economy, including how far they were advantaged under the Bretton Woods system. Following the breakdown of this system in the early 1970s, questions relating to the design of a New International Economic Order (NIEO), more beneficial to the developing world, have been raised. Effects on these countries of the international financial arrangements that superseded the Bretton Woods system have also been debated. Such questions have frequently been discussed in relation to the notion of a North–South divide.

This chapter is concerned specifically with monetary matters. It reviews how the developing countries have fared since 1973, when the Bretton Woods monetary arrangements were replaced by generalised exchange rate flexibility as well as by a move to the private capital market as the principal means of providing balance of payments finance. The question of whether the 'South' currently constitutes a special case, with clearly delineated problems in terms of the size and nature of its balance of payments, is raised. Various options for future international financial arrangements are considered: first, an NIEO involving far reaching, radical, though inter-temporally discrete, reforms to a wide range of issues; secondly, a more piecemeal, marginalist, or incremental reform of existing institutions and arrangements; and thirdly, the introduction of a more exclusive set of Southern solutions. The final section offers a few concluding comments on the political economy of international financial reform of relevance to developing countries.[1]

Trade issues and policies are not discussed directly, but any discussion of international financial problems almost unavoidably involves indirect reference to trade. Yet, at the same time, it is no longer valid to see international finance simply as the hand maiden of trade. Financial flows now tend to over-shadow trade flows in terms of their quantitative significance and it may therefore be appropriate to concentrate on them.

THE POST BRETTON WOODS ERA

Lack of space precludes a detailed discussion of the Bretton Woods system; a knowledge of the basic assumptions and workings of that system are assumed here. Suffice it to say, that while the developing countries derived some significant and in certain ways increasing benefits from the system, they might have derived more had the system been modified in certain ways. For example, it is possible that developing countries would have done better had the Keynes Plan been adopted in 1944, with its advocacy of greater exchange rate adjustment, the introduction of an International Clearing Union, and a new international reserve asset, bancor, which might have been used to help finance economic development in poorer countries as well as commodity stabilisation schemes.[2] However, it is more difficult to see how simply opting out of the system would have yielded any advantage to developing countries.

Following the dollar crisis of 1971 and the related collapse of the Bretton Woods system, the trend towards greater recognition of the balance of payments problems of developing countries initially continued. However, in the 1980s there is evidence to suggest that this trend was, at least temporarily, reversed. Here, some of the organisational changes that occurred are outlined, along with the principal changes in the general operation of the international 'system' (or 'non-system') during the period since the early 1970s, especially as these impinged on developing countries.

Institutional changes specific to developing countries

The failure of the Smithsonian Agreement in 1971 to shore up the Bretton Woods system led to an attempt at a full assessment of the international monetary system, under the auspices of the Fund in The Committee on Reform of the International Monetary System and Related Issues (The Committee of Twenty or C-20). The interests of less developed countries (LDCs) were well represented on the Committee, with nine out of twenty members. Two technical groups set up by C-20 looked at issues of specific concern to LDCs, namely the SDR/aid link and the transfer of real resources. The Committee's report and 'Outline of Reform' urged that future international monetary arrangements be organised so as 'to give positive encouragement to economic development and to promote an increasing net flow of real resources to developing countries'.

The report and 'Outline of Reform' of C-20 are significant landmarks in the evolving relations between the International Monetary Fund (IMF) and LDCs. Although for some years eight or nine Executive Directors from LDCs had sat on the Fund's Executive Board, for the first time LDCs now participated fully in an attempt to remake the international monetary system, and the proposed changes envisaged that the system should specifically cater for the problems of development. Some distance had been travelled from Bretton Woods.

Although, subsequent to the C-20 discussions, the IMF has maintained its concern for LDCs' problems, the move towards flexible exchange rates and the increasing significance of private financing eroded the central position of the Fund in the international monetary system. Even so, the momentum generated by C-20 was not totally dissipated. Indeed, concern with the problems facing LDCs was enhanced by the rising price of oil and its implications for non-oil LDCs. The economic situation of the developing countries and ways of protecting their economic growth from the effects of world inflation and recession became recurrent themes at annual meetings, and resulted in modifications to the operation of the IMF.

Following a suggestion of C-20, a Joint Ministerial Committee of the Boards of Governors of the Bank and the Fund on the Transfer of Real Resources to Developing Countries (Development Committee) was set up, thus institutionally linking international monetary matters to economic development. The Committee has concerned itself with the transfer of real resources of LDCs, paying particular attention to the least developed countries and those LDCs most seriously affected by payments difficulties. Further suggestions made by C-20 resulted in the establishment in 1974, for a two-year period, of an Oil Facility (OF), the specific purpose of which was to assist countries to cope with the payments implications of the increased cost of oil. To reduce the interest rate burden associated with OF drawings the Fund also established a Subsidy Account to make concessionary assistance available to low-income LDCs that had been most seriously affected by the oil crisis. The partial insulation from the implications of increases in import prices provided by the OF, and the subsidisation of interest rates, were significant changes in the relationship between the IMF and developing countries.

As a further response to the deterioration in the world economic situation the CFF was liberalised in 1975 and again in 1979. In 1981 it was integrated with a scheme to assist countries facing balance of payments problems as a result of excess cereal imports; furthermore the percentage of quota that could be cumulatively drawn from the Fund, exclusive of the Compensatory Financing Facility (CFF) and Buffer Stock Financing Facility (BSFF) drawings, was raised.

Other institutional changes within the IMF were the introduction of the Extended Fund Facility (EFF), the Trust Fund and the Supplementary Financing Facility (SFF). In principle the EFF provides a significant extra dimension to Fund involvement with the formulation of economic policy in member countries, since, prior to its introduction, the Fund had appeared to be more narrowly interested in short-term financial stabilisation policies. The EFF gives some recognition to the fact that payments difficulties may constitute the monetary manifestation of structural misallocation, and specifically views the balance of payments in the context of development policy. The main purpose of the Trust Fund was to provide eligible LDCs, basically the least developed countries, with low conditionality and concessionary balance of payments assistance. Its establishment demonstrated a willingness by the IMF to use international monetary reform, in this case a reduction in the role of gold, as a way of benefiting the poorest countries. The Supplementary Financing Facility, set up in 1979, offered a repayment period on drawings longer than that associated with conventional stand-bys, so it could be expected to be of particular help to developing countries in which adjustment is relatively slow. Furthermore, a concessionary element to drawings under SFF was provided to low income countries by a two-tier Subsidy Account designed to reduce the associated interest rate. Subsidy arrangements were, however, not applied to the policy on Enlarged Access to Resources which superseded the SFF.

In the early 1970s there also seemed to be the beginning of a reappraisal of the Fund's involvement in economic stabilisation. The outcome of this, made more necessary by events in the 1970s, was, one suspects, reflected by changes in policy regarding the content and repayment period of programmes made at the end of the 1970s. Previously the IMF had tended to respond to pressures from developing countries by enlarging the range of its facilities rather than by changing its policy conditions. However, in the late 1970s and early 1980s there were some potentially significant changes, such as lengthening the possible programme period for stand-bys and the 1979 Review of the Guidelines on Conditionality. The former appeared to offer countries the chance to pursue rather longer-term balance of payments policies, thus allowing the Fund to put greater emphasis on structurally oriented policies and on supply, as opposed to demand, management. The latter, while endorsing the Fund's belief in conditionality, included what seemed to be certain changes from the previous position. The most frequently quoted example of liberalisation was the statement in the Review that 'the Fund will pay due regard to the domestic social and political objectives, the economic priorities, and the circumstances of members, including the causes of their balance of payments problem'. However, the Review also emphasised the need to encourage members to adopt corrective measures at an early stage in their balance of payments difficulties and recognised that in many cases a longer period of adjustment is required than normally associated with a stand-by arrangement. In fact neither change turned out to be of great practical importance. Apart from a brief interlude discussed later, the Fund's preference remained strongly for short-run programmes, even though a series of them might be negotiated. Meanwhile, the 1979 Review was, in retrospect, much more an attempt to clarify and codify existing practice on conditionality than to break new ground, and the reference to social and political factors had little discernible effect on actual lending policies. The Fund clearly retained its views concerning, first, the need for countries to adjust irrespective of the origin of their balance of payments problems and, secondly, what policies were, generally speaking, most useful in bringing about such adjustment. The logic of a more supply oriented approach to adjustment was largely rejected by the Fund for a series of theoretical and operational reasons, and sound demand management remained the centrepiece of Fund-supported programmes.

However, while downplaying the practical significance of the 1979 Review in changing the nature of conditionality, there have undeniably been variations over recent years in the stringency with which conditionality has been exercised. For a time at the end of the 1970s and the beginning of the 1980s there was a move towards a rather more liberal approach. Programmes that in previous years might not have been were approved by the Executive Board, longer programme periods were used, loans were more heavily front-end loaded, waivers were more easily available, and borrowers were not always required to eliminate negative real interest rates or cut the fiscal deficit significantly. However, with political changes in certain important member countries, notably the US, and some feeling within the Fund that the changes had not been successful, this relaxation proved to be short lived.[3]

The reversal of the attempt to liberalise conditionality was not the only thing that weakened the Bretton Woods institutions from the viewpoint of developing countries in the early 1980s. In addition, the CFF was deliberalised by making its resources more conditional, representing a clear departure from its original purpose.[4] In real terms the size of resources available from the Fund fell. Special Drawing Rights (SDR) allocations failed to be made on a regular basis. Surveillance did little to reduce exchange rate volatility or to encourage industrial countries to pursue policies which were more helpful to developing countries. Moreover IDA replenishments were regarded by many outside the US as inadequate. Against this, the Fund became heavily involved in dealing with the developing countries' debt problems, and the tabling of the Baker proposals[5] on debt put forward by the US could mark some small reassertion of the earlier trend.

General operational changes, and their implications for developing countries

A number of differences between the Bretton Woods system and the set of international financial arrangements that superseded it have had important implications for developing countries. Most importantly amongst these are: first, the move away from generalised fixed to generalised floating exchange rates; secondly, the move to the market place as a means of providing balance of payments financing; thirdly, the lack of effective policy coordination between industrial countries; fourthly, the move away from a structured international financial system implied by these first three changes; and fifthly, the rise of the 'new protectionism'. Along with, and perhaps in relation to these developments, political changes in a number of important industrial countries around the end of the 1970s and beginning of the 1980s brought with them a change in economic philosophy. This involved a much stronger belief in the efficiency of private markets and therefore a much weaker commitment to the need for government intervention. In addition, macro-economic policy in industrial countries became much more firmly based on an attempt to reduce inflation through the pursuit of restrictionary monetary and fiscal instruments; although fiscal constraints were fairly dramatically relaxed in the US as the 1980s proceeded. How did these changes effect developing countries?

In the case of floating exchange rates, developing countries were largely opposed to the introduction of generalised floating for a number of reasons. First, it was felt that through the uncertainty that would be associated with them they would have a globally anti-trade bias. Secondly, and more specifically from their own perspective, developing countries feared that they would have insufficient access to forward cover and would therefore be in a particularly disadvantageous position with regard to such uncertainty. A third concern was that, since many developing countries might continue to peg the value of their currencies to one specific, though not necessarily the same major world currency, variations in the value of these major currencies *vis-à-vis* each other might be inappropriate for developing countries, leading to disequilibrium in developing countries' real effective exchange rates – the so-called 'third currency phenomenon'. Related to this phenomenon was the worry, fourthly, that generalised exchange rate flexibility would increase the need for international reserves in some developing countries, even though globally greater flexibility in exchange rates would be seen as reducing the need for reserves. Moreover, exchange rate flexibility, it was feared, would have implications for the optimum composition of reserves, since an additional risk of loss through a depreciation in the currency in which reserves are denominated is introduced, calling for more sophisticated reserve management. Fifthly, where debt is denominated in currencies which appreciate, its real value may rise and debt management also becomes more of a problem.

Although it is true that an attempt to maintain generalised fixed exchange rates during the post 1973 period would have resulted in the pursuit of domestic economic and trade policies in the developed world which would have been unfavourable to developing countries, and that, to some extent, the cost of generalised exchange rate flexibility can be minimised through developing countries' own exchange rate policies,[6] there is considerable empirical support for claiming that at least some of these fears were justified. Third currency instability has caused changes in real effective exchange rates, and exchange rate flexibility may well have constrained the growth of trade.[7] At the same time there is little causal evidence to support the claim that flexible exchanges have enabled countries to pursue policies of demand expansion and trade liberalisation.

While these observations suggest that developing countries have a common interest in reforming the global exchange rate regime to remove excessive flexibility, it is also the case that some developing countries have been more adversely affected than others, depending on the pattern of their trade, the currency denomination of their reserves and debts, their access to forward cover, and their own exchange rate policy.

Regarding *private market financing of payments deficits*, it was in the 1970s and early 1980s that the private banking sector took over the principal role in providing balance of payments financing to developing countries. However, the pattern of lending was heavily skewed. Recipients of bank loans, essentially the middle-income exporters of manufactures (and oil), were able to de-emphasise adjustment or to select longer term adjustment strategies. Non-recipients were, however, often forced to turn to the Fund where they became subject to conditionality which favoured short-term balance of payments stabilisation. The attitudes of different developing countries to this alteration in the provision of international finance was therefore clearly not uniform.

More recently the banks have endeavoured to extricate themselves from lending to even those developing countries previously seen as creditworthy and have therefore, in a sense, exacerbated the debt problems which many countries have been encountering. Without delving into the various causes and consequences of the global debt problem we can note that a broad range of developing countries might be expected to be unhappy with the existing status quo. However, while the formerly creditworthy developing countries might be looking for measures from the official sector to support private lending, the least developed countries will tend to favour more direct lending by the official agencies. Again, there is little reason to presume that all developing countries will have similar interests with regard to the nature of reform.

In terms of *policy coordination*, while economic summits give the image of a degree of coordination in terms of the design of macro-economic policy in industrial countries, the hard evidence suggests that this image is misleading. Most notoriously the 1980s have witnessed a significant misalignment of policy between the US and the major European economies. This has itself led to exchange rate problems and to protectionist pressures. The design of US macro-economic policy, which has involved a largely bond-financed fiscal deficit, has pushed up world interest rates, and this has had implications for heavily indebted countries with a large amount of floating interest rate debt. At the same time, of course, while some developing countries have enjoyed benefits from US expansion in terms of higher exports, many other developing countries produce exports that remain essentially unaffected by expansion in the US. More generally, fears amongst the governments of industrial countries about the effects of isolated and independent demand expansion on the domestic rate of inflation and balance of payments means that an uncoordinated approach to macro-economic management imposes a restrictionary and demand deflationary bias on the world economy.[8]

A *destructuring of the system* has accompanied the moves to generalised floating and to the private sector as the principal source of balance of payments financing. Much of the underlying structure of the Bretton Woods system fragmented after 1973, although the debt problems of the 1980s, which in part resulted from this fragmentation, led to a certain amount of restructuring. Some developing countries initially did quite well from this evolution but other, essentially poorer, developing countries did much less well. The impression that exchange rate flexibility and the private provision of international liquidity removed the need for additional reserves militated against their interests. While, by the mid 1980s, there might be much more agreement amongst developing countries concerning the need for a move back towards a more structured system, their views on the precise details of such a restructuring might be expected to differ for the reasons discussed already.

Many of the developments of the post 1973 era imply trade deliberalisation, and this has been observed, with many studies cataloguing the rise of the new protectionism; 'new' in the sense of being based on non-tariff barriers.[9] While protectionism in developed countries is, in general, against the interests of developing countries anxious to expand exports and earn more foreign exchange, not least to help service their debt obligations, developing countries will be differentially affected by it depending upon its precise form.

This section has sought to demonstrate that in the early part of the post Bretton Woods era international financial developments were not uniformly against the interests of all developing countries. Institutional changes continued to be made which were in some ways helpful, while the overall reduction in the importance of the official sector was not immediately unhelpful to those developing countries viewed as creditworthy by the private international banks. During the 1980s, however, the situation changed and developments became much more uniformly hostile towards the interests of developing countries. This increasingly hostile environment was reflected not only in a number of key institutional and operational changes but also in various trends in the world economy. The section has also shown that throughout the period not all developing countries or groups of developing countries experienced similar problems. Before moving on to say a little more about these dissimilarities in the following section, we may note, at this point, that there is little reason to believe that the overall position of developing countries within the world economy will improve in the foreseeable future. Assuming that there is no sudden rise in the supply of domestic financing, the continuing stagnation or decline in international financing implies that economic growth will be severely constrained. In many instances the prospects for developing countries are of negative net financial transfers and negative net real transfers. In the section after next we turn to the question of what strategy developing countries might adopt in order to minimise their plight. But first, can developing countries legitimately be grouped together in terms of their international financial problems?

DEVELOPING COUNTRY HETEROGENEITY

Although initially classified into hardly any sub-groups in official statistics, recent years have observed a very significant change in the presentation of data relating to developing countries. The IMF and the World Bank have used an ever increasing range of sub-groupings, including those covering different income levels (low income and middle income), different structures of trade (major exporters of manufactures, oil exporters, oil importers), different usages of external borrowing (major borrowers), different geographical locations (Western Hemisphere, Africa, Asia). The official agencies recognise that there is no such thing as a 'typical' developing country.

This apparent heterogeneity is confirmed by the discussion undertaken so far in this paper. For example, only a relatively small sub-group of developing countries had significant access to private capital markets in the 1970s and early 1980s. Only certain developing countries benefited from the US expansion in 1984. This tended to assist exporters of manufactures while doing little for primary product producers. To the extent that low income countries are deemed uncreditworthy and also have undiversified export bases which rely on one specific primary product, it may be argued that it is this group of countries that has been particularly disadvantaged by recent international financial developments. Moreover, a case may be made that the nature of IMF conditionality, with its emphasis on exchange rate devaluation and domestic demand deflation, is particularly inappropriate for these countries.[10] More formal analysis of the various aspects of developing countries' balance of payments problems covering export and import trends, the commodity terms of trade, export concentration and export instability, holdings of, and the adequacy of international reserves, access to private capital, debt, and the scope and costs of adjustment confirms that it is unwise and inaccurate to classify all developing countries together.[11]

The fact that different developing countries have different international financial problems means that they will have different interests in international financial reform. This, in turn, has implications for the likely viability of the alternative approaches to reforming the international economic order, some of which will be drawn out in the following section which examines these approaches.

REFORMING THE INTERNATIONAL ECONOMIC ORDER: THE POLICY ALTERNATIVES FOR DEVELOPING COUNTRIES

This section looks at three approaches to reforming the international economy from the viewpoint of developing countries.

A new international economic order and the North–South debate

The first possibility is to build a new order which would involve new, or reformed international agencies. The basic idea behind such a new order is that it would more fully reflect and serve the needs of 'the South'. The broad prospectus of the new order would cover: trade issues, particularly encouraging manufactured exports from developing countries, improving the terms of trade of primary product producers, and reducing export instability; multinationals; aid; debt; other aspects of international finance; and developing country representation in international agencies.

Claims for an NIEO were frequently made during the 1970s and early 1980s through, inter alia, the Special Assembly of the United Nations, UNIDO, UNCTAD, the Paris Conference on International Economic Cooperation, and the Brandt Reports. However, these deliberations resulted in little tangible progress. The North/South debate atrophied, and little changed with respect to the distribution of power and influence as regards international financial issues. Indeed, far from there being a movement towards the objectives of the new order, the movement was in many ways in the opposite direction. While some 'positive' modifications were made in international financial arrangements, as catalogued earlier in this chapter, these hardly constituted evidence of a NIEO.

How can this lack of progress towards a new order be explained? The short answer is surely that the bargaining position of those seeking it was insufficiently strong. The longer answer comprises a number of points.

First, the North–South distinction is too simplistic. Different countries within the South – and indeed within the North – have different interests and different views as to how these interests are likely to be best served. Even for individual Southern countries or groups of countries there may be internal inconsistencies in their position with regard to reform. Debt relief, for example, may have some short-term appeal, but at the same time recipients of such relief will worry about damaging their long-run creditworthiness. Or again, while many developing countries may stand to gain from a more structured system of international liquidity creation based on the SDR, they may be reluctant to give up the flexibility that the Euro-currency market offers, or to abandon the scope for reserve management.

Secondly, the international environment most conducive to evolutionary reform is a structured one. In practice the world moved away from a 'system' in the 1970s. The old order was replaced by no order rather than a new order.

Thirdly, commodity market conditions changed. There was a move from excess demand to excess supply, and from a sellers' to a buyers' market. To the extent that bargaining strength reflects market position, it is not surprising that the momentum for an NIEO initially generated by the increase oil prices subsequently petered out. In effect the response of the developed world to the claims for a new order were: to move into recession, economise on the use of oil, adopt more inward-looking trade policies, and thereby undermine the bargaining strength of the South. Of course, this was probably not the motivation for these policies. Instead they reflected a preoccupation with reducing the rate of inflation and payments deficits. With respect to inflation, many elements of the NIEO, such as the SDR link and the Integrated Programme for Commodities, were seen by countries of the North as making it worse. Furthermore, it is interesting to note that the increase in oil prices which stimulated the South's interest in a NIEO, and which initially improved their bargaining position, also contributed to worldwide inflation and to attitudes which were hostile to the proposals for a new order. As far as the balance of payments is concerned, measures taken to strengthen the North's position almost inevitably weakened the South's and pushed many developing countries into a situation where they had little option other than to turn to the Fund, an institution which many of them see as a bastion of the old order. The strength associated with being a surplus country and one of the Fund's creditors was really attained only by Saudi Arabia.

Fourthly, the 'mutuality doctrine' that is so much a part of some (though by no means all) of the proposals for an NIEO has essentially been rejected by governments of the North. It is seen as being based on out-moded Keynesian notions that have been replaced by a more monetarist approach to economic management. In many cases governments have no doubt viewed many aspects of the NIEO, for example increased aid, as politically not feasible in circumstances where the thrust of domestic economic policy is contractionary.

Given the rejection of mutuality, Northern governments have seen nothing for them in the NIEO, particularly after oil became of less pressing concern. Their short-term interests appeared to be best served by participating in discussions from which nothing much would emerge. This approach by the North was facilitated by developing countries identifying commodity price stabilisation and the Integrated Programme of Commodities as the symbolic centre-piece of the new order. Economic analysis reveals that there are numerous problems associated with attempts to stabilise prices. It is not even self-evident that developing countries will benefit greatly from such stabilisation.[12] In retrospect the 'South' would have been better advised to de-emphasise the role of buffer stocks and emphasise more fully the role of compensatory financing. Similarly, it is unclear whether some of the most extreme plans for debt relief stand up to detailed economic analysis or indeed whether they would be of much benefit to the 'South'.[13] In the longer term the 'North' effectively withdrew from the discussions.

The Southern alternative

The above factors make it unlikely that a 'grand design' approach based on global negotiations will prove successful. Indeed there is a fundamental 'Catch 22' dilemma. For the South to be in a strong bargaining position it needs to have been relatively successful economically. However, economic success under the old rules will reduce the desire for change. The motivation to change the system will only be strong in conditions where the South's bargaining power is weak.

If there is not much mileage left in global negotiations involving the North and South, what about the scope for South–South cooperation? In one sense the heterogeneity of the South in terms of comparative advantage provides the opportunity for intra-South trade and investment, yet by the same token the heterogeneity of interests makes it likely that a South–South dialogue will generate as few positive benefits as the North–South one has done. When, for example, thought is given to schemes for an exclusively Southern version of the IMF or the World Bank, a key question is where is the finance to come from? The short answer is that it will have to come from countries that have been relatively successful under existing arrangements. But will these countries be anxious to foster Southern arrangements? They may, of course, be rather more interested when they themselves become less successful, but then they are unlikely to possess the necessary finance.

The conclusion is that, while frustration with the lack of action on the North–

South front is understandable, the chances of success on the South–South one can easily be exaggerated. It should be emphasised that this general conclusion does not mean denying that there may be opportunities for greater Southern cooperation than has been achieved in the past. What it does imply, however, is the need to get away from the banner-waving type of advocacy of vague South–South solutions and towards a more reasoned and thorough analysis of specific proposals for reform. One cannot escape the fact that attempts to apply the logic of cooperation, as can be found in various Southern trading blocs, have often been rather less than successful. It should not simply be assumed, therefore, either that Southern solutions are automatically desirable on economic grounds – some may be, others may be not – or that they can be made to work.[14]

Incremental and evolutionary reform of the old order

So what is left if both a NIEO and a Southern solution are ruled out? Must developing countries resign themselves to existing arrangements with no chance of reform? The answer to this second question is 'no'. As noted earlier, one of the features of the 1950s, 1960s and 1970s was the gradual modification of the Bretton Woods system and institutions directed towards assisting developing economies. Although this trend has been reversed somewhat in the 1980s, there may be some hope for reasserting it; this will be discussed in the next section.

What sorts of modification might be made? These could relate both to adjustment and financing. With regard to adjustment, there is still considerable scope for reforming Fund conditionality in such a way as to make it more appropriate to the balance of payments needs of many developing countries, with more emphasis being placed on structurally oriented and supply or growth based adjustment.[15] To some extent such a change could be achieved by returning to the original rationale of the Extended Fund Facility. Appropriate adjustment might similarly be encouraged by extending structural adjustment lending by the World Bank. However, adjustment may not always be apposite. In these circumstances, and where adjustment is most appropriately brought about over a relatively protracted period, international financing is required. Hence measures to expand the lending capacity of the Fund (and the World Bank), to reform and reliberalise the Compensatory Financing Facility (thus raising the proportion of low conditionality Fund finance), to strengthen the role of the SDR in the international financial system and to modify the distribution formula so that a larger proportion of any given allocation goes to developing countries, would be beneficial to the 'South', especially to the least developed countries. These countries could also be assisted by the extended use of interest rate subsidisation.[16]

The better-off developing countries might, of course, prefer to see a larger proportion of official finance being used to support enhanced private capital flows. Here again there are proposals for loan insurance and guarantees, and the provision of lender of last resort facilities that are worthy of close consideration.[17]

Many of the proposals mentioned above would contribute to the easing of the debt problem, but there is also a range of other, individually quite modest proposals, which could also be beneficial and usefully considered including the reform of rescheduling packages. Although many of the reforms outlined here would not seem out of place in a programme for an NIEO, the approach to (and in some cases design of) reform is significantly different in the incremental alternative. The design takes existing institutional arrangements and works within the general framework that they provide. The approach does not involve a sudden root and branch change but rather a gradual series of modifications, each of which, on its own, may seem relatively modest, but which, in aggregate, sum to significant reform. Of course, while each individual element of reform may be modest, it would be wise for developing countries to have a notion of what their long-run policy objectives were and of what type of 'system' they would like.

CONCLUDING REMARKS: THE POLITICAL ECONOMY OF REFORM

If developing countries want to bring about changes in the international economy they have to decide two things. First, what changes do they want to achieve? Secondly, what approach stands the best chance of getting these changes implemented? This chapter has demonstrated that there are problems in relation to each of these questions. With regard to the first, the heterogeneity of developing countries, and in particular the division between the middle and low income countries, means that they do not possess uniformly consistent interests. This creates a challenge for the 'South' to come up with a set of agreed policies. The challenge does not evaporate within the context of exclusively Southern reform. Besides, there are important doubts about just how large would be the benefits from Southern solutions, particularly where these are regarded as a replacement for some form of North–South reform. Turning to the second question, North–South reform based on a NIEO seems unlikely to succeed. The design of the specific NIEO favoured by the South in the past may in any case be criticised on grounds of its underlying economic deficiencies. But the deciding factor is that it has failed to generate the degree of support needed from the North, where such fundamental reform is not seen as necessary and even as counter-productive to Northern interests.

Possibly the only chance of progress with a NIEO exists if the 'South' can exploit the vulnerability of the 'North' in the context of global debt. A debtor cartel may exert some bargaining power. But would this power, in practice, necessarily be used to achieve a NIEO? Furthermore, and for well-established reasons, cartels are notoriously fragile. What is more, where developing countries have adopted a more aggressive and militant approach to reform in the past, this has had little lasting impact. After the first oil price increase there was an attempt to exploit the concern and apparent vulnerability of the North to the oil threat, and there was some talk of more generalised commodity cartels and of 'commodity power'. But the era of greater militancy was short lived and achieved little other than an effective undermining of the power base of the South. Evidence seems to support the view that there is little mileage left in a NIEO.

Evidence also suggests, however, that there is scope for more gradual and piecemeal reform. Even during a period when the environment has been hostile politically there has been some, albeit very limited, progress on the handling of debt and on the provision of Fund finance to the least developed countries through the recently introduced Structural Adjustment Facility (SAF). If developing countries can identify areas of shared concern with industrial countries, as in the case of debt, or if they can agree to push for specific marginal (and inexpensive) reforms, there may be a reasonable presumption that they can make worthwhile progress.

Within this overall picture it needs to be recognised that some developed countries may offer more support for schemes that assist certain developing countries than others. The US may, for example, be more concerned about the plight of Latin American economies than those of Africa, and this will be another element in the negotiating process.

Finally, it needs to be said that, while the international economic environment has an important bearing on the economic development of developing countries, it should not be regarded as the only significant factor. Developing countries exert significant control over their own destinies through the domestic economic policies which they pursue. Governments which persistently defend over-valued exchange rates or, through an understandable desire to increase government expenditure designed to improve living standards, create large fiscal deficits are likely to encounter payments problems which adversely impinge on economic development irrespective of the nature of the international economy within which they find themselves.

NOTES

1 The discussion in this paper draws heavily on two books by Graham Bird, *The International Monetary System and the Less Developed Countries*, 2nd Edition (London: Macmillan, 1982); and *International Financial Policy and Economic Development: A Disaggregated Approach* (London: Macmillan, 1987). Many of the arguments, only briefly mentioned in this paper, receive much fuller discussion in these books which should be consulted for greater elucidation.

2 See A. P. Thirlwall (ed.), *Keynes and Economic Development* (London: Macmillan, 1987).

3 Confirmation of this relaxation in conditionality is provided by John Williamson, *The Lending Policies of the International Monetary Fund* (Washington: Institute for International Economics, August 1982). For an interpretation of the modifications in conditionality and their subsequent reversal see G. Bird, *International Financial policy and Economic Development*, where there is also a more detailed review of the institutional changes alluded to in the text. This book also contains a statistical analysis of the use of Fund resources by developing countries.

4 For a review of this see Sidney Dell, 'The fifth credit tranche', *World Development*, February 1985. See also Stephany Griffith Jones, *Compensatory Financing Facility: A Review of the Operation and Proposals for Improvement*, UNDP/UNCTAD, project INT/P1/06, January 1983, and Bird, *International Financial Policy and Economic Development*.

5 These were, albeit rather vague, proposals put forward to the annual meeting of the Fund and Bank in 1985 by the US Treasury which envisaged a somewhat enhanced role for the Bank and Fund. Views differ about just how significant these proposals are.

6 For reviews of developing countries' exchange rate policies see, for example, Bird, *The International Monetary System and the Less Developed Countries*, John Williamson, 'A survey of the literature on the optional peg', *Journal of Development Economics*, August 1982, and R. Wickham, 'The choice of exchange rate regime in developing countries: a survey of the literature', *IMF Staff Papers*, June 1985.

7 For a discussion of these effects see D. Brodsky, G. K. Helleiner, and G. Sampson, 'The impact of the current exchange rate system on developing countries', *Trade and Development*, Winter 1981. See also D. O. Cushman, 'The effects of real exchange rate risk on international trade', *Journal of International Economics*, August 1983.

8 For a more detailed discussion of global economic management see Graham Bird, 'Beyond the Brandt Report: a strategy for world economic development', *Millennium: Journal of International Studies*, Spring 1980.

9 For a discussion of the rise in new protectionism see, for example, David Greenaway, 'Multilateral trade policy in the 1980s', *Lloyds Bank Review*, January 1984.

10 Tony Killick (ed.), *The Quest for Economic Stabilisation: The IMF and the Third World* (London: Heinemann, and ODI, 1984); and John Williamson (ed.), *IMF Conditionality* (Washington: Institute for International Economics, 1983), provide in depth critical studies of the Fund's conditionality.

11 See Bird, *International Financial Policy and Economic Development*.

12 See Bird, *International Financial Policy and Economic Development*. For a detailed and rigorous analysis of commodity stabilisation which reaches broadly similar conclusions see David M. G. Newbery and Joseph E. Stiglitz, *The Theory of Commodity Price Stabilization: A Study in the Economics of Risk* (Oxford: Clarendon Press, 1981). See also, Max Corden, *The NIEO Proposals: A Cool Look*, Thames Essays, No. 21.

13 See, for example, William Cline, *International Debt: Systematic Risk and Policy Response* (Washington: Institute for International Economics, 1984), for a review of such plans.

14 Bird, *International Financial Policy and Economic Development*, provides a more thorough critical review of certain specific proposals for greater economic cooperation amongst developing countries, including a clearing union, reserve pooling, a credit union, and a Southern currency.

15 Tony Killick (ed.), *The Quest for Economic Stabilization* fully develops this argument. See also Bird, *International Financial Policy and Economic Development*.

16 For a more detailed explanation and defence of this stategy along with a larger bibliography see Bird, *International Financial Policy and Economic Development*.

17 As note 16 above.

Part III: Alliances, bases and security

5 A Southern perspective

P. Saravanamuttu

It may well strike an observer of contemporary international relations that the issue of foreign bases has been substantially modified or indeed transformed out of all recognition by developments in the post World War Two era. Whilst advances in military technology, it is maintained, have rendered bases increasingly irrelevant, decolonisation has made them untenable. Certain qualifications, however, are in order before the issue is divested of political controversy and thereby dropped from the agenda of security concerns germane to the North/South debate.

Technological advances, whilst obviating some of the traditional military requirements for bases, have nevertheless produced new ones. As Robert Harkavy points out in his study of the subject – 'Emerging technology, for instance, seems to be *diminishing* but not eliminating the *quantitative* requirements for naval and air bases: rather, retention of a small but critical number of access points remains essential' (emphasis in original).[1] This is because, as he notes earlier on, though

increased transport aircraft ranges (in great measure due to improved tanker refuelling), greater utilization of nuclear engines for ships, and perhaps also enhanced at-sea fleet support capabilities (at a cost) all should act to reduce the major powers' facilities requirements . . . [they are] counter-balanced by the enhanced requirements for access related to technical functions (surveillance, satellite tracking, ASW (anti-submarine warfare), which themselves, however, may later be reduced by still newer satellite capabilities, at least in same areas.[2]

However, as Harkavy then goes on to conclude, the 'looming Superpower competition for access to Persian Gulf oil seems to augur more rather than fewer needs for basing access'.[3] Nevertheless, technological advance and the impact of decolonisation, both in reducing the number of bases retained by ex-colonial powers and through the introduction of sensitivity towards host country sovereignty in future arrangements, have made possible – ironically in the latter case – a change in the terminology associated with the issue. This in turn has had the effect of reducing its potential for controversy.

What was hitherto known as a base is now a 'technical facility' under the sovereignty of the host country. 'Access' to it is therefore not unrestricted but limited to certain circumstances and objectives. In practice, needless to say, things are different. With the exception of Egypt's refusal to provide a written guarantee for US access to Ras Banas, the other possible examples of Washington's limitations in this respect suggest more a need on the part of the host government to publicly affirm its nationalist credentials than an effective constraint on the superpower's freedom of manoeuvre. Following the 1979 US–Philippine bases agreement, Marcos made a virtue out of restoring Manila's sovereignty over Clark Field and Subic Bay, but as a State Department officer claimed, the agreement was '. . . designed above all to preserve the status quo' or alternatively in the words of a departmental fact sheet on the subject, its objective was to ensure 'unhampered United States military operations'.[4] Indeed the concessions obtained by Marcos were superficial; to name one – the appointment of a Philippine base commander was devoid of any real significance, since his authority did not incorporate the US 'facilities' in the bases, which remained 'under the command and control of US Facility Commanders, whose freedom to conduct military operations continues as before'; or to name another one equally denuded of substantive import – the return of some base lands, which nonetheless were kept on offer to Washington for 'operational purposes and which in any event cannot be used in a manner prejudicial to US military operations'.[5]

Much too has been made about current US difficulties concerning its Rapid Deployment Force (RDF) or Central Command (US CENTCOM) contingents in the Gulf. In particular it is argued that stringent host government prerogatives have been observed over rights of access and no written guarantees for them obtained. Notwithstanding this and the question of an intimate or immutable congruence between host country and foreign power strategic perspectives – which will be addressed later – at least one authority concerning the issue notes that Washington's war plans do not consider this a problem and points to the possibility of secret understandings as the source of such confidence.[6] Martha Wenger in a *Middle East Research and Information Project* (MERIP) Report notes that US arms transfers to the region as well as its military installations are devised to specifications 'more suited for hosting a US intervention force than for self defence'.[7] She too contends that 'US access to such facilities in a crisis is not publicly acknowledged for political reasons, but is certainly tacitly assumed by Pentagon planners'.[8] This was confirmed in a New York Times article, dated 6 September 1985. It cited a confidential administration policy document on arms sales to the Middle East, which stated that 'access to [Saudi military facilities] will be forthcoming for US forces as necessary in order to counter Soviet aggression or in regional crises which they cannot manage on their own'. Further arguments discounting 'access' problems at the present time can be discerned in the 30 May 1986 issue of *Middle East International*. Extrapolating from information uncovered by defence analyst Anthony Cordesman, Rex B. Wingerter points out that the Saudis have granted Washington access to 'prepositioned equipment and munitions sufficient to sustain US forces during intensive combat for 90 days or more'.

Though this may well relate to the congruence of strategic perspectives referred to above, the overall argument that needs to be emphasised is that problems of access in this vitally important US security network are not as large as sometimes made out. Moreover on the issue of the changed strategic environment for access and its corresponding terminology, as the foregoing indicates, the nature and function of those 'facilities' are *not* markedly different from those that were associated with bases. They are geared towards the exercise of influence and the securing of vital resources; more importantly they are means through which congenial regimes in host countries are sustained and as such serve to keep the forces of social change at bay on the grounds that they are inimical. The continuity in the nature and function of 'facilities' as opposed to 'bases' is best illustrated in a 1979 Congressional Research Service paper for the Senate Foreign Relations Committee (SFRC) entitled 'United States Foreign Policy Objectives and Overseas Military Installations' which candidly declared that, as far as its subject matter was concerned, the Pentagon 'would probably consider them bases if the Soviets enjoyed the same rights in lieu of the United States'.[9] Given the North/South context of these discussions and the extent of Washington's basing network relative to that of its rival superpower, this presentation of the Southern perspective will concentrate on the issues raised by US bases in Diego Garcia, the Gulf and the Philippines. Its essential thesis will be that this existing network and its potential for expansion conflicts with any one of the various elements that make up the Southern perspective and accordingly compounds the problem of international security. These elements characterised as 1) Non-alignment and Southern conceptions of security, 2) The danger of host governments being 'short-changed' and 3) Social and political change in the South, will be addressed in turn.

NON-ALIGNMENT AND SOUTHERN CONCEPTIONS OF SECURITY

The argument in this section, as indeed in others, is that bases symbolise the imposition of an extraneous East–West political divide upon the predominantly

North–South concerns of the developing world with the consequence that some of these states accept a pre-ordained agenda of security and abnegate the responsibility to define their own priorities. The effect in short is that of a self-fulfilling prophecy about the ability of developing states to provide for their own security.

Non-alignment, seen as the available reference for Southern identity in international relations, was specifically defined by its architects in opposition to this. Included among the criteria governing membership drawn up by Foreign Ministers at the June 1961 Cairo Preparatory Meeting for the First Non-Aligned Summit was the following:

iv) in case of bilateral military agreement with a Great Power, or membership of a regional defence pact, the agreement or pact should not be one deliberately concluded in the context of Great Power conflicts; and

v) in case of lease of military bases to a foreign power, the concession should not have been made in the context of Great Power conflicts.[10]

These were reiterated in the Declaration of Peace issued at the 1970 Lusaka Conference as amongst the basic aims of the movement. Furthermore all other collective attempts by Southern states to define regional security in terms of their own priorities have reaffirmed this position.

Before Diego Garcia assumed its current importance for the United States, the United Nations in December 1971 passed General Assembly Resolution 2832, on which the two superpowers abstained, designating the Indian Ocean 'for all time as a zone of peace'. The resolution called upon states to eliminate,

all bases, military installations, logistical supply facilities, the disposition of nuclear weapons and weapons of mass destruction and any manifestation of Great Power military presence in the Indian Ocean conceived in the context of great Power rivalry.[11]

This is a position that has been subsequently reaffirmed in other regions as well with regard to bases, and on Diego Garcia specifically has been underlined by the Organisation of African Unity's (OAU) unanimous 1980 demand that the atoll be returned to Mauritius and its denunciation of the base as a 'threat to Africa'.[12] In Southeast Asia too, member states of the Association of Southeast Asian Nations (ASEAN) see their long-term security being fulfilled through the creation of a Zone of Peace, Freedom and Neutrality (ZOPFAN) that explicitly entails the removal of foreign bases. The Gulf states are no exception either. At the first Heads of States Meeting of the Gulf Cooperation Council (GCC) on 25–6 May 1981, the rulers in a final statement recorded their 'absolute rejection of any foreign interference in the region from whatever source and their desire to isolate it from international conflicts and particularly the presence of military fleets and foreign bases'.[13] Nevertheless they persist and provide some evidence of the complicity of regional states in their retention, despite the pious declarations of these states to the contrary.

The paradox this gives rise to underscores the dilemmas of rule in the South. The ZOPS, though an assertion of independent identity inspired by the enduring demands for political legitimacy, are nonetheless relegated to the aspirational or declaratory realms of policy and remain unrealised; the bases necessitated by the dynamics of superpower conflict attest to an extra-regional conception of security that is. Yet aspirations perform important functions in international relations too.

On the other hand it may be averred, as it has been in the case of Marcos and the Philippines, that under the 'permissive environment' favouring the host country and its establishment of the principle of rent, North/South concerns in terms of resource transfers can be facilitated by bases. This, however, must be rejected as a perversion of the resource transfer idea, suggesting a certain legitimacy for transactions that involve in essence an exchange of favours that buttress the dependent nature of security in the South. Indeed, though Marcos successfully raised the price for the US bases and though the monies received went to prop up his decrepit regime, the salient feature of the whole bargain was that his options were always conditioned by Washington's evaluation of the bases' strategic worth, an evaluation which belied the supposedly Kantian norms of non-intervention – i.e. to say, the security of the Philippines was not seen as an *end in itself* and therefore a contribution towards global security per se, but was seen *in terms of the bases* defined as an indispensable contribution towards the prevalence of a US conception of security. This in turn was indistinguishable from the global objective.

HOST REGIME INTERESTS AND THE RISK OF BEING SHORT-CHANGED

The preceding arguments bring one to the relationship between host regimes and the foreign power, particularly to the question of whether the former is short-changed by the latter. What needs ascertaining here is whether the apparent coincidence of strategic perspective exemplified by the bases is a camouflage for the real, though unclarified or undeclared functions conceived for them by the foreign power and beyond the control of the host country. From a Southern perspective what this implies is that the relationship entered into over bases is not underpinned by genuine partnership but on the contrary one in which the interests of the *host regimes* as well as that of its people are peripheral. If this is disputed, then the equally damaging concession must be made that the bases are intended to secure a particular political orientation from the host country. Either way their essentially interventionist character cannot be ignored.

This section looks at the question in the context of the host regime's interest. It will leave aside for the moment arguments about the political legitimacy of these regimes and take as its basis the assumption that, if it is not a regime's exclusive prerogative to define a country's security, it is nevertheless the task of a regime to articulate it. Therefore in the interstate bargain for bases the host country's interest will be represented by the ruling regime. Do US bases guarantee the position of the ruling regime or do they constitute a vested US interest in controlling the bounds of acceptable regime change in the host country that is not predicated upon the fortunes of a specific ruler?

The answer to this question in the case of the Philippines must be the latter. From Washington's perspective, the replacement of Marcos in the Malancanang Palace by Mrs Aquino did not portend the imminent loss of Clark Field and Subic Bay, but rather holds out the prospect of their future retention. Given the past association, there is some justice too in Marcos's current grievances against the US; after all it was action by one arm of the mainstay of US influence in the country, the army, that forced him to relinquish power to a member of the other – the feudal aristocracy. Washington has subsequently managed to present itself in a good light over this transfer of power, but the question remains as to whether Mrs Aquino too would be sacrificed to ward off the fundamental political change promised by the Communist New Peoples Army (NPA). It is worth noting that Washington's position would have been quite different if the transfer of power was from Marcos to the NPA, and may well be different if it is from Mrs Aquino to the NPA. Indeed, as far as Mrs Aquino is concerned, her dilemma springs from the inability to strengthen her position without some measure of US support, expressed either indirectly through the army or directly in economic assistance. Stabilisation of the Aquino Government must ultimately reside on economic development and radical land reform to blunt the NPA challenge. In both instances US support will be crucial. It may not be given however to the degree needed as progress on the first may be curtailed by what Washington determines to be too much movement on the second.

Perhaps this is a position confined to the conservative elements of the Reagan Administration and would not last beyond 1988 when another bases agreement has to be negotiated. Moreover, it may well be that a process of reverse leverage does apply and that Washington has concluded that, if the bases are to be kept, they can only be kept with Mrs Aquino in power – any other regime would only call for their removal or hasten that eventuality. Suffice it to say that talk about base relocation, tremendously costly and prolonged in itself (between \$3–4 billion and ten years, according to one estimate), has subsided.[14] However, no decision on them seems to have been taken, as arguments about their indispensability continue unsettled.[15] In addition, it should be pointed out that the past record of US foreign policy does not indicate that opposition to radical land reform is confined to the present administration. Even the Solarz position amounted to regime change within acceptable limits, but limits nevertheless on the nature of socio-economic and political change.

Clark Field and Subic Bay, the largest US military installations abroad, assure the US dominance over the South China Sea and the Eastern Indian Ocean – their significance being heightened accordingly with that of the Gulf and by the Soviet base at Cam Ranh Bay. They provide important facilities for the conduct of conventional and nuclear war as well as for deterrence; worthy of mention in this respect is that Clark is integrated into the global communications system for the Strategic Air Command, whilst Subic is the largest logistical support base for the US Navy in the Western Pacific.[16] It can serve all types of ships in the US Navy, nuclear aircraft carriers included. Furthermore, in the words of one expert source, Clark and Subic are 'the main storage point for tactical nuclear weapons in the Pacific'.[17] Consequently, because of these and other facilities provided by the bases, Soviet SS-20 missiles are targeted on the Philippines.[18] The relative importance therefore of US interests in the Philippines stem from the bases maintained to satisfy the wider geo-strategic imperative that informs US policy. Thus, if a particular Philippine regime is not being short-changed by the absence of a guarantee for its security, the Philippines is laid open to nuclear attack from the Soviet Union with whom it does not have a conflict of interest. The bases constitute an *invitation of threat* rather than carry with them an *insurance against threats* and one can be sure that, as long as they are available, the US military rationale for the bases will not change, unless of course technology deems otherwise or an indefinite renaissance in detente concludes the cold war in all its phases.

As far as the Gulf is concerned the question of US indifference to the fortunes of a specific regime does not apply because Washington sees this as synonymous with its interest in maintaining the status quo of political orientation in the region from which the Western Alliance's crucial oil supplies are obtained. President Reagan has declared that he will not permit Saudi Arabia 'to be a Iran' and as Cordesman notes in his authoritative work, *The Gulf and the Search for Strategic Stability*, both the Carter and Reagan Administrations have conveyed to the USSR that 'the US would use nuclear weapons rather than suffer a decisive loss of Gulf oil'.[19] Numerous administration officials and the President himself have reiterated this on subsequent occasions. It would seem then that regime stability is assured against external attack from the Soviet Union. However, the point not clarified is whether these regimes will have any control in determining the circumstances in which nuclear weapons will be employed in their defence. As a writer in the January 1983 MERIP report avers, US CENTCOM 'represents a key ingredient in an overall strategy that rests more than ever on a doctrine of first use of nuclear weapons'.[20] Two years on in another such Report, Scott Armstrong reviewing Cordesman's book poses the question,

If during a multi-regional war, the United States is prepared to prevail over the Soviet Union in the Gulf – particularly the bomber force based inside Soviet territory – is it not prepared to use offensively what it is ready to use defensively?[21]

His subsequent answer to this question is,

In short the most important implications for American military strategy in the Gulf in the decades ahead have much more to do with American abilities to 'project power' across the Soviet southern border than with Gulf regional stability per se.[22]

The only conclusion that can be drawn from this is that the apparent coincidence of strategic perspective notwithstanding, the host government has been enmeshed in a spiral of escalation purportedly to ensure its security but vastly disproportionate to the degree of control it can exert in that exercise. What this also confirms is that the absence of formal agreements that characterise the 'permissive' environment for basing arrangements does not necessarily favour the host government but can just as easily be manipulated by the foreign power. On the other hand it may well be argued that nuclear deterrence works as the Sheikhs know full well. Needless to say, if it has worked it does not follow that it always will.

What is being argued here is not the legitimacy of a US interest in obtaining vital energy supplies and ensuring open sea lanes of communication, but that the manner in which it is prosecuted still betrays an inability and/or unwillingness to comprehend the dimensions of security in the South. It strongly reflects the belief that security in the South is almost entirely beyond the competence and control of the South and that Southern governments are only mature enough to be junior partners in the search for security. After all, though US CENTCOM might testify to the convergence of US and Gulf state interests in protecting oil supplies it also does imply US lack of faith in the ability of these regimes to provide for their own security and defend their valuable energy source. Admittedly these are criticisms of US alliance policy not exclusive to the South but pertinent to Europe as well. However, it must be emphasised that there are important differences, particularly, the degree of consensus obtained over threat perceptions in Europe by NATO is not replicated in the Gulf where US and regional views on Israel for one are dramatically opposed. These bases attest to the engraftment of a wider and hypothetical threat upon the either incipient or regionally defined Southern security perspectives and promote reliance upon the military instruments of policy. That this may in the end be self-defeating for the

United States provides little comfort for the South, which in the meanwhile is marginalised to a minor role in its own destiny.

Social and political change in the South

As contended earlier, irrespective of treaties and official pronouncements stipulating otherwise, bases constitute a symbol if not an instrument of the enduring US interest in managing the process of social and political change in the South. Congenial regimes willing to entertain a measure of alignment and far removed from the liberal-democratic ideal are an indispensable prerequisite for them. These regimes in turn are rewarded with economic assistance and armaments, the impact of which outlast them for the intention is not to *mortgage interest* but to *institutionalise influence*. Nevertheless, in the short term at least bases contribute, as former Senator and spokesman of the Anti-Bases Coalition in the Philippines, Jose Diokno, has charged, towards sustaining authoritarianism. According to him there was a direct correlation between the Clark Field and Subic Bay bases and the Marcos dictatorship. Diokno even accused the US of instigating Marcos's rule by martial law:

In fact martial law was imposed and our democratic system was totally subverted among other reasons because there was a very strong and growing demand from the Filipino (sic) people that the bases be removed. This was one of several demands which affected the interests of the United States government. Which is why the United States government favoured the imposition of martial law. If it did not instigate it.[23]

As Diokno himself concedes there were other reasons for martial law rule in 1972 and the dictatorship that ensued. Nonetheless US interests militated in Marcos's favour as they eventually did to his detriment, because of the bases.

With respect to Saudi Arabia, President Reagan as cited above, declares (in language akin to that used over China some forty years ago) that he will not '*permit*' that country to undergo the type of political transformation that occurred in Iran. Of course he is not suggesting that if need be the US would steer the House of Saud away from indulging in the worst excesses of the Peacock Throne, or is he? An obliging colonel or disgruntled prince may someday find that his hour has arrived. A more plausible interpretation of the President's remarks is that the US would act to suppress indigenous revolution determined to proclaim and consolidate an independent identity. Under either scenario what this amounts to is that government and political development in Saudi Arabia will be tutored and tempered from Washington, regardless of whether they need direction or moderation. In the meantime one can justifiably assume that Reagan's declaration provides coherence to current US policy.

The Secretary of Defense classified *1984–88 Defense Guidance* document states:

It is essential that the Soviet Union be confronted with the prospect of a major conflict should it seek to reach oil reserves of the Gulf. Because the Soviets might induce or exploit local political stabilities, their forces could be entered into the area by means other than outright invasion. *Whatever the circumstances*, we should be prepared to introduce American forces directly into the region should it appear that the security of access to Persian Gulf oil is threatened.[24] (Italics taken from printed secondary source.)

Noteworthy too in this connection are reports that the Pentagon has strengthened its Special Operations Forces (SOF) including the Green Berets and the Navy SEALS (Sea, Air, Land) 3,500 of which can be called upon by the US CENTCOM.[25]

Yet the nature of a Southern policy is such that it is not amenable to being ossified in some permanent political orientation, but by and large is enveloped in a state of flux – not surprising, one might add, after four decades at the most of decolonisation. It is characterised by competing claims to political legitimacy and the tenuous relationship between nation and state, ruler and ruled, however defined. The level of political stability and economic development obtained elsewhere is absent here, as often observed. Hence the prognosis must be one of more not less change and of movement from within to establish the boundaries of that change. Threats being internal need to be managed or dissipated locally. Bases therefore do not help but compound the problem of security.

CONCLUSION

The question of bases cannot be separated from the wider issue of intervention in the South and the enduring Northern belief that the over-arching demands of international order legitimise it. Yet, if international order is supposed to be predicated upon the observance of national sovereignty, the bases attest that decolonisation notwithstanding the modes of thought that characterised the preceding era have not been exhausted from contemporary international relations.

It is fashionable in some quarters to deride non-alignment as the sanctimonious outpourings of a movement better known for its pretensions than for its accomplishments. The movement is as unreal, the argument goes, as its objectives are unrealisable; if it serves any function at all, it answers the South's need for collective self-identity in international politics in a manner that reinforces perception of victimisation and injustice. The non-aligned, in short, are pursuing vain hopes and past grievances, neither of which have any positive bearing on their present predicament or future position. Likewise, with social and political change in the South, it has been contended that this process is too delicate a task to be entrusted to management from within and that in any event does not allow this change to be cocooned from the world outside. These societies are penetrated and bases merely register this fact.

The validity of these judgements apart, self-perceptions should not be discounted. They inspire attempts to structure the agenda of international relations which after all is what the North–South debate is about. The need for bases, rights of access to a state's territory, the airspace above it and the water that surrounds it, will not go away unless the Hobbesian notion of international relations is invalidated. The point however is that in the meantime, if bases are to remain even as symbols, they must have new meaning.

NOTES

1 Robert E. Harkavy, *Great Power Competition for Overseas Bases, The Geopolitics of Access Diplomacy* (London: Pergamon Press, 1982), p. 344.
2 Ibid., p. 339.
3 Ibid., p. 339.
4 Officers claim cited in Robert Pringle, *Indonesia and the Philippines: America's Interests in Island Southeast Asia* (New York: Columbia University Press, 1980), p. 77. The other quotation is from an *US State Department*, 'Fact sheet: amendment of the 1947 US Philippines Military Bases Agreement' (undated), p. 1, cited in Walden Bello, 'Instruments for intervention, instruments for nuclear war', *Southeast Asia Chronicle*, Issue No. 89, p. 13.
5 Ibid., *US State Dept* Fact sheet cited in Bello.
6 *Middle East Research and Information Project (MERIP)* Report No. 128, November/December 1984, p. 29.
7 Ibid., p. 22 in Wenger, 'The Central Command: getting to the war on time', pp. 19–23.
8 Ibid.
9 Ibid., p. 24.
10 Cited in Peter Willets, *The Non-Aligned Movement: The Origins of a Third World Alliance* (London: Frances Pinler Ltd, 1978), p. 19.
11 Cited in Dieter Braun, *The Indian Ocean-Region of Conflict or 'Zone of Peace'?* (London: C. Hurst & Co. [Publishers] Ltd, 1983), pp. 214–15.
12 *International Herald Tribune*, 5 July 1980.
13 *Keesings Contemporary Archives*, 24 July 1981.
14 This estimate is taken from a testimony given before the *US House of Representatives SubCommittee on Asian and Pacific Affairs*, Hearings: United States–Philippine Relations and the New Base and Aid Agreement, 17, 23 and 28 June 1983 and is also cited in Sheldon W. Simon, 'The great powers and Southeast Asia', *Asian Survey*, Vol. XXV, No. 9, September 1985, p. 929. The opinion expressed is the author's own and is based on State Department and Pentagon interviews in July–August 1986.
15 Ibid., author interviews.
16 Bello, Instruments, pp. 3–4.
17 Robert Berman and John Baker, *Soviet Strategic Forces: Requirements and Responses* (Washington DC: Brookings Institution, 1982), p. 21. Also cited in ibid., p. 11.
18 Ibid.
19 Reagan quote in *New York Times*, 18 October 1981. Cordesman quote from Anthony H. Cordesman, *The Gulf and the Search for Strategic Stability* (Boulder, Co.: Westview Press, 1984), p. 862.
20 Christopher Paine, 'On the beach: the rapid deployment force and the nuclear arms race' *MERIP* Report, January 1983, p. 4.

21 February 1985, *MERIP* Report, No. 130, p. 26.
22 Ibid.
23 *Southeast Asian Chronicle*, Issue No. 89, Diokno Interview, p. 17.
24 Paine, *On the beach*, pp. 10–11.
25 M. Wenger, *MERIP* Report No. 128, pp. 21, 22.

The author would like to acknowledge the research assistance given to him by Mr Darryl Howlett in the preparation of this paper.

6 A Northern perspective

Christopher Coker

In the immediate post-colonial period it was generally believed that the presence of foreign bases compromised the sovereignty and security of the new powers. On this question, if little else, there was a striking consensus within the Non-Aligned Movement which was reinforced by an equally striking unanimity of opinion in the academic community.

Bases remained in the public eye because strategic decoupling from the Third World followed on many years after political disengagement. Both the British and French retained base rights in many of their former colonies after granting them independence, even rights of access in an emergency. They may have lost an empire but they maintained part of its original infrastructure well into the late 1960s and beyond. Partial withdrawal may have been important but it bore no relation to total withdrawal and although the one experience may have preceded the other it in no way prepared the ground for the final pull-out.

By the end of the 1960s circumstances had changed radically. Where bases survived at all they were either seen as historical curios like the naval base at Mers-el-Kebir which the French finally evacuated in February 1968, seven years ahead of schedule, or part of a global network of power projection for the superpowers rather than the Europeans, the new 'imperial' powers of the modern era.[1] But circumstances changed also for the superpowers as well with the result that even their base rights lost much of their importance, a development particularly well-illustrated by the fate of the US base at Kagnew, Ethiopia.

In 1970 there were over 3,000 American personnel working in the communications centre. By 1976 the number had fallen to 35. The principal reason for the decline was technological advance. The growth of satellite communications, tracking and photography replaced many of Kagnew's most important functions. While the USN admittedly had no plans to cease operations before the lease terminated in 1978, it made no secret of the fact that there would be no attempt to renegotiate a new lease on its expiry.[2]

America's reluctance to continue operations in the area also reflected a broader shift in American strategy. By the mid 1970s the United States had begun to recognise that its global network of military bases was becoming politically sensitive in many Third World countries. The growth of Third World nationalism accelerated the search for more remote atolls or anchorages, or even residual colonial territories like Diego Garcia which – to quote a Defence Department spokesman in 1974 – would not require 'abrasive discussions or potentially abrasive discussions involving the sensitivities of littoral states when a requirement comes to use it'.[3] This was one reason why the United States decided to sharply limit its presence in the Horn of Africa (even before the military coup which toppled Haile Selassie). According to a former American ambassador Kagnew was relegated fairly early on 'to outer fringes' of American security.[4]

It may seem that Kagnew constitutes a special case, but in fact the waning American presence, if particularly well documented, was merely part of a general disengagement that held true for all the Western powers, not only the United States. Strategic decoupling may have been a protracted and intermittent process which continued for many years but it seemed almost complete by 1973.

The world, of course, has changed dramatically since then. New bases have sprung up throughout the 'arc of crisis' described by Zbigniew Brzezinski in 1979. Subic Bay in the Philippines remains more vital than ever for US military operations in the Indian Ocean as well as East Asia. What has happened in the last ten years is the strategic recoupling by the West in response to geo-political and geo-strategic factors for which it could not have been less prepared. By the mid 1970s the United States had right of access to only three ports in the whole of sub-Saharan Africa – Dakar, Monrovia and Mombasa and no bases at all. Today the Rapid Deployment Force (RDF) involves the most extensive network of base rights and military understandings outside Western Europe. Its existence has also promoted one of the most intense discussions of Third World security since the outbreak of the cold war.

STRATEGIC RECOUPLING BY THE WEST

On the geo-strategic front the United States and its allies have been confronted with a development which took them by surprise in the mid 1970s; the projection of Soviet military power in areas of the world where hitherto the Soviet Union had never played a role. The period 1974–8 witnessed the emergence of Marxist-Leninist regimes in Southern Africa and the Horn, the two regions considered most vital to Western security. The invasion of Afghanistan in 1979 also appeared to bring the Soviet Union within striking distance of the Gulf, to present the first real military threat to the supply of oil since the appearance of Field Marshal Kleist's First Panzer Group in the Caucasus in the Summer of 1942.

But strategic recoupling was much more than merely a reflex response to Soviet actions; it reflected a much more acute concern about geo-political developments over which the Western powers perceived they had little control. By 1979 they had to face several unpalatable facts: that the demand for OPEC oil would begin to rise, that the trend towards lower energy consumption sparked off by the OPEC embargo of 1974 would soon become recessionary rather than efficient, that non-OPEC production would soon peak and that the Gulf would become an increasingly important market, producing 89 per cent of OPEC oil by the mid 1990s, compared with 50 per cent or less prior to 1973.

Inevitably, these considerations influence military thinking. For much of the 1970s the prevailing academic wisdom in the West especially in Europe was that military power was often a poor instrument compared with a variety of non-military responses, including economic aid.[5] But as 'The Age of Affluence' gave way to 'The Age of Uncertainty'[6] as the Western economies themselves plunged into recession induced partly by the tripling of OPEC prices between 1979–81, economic power, while still important, seemed much less important than once imagined, indeed increasingly transparent in a neo-mercantilist age.

Economic development no longer appeared to offer a reliable remedy for political instability, an implicit guarantee of security for the future, as under the stress of the oil price increases many poorer Third World states found that income distribution became more inequitable not less; while some OPEC members, notably Iran, grew considerably richer only to discover the political penalties of developing too fast.

Finally, the rise of Islamic fundamentalism fuelled these concerns by producing a peculiar brand of Shi'ite terrorism which represented a long-term threat to the secular state system which the West had created out of the detritus of the Ottoman Empire, sixty years before. Since the United States had taken upon itself to underwrite that system it found it necessary to 'prove' that terrorism, whether state sponsored or not, could be dealt with by the application of military power. The critical episode, if only for its symbolic significance, perhaps was the bombardment of Druze positions in the Lebanon in October 1983 by the 16 inch guns of the USS Jersey, an old battleship of Second World War vintage. As the Long Commission later noted, the decision to bombard the Chouf mountains was intended to demonstrate to the world that military force *could* bring order to the anarchical society the Lebanon had become.

Such in broad outline are the developments that have led to Western strategic recouplement. It remains to ask whether it has had an adverse affect on Third World security. In this paper I shall focus entirely on the United States, not because it is the only actor but because the Europeans have largely acted on 'sub-contract', when at all,[7] and because the US global network of bases is still more extensive and important than its Soviet counterpart.[8]

With this in mind, we might well question how far the United States has managed to remain a free agent; how far its Third World allies have succeeded in retaining their independence, how far either is in control. We may agree that new geo-political realities have contributed a renewed interest in base rights, and that such a development must have security implications for all the powers involved. The fact that the bases are important is a matter surely beyond dispute. The question is whether they have added to regional security, or the security of the United States. When it comes to answering this question there seems to be some point to the arguments put forward by the most recent generation of US strategists who would claim that their profession has taken a strange turn in recent years since the United States has rewarded governments for 'bases' that the Pentagon has managed to conceive but never quite construct.

STRATEGIC RECOUPLING AND THE 'PERMISSIVE ENVIRONMENT'

To begin with strategic recoupling has taken place within what has come to be termed 'a permissive environment'. Addressing the Senate Committee on Foreign Relations in 1980 the former Undersecretary of State David Newsom readily acknowledged that 'in all countries there are images and political cliches about past colonisation and intervention which come to the fore when a Western country talks of securing facilities or establishing bases'.[9] Their experience of the colonial era still remains the most enduring memory of nations caught up in the Second Cold War, the dimensions of which many of them have difficulty in conceiving. Longing for a regime which will bestow some protection they have promoted a new orthodoxy which has shaped the context within which military re-engagement has taken place.

The United States has found its freedom of action severely constrained in three areas: its ability to intervene in the affairs of the host nation; its right to use bases for military operations against other Third World states; and its right to compromise the essential non-aligned status of those countries which have been willing to provide base facilities. In permitting the US to use former British facilities in Bahrain, or the former Soviet naval base in Berbera, the countries concerned have acted with a great deal more circumspection than they have often been given credit.

Interference in host countries

Political interference can take many forms but there has been very little evidence of it in recent years, certainly not in Cuba or Cyprus where the United States and Britain enjoy sovereign control of Guantanamo base and Akrotiri. The former is used only as a training base, a card which might one day be negotiated away if relations with Cuba were to improve. During the coup which toppled the Cypriot government in 1974 the 8,000 British troops on the island remained strictly in camp, not perhaps surprisingly when one considers that most were concerned with the management and control of military airfields, and that only 2,500 were actually trained and equipped for combat.

Elsewhere in the Third World, nevertheless, bases still exercise an extraordinary hold over the imagination. It was America's perceived support for Ferdinand Marcos arising from its presence at Subic Bay which led to the formation of the Anti-bases Coalition in 1983. The Declaration which the movement issued in its first year made several claims, most of which were difficult to substantiate when looked at closely: that base rights gave support to an 'inequitable status quo', that they strengthened authoritarian rule, intensified the violation of human rights and the 'degradation of national values'.[10]

True, without the risk of losing Subic Bay Carter's human rights programme might have carried greater weight but many countries, the Soviet Union included, found the programme an intolerable intrusion into a country's internal affairs. America's tacit acquiescence in Marcos's decision to declare martial law in 1972 did not betoken any indifference to political freedom in the developing world as opposed to the developed, *vide* its equally muted response to the military coup in Greece in 1967.

If the 1983 bases agreement brought Marcos an 80 per cent increase in the security assistance budget, it was the army which finally removed him from power. Indeed, Third World regimes court the superpowers at their own risk. Base agreements do not lead to the 'militarisation' of society, but they do promote the military in society. The latter are an enclosed, frequently unrepresentative caste, closely linked to the United States by what Johann Galtung once described as 'bridges of dependency', military aid and exchange programmes and joint manoeuvres which enable Washington to penetrate the military establishment and establish close personal links with Third World generals. Arbenz in Guatemala, Bosch in the Dominican Republic, even Diem in South Vietnam were all removed in American sponsored coups.

Marcos too, in the end paid dearly for his relationship with the United States; not because it made him an unpopular leader at home, but because it enabled the United States to countenance his fall, knowing full well that the new government would only be as strong as the support it received from the armed forces.

The Anti-bases Coalition was on somewhat stronger ground when it indicted the United States for the social costs of its military presence; the squatter camps around Clark airfield with their 23,000 inhabitants, the high incidence of child prostitution, the denial of union representation to the 40,000 Filipino workers employed in the base facilities and who were segregated from all American non-military personnel and paid markedly smaller wages.

As Senator Jose Diokno insisted, the bases may have stabilised the regime, but not the society. For the Philippines real stability meant economic and social development.[11] Very little of the $500m which Marcos received in 1979 in payment for the bases was spent on the Filipino people, even though it represented an amount roughly equivalent to the cost of American bases in Turkey, Greece and Spain.[12]

Yet such criticisms while true are often irrelevant. Diokno's claims betray a resentment at exploitation, a quest for self-esteem by a country that has been exploited by its own rulers with very little encouragement by the Western world. The huge sums involved in rental may well pose dangers for regimes who are oblivious to the social consequences of a foreign military presence, but there is an equal danger of opposition politicians attributing those problems to external factors alone. Once a government has fallen they often find that the real world conforms hardly at all to the world to which their followers have been promised swift passage.

Indeed, given the informal nature of today's military agreements which have attracted so much criticism in the United States, it is difficult to see why external power should be held responsible for governments which it neither controls nor influences as much as it would like. This is part of the permissive environment which makes it possible for base rights to be transferred to a foreign power; that is the reason why the RDF – to cite a specific case – is permitted, it is too weak to pose a serious threat to the Arab states on whose support the United States ultimately relies.

It is interesting to recall that when the Johnson administration first proposed such a force in 1967 Richard Russell, the then chairman of the Senate Armed Services Committee, warned, with the experience of Vietnam much in mind, that 'if our involvement in foreign conflicts can be made quicker and easier there may be a temptation to intervene in many situations'.[13] In the Carter administration's last year, even pro-American Saudi officers expressed concern that the RDF might be employed one day not to defend Riyadh but to seize the oil fields in the north east of the country, as Washington had originally planned to do in the event of another embargo.[14] Some Saudis still see the RDF as a threat to the dynasty, but not as many as before.

A more immediate danger for Saudi Arabia derives not from its association with the United States, but from the fact that the association is so loose; that in the absence of a strategic consensus the relationship has only a spurious legitimacy; that the host government is likely not to be overturned, but short-changed.

While he was still Secretary of State Alexander Haig often spoke of the need to convince the Saudis that the United States was a 'reliable security partner' with whom it was possible to establish a 'regional partnership'.[15] The Americans may still see the Arab states as an enclosed order, often unresponsive to the Soviet threat, obsessed with their own preoccupation with Israel, but, for their part, they have shown little genuine capacity to respond to the societies they are trying to coopt.

As Anthony Cordesman notes, the complaint among Saudi officers is not that relations with the United States are *too* close, but that they are not close enough. 'The lack of teeth' Saudi Arabia has obtained in proportion to its vast expenditure on 'tail' has become a political issue within (the country) especially with students and younger military officers.[16] Although the regime even went so far as to establish a joint military committee with Washington, the narrow vote on the sale of AWACS and the formal limits Weinberger tried to put on their use, which if accepted would have severely compromised Saudi sovereignty in the eyes of its own people, seem to show that the Americans have no intention of treating the country as an equal partner.

They are not even above exploiting it commercially. The $15bn which Saudi Arabia intends spending on enhancing its air defence system before 1994 may well be an artificial figure inflated by the American defence industry. As the Vice President of Boeing observed after the AWACS sale had been agreed the USAF could always 'load it onto the Saudis' by pricing up the E3A.[17] Fortunately for Riyadh, it can engage in countertrade deals, purchasing goods and services with oil shipments or scheduling payment in years when the demand for oil is likely to rise. Other countries like Mubarak's Egypt have not been so fortunate.

The real threat to local regimes is not association with a superpower, even less the prospect that it might interfere in local politics, but the perception by the population at large, and more importantly the army, that thirty years after decolonisation Third World states are treated very differently from the Europeans. As long as this remains the case America's capacity for arriving at a genuine strategic consensus will be limited; its capacity for conceiving grand designs like the RDF will continue to be matched by its incapacity to carry them through to a successful conclusion. Its alliances will remain compromises of the moment, tactical arrangements, to use a phrase of Henry Kissinger's (in one of his periodic snipes at NATO) 'an accidental array of forces in search of a mission'.

In these circumstances some Third World regimes might question the wisdom of entering into any association with a power such as the United States. In time American support may prove to be a wasting political asset, a promissory note which can never be cashed. Episodes such as the AWACS debate which very nearly turned into a major crisis might have prompted the Saudis to question Churchill's dictum that 'the only thing worse than fighting with allies is fighting without them!' If there is any fighting to be done they might look to allies closer to home.

Rights of intervention

As late as the early 1960s the United States operated a vast network of bases and facilities, nearly 3,000 in all which enabled it to intervene anywhere at comparatively short notice. Today it must seek approval for any actions mounted against third parties, one reason why it tends to hide behind large pronouncements and even larger gestures.

In 1978, for example, as relations with Nicaragua deteriorated the small USAF contingent in Costa Rica was ordered out of the country within twenty-four hours. The Turkish government placed severe restrictions on the use of Incirlik during the Iranian revolution, a base from which US troops had been airlifted into the Lebanon in 1958.

Even the closest of American allies have been highly sensitive to the charge of complicity in operations against other Third World states. In the 1960s Marcos threatened to deny Australian war ships the right to use Filipino ports en route to help the United States in Vietnam.[18] He even refused to allow B52 bombers to use the Clark airbase; instead the Americans had to build airfields in Thailand at great expense, five times more than it would have cost to have extended the Clark runway. When the US base agreement was renegotiated in 1979 the government of the Philippines immediately assured Hanoi that the Americans would not be allowed to use Subic Bay for operations in any part of South-East Asia.

Perhaps, the main conclusion to be drawn from Marcos's behaviour is that his attitude seemed out of all proportion to his dependence on the American presence. On this vital issue, however, Subic Bay epitomises the permissive environment within which the United States has to work, in the Middle East even more than the Western Pacific.

The RDF may enjoy the most extensive set of basing rights recently granted a single power, an airfield in Oman, facilities at Seeb, a naval base in Somalia, as well as Ras Banas on the Red Sea, but the United States has no automatic right of access to any of them and would probably be denied access if it tried to intervene against another state in the region, without the express invitation of the host country.

Should Iranian air attacks on tanker traffic escalate in the straits of Hormuz or against the oil refineries along the Arabian peninsula, it could not attack Iranian airfields in response or even carry out normal aerial reconnaissance to assist in the protection of allied shipping without Arab support. The use of Saudi AWACS under US supervision could play an important and visible role; indeed the information gathered by such planes is normally shared among the members of the Gulf Cooperation Council. According to a Pentagon source, the United States has had contingency plans for such operations for some time.[19] Because of the distances involved the participating airforces would have to utilise the airfields in the GCC states; and that would depend on prior agreement of its members.

The United States has had to accept the limitations of operating in a permissive environment, the use of staging rights not bases, the prepositioning of equipment not men, reliance on precedents rather than formal agreements. As a result it has been persuaded that the RDF's proper mission is not to replace but to supplement the efforts of the Gulf states themselves, to defend interests common to the oil producers and consumers.

The joint military committee set up with the Saudis has not become a vehicle for joint military planning, or joint military exercises, but its existence did make possible the rapid transfer of aircraft to Riyadh in the summer of 1984 when the Iran–Iraq war entered a new and more dangerous phase. The sale of AWACS E-3As enables the Saudi airforce to coordinate American operations, to handle, if necessary, an entire US carrier or Marine Corps airwing, or up to two wings of fighters, in the absence of the sprawling logistical presence on the ground which was such a feature of the Vietnam war.

The sale of naval patrol boats to the GCC has provided the Gulf states with a military presence which can be used to complement US forces in precisely those areas in which the RDF is likely to serve both American and Arab interests. Conversely it has become almost impossible for the United States to act independently of its Arab allies without enormous cost.

This reality makes it impossible to stereotype Oman or the UAE as traditional American clients, over-sensitive to American interests, insensitive to their own. The development of the RDF suggests that the story needs retelling.

Non-alignment

If there is one place darker to the more radical non-aligned countries than the East–West struggle it is their own painful introspection. With the passage of time their concern about their involvement in the cold war has appeared increasingly remote and unreal; yet it still persists in their opposition to bases such as Diego Garcia.

Apart from Diego Garcia, the only overseas base outside Europe which is vital to US interests is Subic Bay, the USN's largest logistical support base in the Western Pacific. Clark Airfield is the largest USAF base in East Asia, a state within a state, as large as Singapore, capable of servicing up to 12,000 traffic movements a month. The San Miguel communications station twenty-five miles north of Subic Bay serves as the key communications station for the Seventh Fleet. Two-thirds of the air routes in the Philippines are reserved for the US military, as is a substantial proportion of the islands' internationally assigned air frequencies.

At times even the Marcos regime seemed to be locked in a posture of political indecision, clearly unwilling to forego the rental payments on Subic yet equally unwilling to entirely forfeit his country's official non-aligned status. In 1977 he seemed to be unsure 'whether the bases do, in fact, provide us with effective protection or whether they pose a danger to our country because of the provocation the bases represent to others'.[20]

Marcos was always more sensitive to the charge that the bases made the Philippines especially vulnerable to a pre-emptive Soviet strike than he was to the criticism that the United States relied on them as a Western springboard for the RDF, as a logistic support for the Seventh Fleet during the Iranian and Yemeni crises. Both Clark and Subic are still used as storage areas for tactical nuclear weapons; Subic still services America's nuclear armed aircraft carriers. When one also takes into account the fact that Clark is part of the Signal Scope Global Communications System for the Strategic Air Command, and that San Miguel also acts as a backup link for the US SLBM fleet, it is clear that the Philippines can hardly be described as non-aligned. The difference between it and Japan (where Sasebo is the USN's only other major ordinance depot in the Pacific) is that Japan is closely allied to the United States by treaty, and plays an increasingly active role in the defence of Western interests.[21]

Once again the RDF owes its success to the fact that the Arabs have been persuaded to see it as a deterrent, not a defensive force. The American presence may be extensive on paper; but in practice it is not large enough to threaten the Soviet Union and therefore invite a pre-emptive strike. It is just sufficiently large to protect an interest vital to both parties – oil – while allowing the United States to respond to an attack in an area of the world other than the Gulf. In that respect the Reagan administration has adhered to President Carter's insistence that the United States should be free to choose the terrain and the tactics to be used in the event of war. The US military presence in the Gulf does not offer a hostage to fortune.

In the past the Arab states could not understand why such an arrangement should be objectionable to Washington, why the Americans should accuse them of being non-political when they merely wished to be non-partisan. Many clearly perceived the dangers of being aligned with one of the superpowers when they were offered no deterrent, and no real partnership, only the prospect of becoming a bit player which might be upgraded in a crisis to a named role. When the RDF was first proposed the Saudis feared that Carter's references to a 'pre-emptive strategy' – of airlifting reinforcements to the region *too* quickly – might commit the United States long before there was any need for such a commitment, that it might provoke the very Soviet attack it was meant to deter. Some Saudi officers were as concerned about the possibility that the force might be used as they were about the possibility it would not be. If that concern has not disappeared, it now figures much less in Saudi thinking.

But that is not the end of the story; it is only part of it. If the Third World politicians of the 1950s were to reappear today much of the political landscape would still be familiar to them – the non-aligned countries are still treated in Washington with suspicion, patronised or cajoled. But much of the landscape is also changing, many of its features are disappearing, possibly for good. One of the questions frequently asked in the West is not whether bases threaten a country's non-aligned status but whether the Non-Aligned Movement threaten the open sea regime, in particular access to the straits at which many bases are located.

If the Third World were ever to turn the Indian Ocean into a Zone of Peace (ZOP) it would go far beyond the permissive environment under discussion. On several occasions in the past the West has been faced with actions by Third World states, not the Soviet Union, which have threatened freedom of passage for its own shipping: the closure of the Straits of Tiran in 1967, and the Suez Canal a few months later, Iran's threat to seal off the Straits of Hormuz at the outbreak of the Gulf War, and Libya's misguided attempt to claim control of the Gulf of Sirte which brought it into open conflict with the United States. In 1983 twenty-three states insisted on prior notification of the movement of all naval vessels passing through their seas, a move which was seen by the Reagan administration as a significant challenge to the traditional rights of free passage, one of the reasons it opposed UNCLOS 3.

Bases are still useful for the United States not as a way of severing communications in time of war, but keeping them open in time of peace, a perspective doubtless shared by the Soviet Union. It is quite possible that if the Soviet fleet had still been in Basra in strength Romanian tankers would not have been attacked during the course of the Gulf war.

The differences and difficulties thrown up by the debate on the Law of the Sea should not be obscured or dismissed. They serve to highlight a very real conflict of interests between the West and the developing world which may not easily be resolved because it involves an implicit challenge to the Non-Aligned

Movement. Far from Diego Garcia presenting a threat to the Zone of Peace, the Americans believe the concept of a ZOP represents a threat to the rights of innocent passage. Since UNCLOS 3 they have tried to redefine 'transit passage' in international law to mean freedom of navigation for all naval vessels with the 'legitimate' interests of the coastal states encompassing only the safety of shipping and protection against pollution, not an assured 'tranquility' of the state guaranteed by law.[22]

The desire of the Non-Aligned Movement to reduce military activity in the Indian Ocean to a minimum is hardly likely to commend itself to the United States, a country that genuinely believes that if the area ever came to be regarded by the coastal states as subject to their exclusive sovereignty the 'sovereign rights of communication' might well be threatened.[23] It is hardly likely to appeal either to the Soviet Union whose commercial trade with the world via the Indian Ocean is greater than the trade conducted between the coastal states themselves.

At the moment, the two sides seem to be cocooned in separate worlds. In the late 1970s one African delegate to the UN complained that in their response to proposals for a ZOP the superpowers insisted on using a vocabulary which meant nothing to the local states with its references to 'strategy, crisis, detente, security'. The representative of Madagascar was far more realistic in suggesting that the whole subject might be more fittingly handled not by the UN but by the Conference on Disarmament based in Geneva.[24] The more one sifts through UN discussions the more one senses a total self-obsession that makes such moments of realism when they do appear all the more compelling.

The weak cannot be blamed, perhaps, for finding fulfilment in what the West often appears to be defects of understanding or unquestioning belief that virtue is its own reward. But they should, at least, be aware of the risks they are courting by travelling their present path. To deny the superpowers right of free passage might provoke them to intervene more forcefully in local affairs, to establish client regimes who could be relied upon to guarantee freedom of transit where it might otherwise be denied. As Eliot Richardson rightly observes 'The Superpowers have trouble enough in an increasingly pluralistic world without being forced into marginal conflicts over the peacetime movement of their military forces'.[25] That will not prevent them from intervening if they are compelled to act, however reluctantly.

In fact, when looked at objectively, the United States has tried to reconcile itself to non-alignment as a position despite a cold war rhetoric which is still cluttered with moral certainties from the Dulles era. Most of its allies in the Third World have not been reduced to ciphers, the arc of crisis bears little relation to Eisenhower's Northern Tier, even the Reagan administration has tended to respect the Kantian maxim of treating others as ends, not means, a measure of how far the United States has travelled since the 1950s.

Indeed, the more one studies the problems it now faces in Europe where base rights are concerned, the more one looks at the tensions between the US and its NATO allies, the more some of the criticisms of the Non-Aligned Movement seem totally self-regarding. Does not reflecting on ones own weakness only compound it? Not only does the Third World insist on recalling its colonial past, it recollects recollecting it. This may act as a form of political exorcism, but a painful and obsessive one. At one point in *In Memoriam* Tennyson despairs that he has 'no language but a cry'. That cry is increasingly echoed in Western Europe as well. The cry is a common one; it is no longer the exclusive property of the non-aligned world.

CROSS CURRENTS

A Third World specialist who knew little of present trends in Western Europe, who was unaware of the concern frequently expressed about the presence of US forces, a concern which extends far beyond the Peace Movement and the parties of the Left, might be forgiven for assuming that the base issue was specific to the Third World. For the United States the rise of anti-American sentiment in Britain following the use of USAF bases for the raid on Tripoli in April 1986 makes the problem infinitely more complex.

Above all the Americans must be especially discouraged by the complaints that Western Europe has sold itself out, that its governments have been coopted, that they have become client states in all but name. On the left many parties have begun to talk of the price of 'Americanism', the military exchange programmes, and close relationship between the intelligence communities of NATO which are also considered 'bridges of dependency', extending back more than forty years in the case of Britain.[26]

In short, many of the issues which are associated with the base issue in the Third World are the common property of all movements or parties that regard association with the United States as a threat to regional security. Only when taken together, only when combined do they present an identikit of the Non-Aligned Movement. As a result, it is difficult in the final analysis not to conclude that the strategic recoupling of the West and the Third World represents much less of a threat to any particular region than to the Non-Aligned Movement itself.

For in reality the movement, like many other institutions in the world, is a political fiction. It is an important fiction, of course, because it unites left and right rather than divides them.[27] It still serves as a point of contact between rulers and ruled, which even Marcos threatened to exploit in 1983, during the last base negotiations with America. Its appeal is universal, not sectarian. It offers emancipation from the neo-colonial condition even though that condition is not military but economic; it promises an escape from the traumatic experience of dependency.

Thirty years on it still acts as an emotional rallying cry for a diverse set of countries which are in fact going their separate ways, some finding in membership of the Fourth World greater dependency than ever, others moving nearer the West, or translating the Western experience into a unique mode of production with which the West cannot compete. In other words, if the base issue is still relevant to the image the Third World has of itself, it is almost entirely irrelevant to its future.

NOTES

1 See my *NATO, the Warsaw Pact and Africa* (London: Macmillan, 1985), for a full discussion of this period.
2 *US security agreements and commitments abroad: Ethiopia*, Hearings, US Senate, Committee on Foreign Relations 1970, p. 7.
3 Cited Dieter Braun, *The Indian Ocean: region of conflict or Zone of Peace?* (London: Hurst and Co., 1983), p. 44.
4 Colin Legum (ed.), *Africa Contemporary Record 1973–4* (London: Rex Collins, 1974), p. B161.
5 See for example Peter Foot, 'Western security and the Third World', in Lawrence Freedman (ed.) *The Troubled Alliance: Atlantic relations in the 1980s* (London: Heinemann, 1983), p. 140.
6 'The age of affluence' is taken from J. K. Galbraith, *The Affluent Society*, 3rd edn. (London, 1977) and 'The age of uncertainty' from *The Age of Uncertainty* (London: BBC and Andre Deutsch Ltd, 1977) by the same author.
7 For the European role see my 'East of Suez revisited: the strategic recoupling of Western Europe and the Third World', in Christopher Coker (ed.) *The United States, Western Europe and military intervention in the Third World* (London: Macmillan, 1987).
8 The USSR has great difficulty securing base rights in the Third World as a Western naval attache was told informally in 1973. See *Soviet Oceans Development* Hearings, US Senate, Committee on Commerce and National Oceans Policy, 94th Congress, October 1976.
9 Cited Braun, *The Indian Ocean*, p. 45.
10 Cites *US–Philippines relations and the new bases and aid agreement* Hearings, House of Representatives, Committee on Foreign Affairs, 98th Congress, 1st Session, June 1983, p. 107.
11 Walter Bello, 'Spring board for intervention, instruments for nuclear war: US military bases in the Philippines' *South-East Asia Chronicle*, No. 89, p. 13.
12 In 1983 Marcos demanded an additional $1.5bn. Half of the $500m allotted in 1979 had been in the form of Foreign Military Sales credits which carried a steep interest of 16 per cent a year. This time Marcos asked for a straight rental, not aid, so that he could administer the funds himself.
13 Cited in Kenneth Walz, 'A strategy for the rapid deployment force', *International Security* 5:4, Spring 1981, p. 68.
14 Anthony Cordesman, *The Gulf and the search for strategic stability* (Boulder, Colorado: Westview Press, 1984), p. 258.
15 Cited Charles G. MacDonald, 'US policy and Gulf security', in Robert G. Davis (ed.), *Gulf security in the 1980s* (Stanford: Hoover Institution Press, 1984), p. 101.
16 Cordesman, *The Gulf and the search for strategic stability*, p. 372.
17 Ibid., p. 383.
18 D. O'Connel, *The influence of law on seapower* (Manchester University Press, 1975), p. 110.
19 *The Washington Post*, 25 August 1984.

20 *The Washington Post*, 9 January 1977.
21 Robert Berman and John Baker, *Soviet strategic forces: requirements and response* (Washington DC: Brookings Institution, 1982), p. 21 report that SS20s have been targetted on the Philippines for some time.
22 George Smith, *Restoring the concept of free seas: modern maritime law re-evaluated* (New York: Kieger, 1980), p. 38.
23 Eliot Richardson, 'Power, mobility and the law of the sea', *Foreign Affairs*, 58:4, Spring 1980, p. 904.
24 Cited *NATO, the Warsaw Pact and Africa*, p. 219.
25 Richardson, 'Power, mobility and the law of the sea', p. 911.
26 See Dan Smith, *The Defence of the Realm in the 1980s* (London: Croom Helm, 1980).
27 The Nigerian government's decision to abrogate the Anglo–Nigerian treaty in 1962 under pressure from the opposition can be taken as a symbolic gesture by the 'right' towards the non-aligned consensus. Britain's only formal treaty with a member of the Commonwealth was concluded with Malaysia (also in 1962).

Part IV: Whose crisis is the debt crisis?

A view from the South

Stephany Griffith-Jones

> The debt bomb of the newspaper headlines has turned out to be more like a debt cancer – less explosive but every bit as traumatic and eventually destructive.
> Sir Shridath Rampal, Secretary General of the Commonwealth, March 1986

> The main dangers are not in disturbance originating in financial markets, but rather in various malfunctions of the real economy. Even though we have not experienced a crisis that seriously disrupted its allocative role, the international capital market still does not appear to be working properly, with the bulk of net flows going from areas of high marginal productivity to areas of lower productivity.
> Barry Eichengreen and Richard Portes in 'The Anatomy of Financial Crisis', September 1986

The widespread foreign debt crises that have emerged since mid 1982 reflect a combination of factors, including fundamental weaknesses in the operation of the international financial system, the slow-down in industrial countries' growth and of inadequate economic policies and strategies in developing countries. The debt crises in their turn exacerbated international and national economic problems, by constraining significantly debtor countries' development prospects, by reducing, as a result, the value of exports from the rest of the world (including the industrial economies) to the heavily indebted nations, and by weakening (though not fundamentally damaging) the international banking system. By focussing attention of all involved on crisis management, the debt problem has distracted attention from the more fundamental long-term issues of designing appropriate development strategies for the debtor nations and of creating a system of international financial intermediation of mutual benefit to both debtors and creditors. As with previous historical experience, one of the first effects of the widespread debt crises of the 1980s has been to significantly reduce new private capital flows of all categories to small developing countries. While an interesting debate on future international financial intermediation to developing countries has begun, mainly in academic circles, any major actions on that front seem postponed until the debt crises are 'resolved'. On the other, solutions are seriously hindered by the lack of major new flows.

The difficult present 'vicious circle' type of situation could however be potentially transformed into a 'virtuous circle'. Several conditions would need to be met, including a clear technical and bargaining strategy by several major debtor governments, a willingness by them to use the yet unexploited 'bargaining strength' which negative net transfers of financial resources from them gives them, and a sympathetic and flexible response from industrial governments and private financial institutions.

This paper examines the key elements which give potential bargaining strength to major debtors; it outlines how the debt crisis has been managed till now, emphasising those aspects which are particularly relevant to the search for more 'positive sum' solutions; it concludes with suggestions on how current short-term debt crisis management can be shifted to a 'positive sum' situation which would lead to a more appropriate system of international financial intermediation to developing countries, and contribute thus more to those countries and to world economic growth.

THE CHANGE IN NET FINANCIAL FLOWS TO DEVELOPING COUNTRIES

In the post-World War Two period, up until 1982, the international financial system was broadly seen as contributing to the development of poorer countries, as it channelled savings from capital rich industrial countries and surplus developing ones to capital poor deficit developing countries. The nature, volume and conditions of the resulting financial transfers were not necessarily appropriate to the development needs of the poorer countries. The Bretton Woods system had not created mechanisms and institutions to channel a sufficient and sustainable level of net external financial resources to developing countries in deficit – from the industrialised countries or other developing countries with large surpluses – *as these countries' growth and development required*. This gap was only partly filled by different actors in the international scene (e.g. foreign investors, official aid agencies and multinational banks), who perceived at particular periods that channelling financial flows to developing countries served well their own economic and/or political interests. Though many politicians and academics, particularly in the Third World, were critical of the limitations and characteristics of the net transfer of financial flows towards their countries, *they broadly welcomed the contribution which foreign savings made to the development process.*[1]

The situation changed quite dramatically in the early eighties, and particularly since 1982. As a result of rapid increases in interest rates coinciding with declining new net flows of capital and increased capital flight from developing countries, the net transfer of financial resources has been dramatically reversed, de facto has now become negative, for many developing countries, particularly but not only in Latin America and for the Third World as a whole. This implies that financial resources now flow on a large scale from South to North, which is inconsistent with commonsense, international equity and economic logic.

The net transfer abroad is particularly large in Latin America, where states have spent around US $125bn more in debt service payments than they have received in foreign finance between 1982 and 1986 (see Table 1). This 'perverse' net transfer has been so large that it has been argued[2] that it has roughly wiped out the entire net inflow of capital generated in the massive petrodollar recycling of the 1970s.

Negative net transfers from Latin America on the scale indicated had two types of effect. Together with the large deterioration in the terms of trade, they contributed to the decline of output that occurred in the region, which implied that in 1986 GDP per capita was on average around 8 per cent below its 1980 level. Furthermore, even the most optimistic forecasters do not expect 1980 per capita GDP to be recovered before 1990, and ECLA as well as others talk of a 'lost decade' for Latin America. Thus *'debt crises management' has been functional to the needs of preserving the survival and stability of the private banks but dysfunctional to growth and development in Latin America*; it has also been dysfunctional to those agents in industrial countries which benefit from growth in the region (see below).

The magnitude and persistence of the negative net transfer of financial resources had a second type of effect, the implications of which have not fully been perceived. This relates to its impact on strengthening the bargaining position of Latin American countries (both collectively and individually *vis-à-vis* creditor banks). When net transfers of financial resources flow towards a developing country, the greater bargaining strength lies in the lenders, as it is they who must ultimately decide to make the new loans and transfer the funds. This implies that the lender can easily impose all types of conditions. When the net transfers are negative, the greater bargaining strength has potentially shifted to the debtor government, as *it might decide not to repay and ultimately not to make the transfer of funds*. Consequently, the debtor is in this case not only in a position to resist the conditions of the lender, but even more fundamentally to impose his own (e.g., fixing limits on its debt service payments as Peru has done and/or demanding a minimum growth target as Mexico did in 1986). Up till now the main question asked in industrial countries is whether Latin American

Table 1: *Latin America*

(US $ billion as a percentage)

Year/s	Net inflow of capital	Net payment of profits and interests	Net transfer of resources	Exports of goods and services	Net transfer/ export
	(1)	(2)	(3) = (1) − (2)	(4)	(5) = (3)
1973–81	21.2	11.0	10.1	64.4	+ 15.8
1982	19.8	38.7	− 18.9	103.2	− 18.3
1983	3.2	34.3	− 13.2	102.4	− 30.5
1984	19.2	36.2	− 27.0	114.1	− 23.7
1985	2.4	35.3	− 32.9	109.0	− 30.2
1986	8.6	30.7	− 22.1	95.2	− 23.2

Source: CEPAL, *Balance preliminar de la economia latinomericana durante 1986*, December 1986.

governments (and those of other developing nations) will use 'debtor power' to disrupt the international banking system. The less spectacular but far more crucial question is whether, and how, could developing countries use 'debtor power' to exert effective pressure for changes to be made in the international financial system that would make it stronger, more stable and more likely to support the development needs of the poorer nations.

The bargaining strength on debt and financial flows is somewhat different as regards the rest of the developing world as net transfers towards them, though they have declined sharply, remain positive or close to zero. From a development point of view, of particular concern is the trend of net transfers towards low-income Africa, which fell from a peak of US $2.8 bn in 1980 to only US $0.7 bn in 1984, recovering only slightly in 1985 (see Table 2). This decline in net transfers is particularly serious as it coincided with a period of severe drought in many SSA countries and sharply deteriorating commodity prices. From a bargaining point of view, those countries still receiving positive net transfers due to official grants and concessional flows are in a different position from the large middle income heavily indebted economies with negative net transfers.

Thus small countries receiving positive net transfers, though they may obtain better financial 'deals' due to their very smallness, tend to be subjected to tighter conditionality on their own economic policies by institutions such as the IMF. They also have far less interest to impose unilaterally limits on their debt payments and far less leverage to use their 'debtor power' to pursue positive sum multilaterally agreed reforms.

MAIN FEATURES OF DEBT RESCHEDULING AND ADJUSTMENT DEALS.

Since August 1982, debt crises and reschedulings have become widespread in Latin America and Africa. This is in contrast with the sixties and seventies when

Table 2: *Net Transfers, 1975 and 1980–5 (US $ billion)*

	1975	1980	1981	1982		1983	1984	1985
All developing countries	20.7	28.2	34.4	16.0		3.6	− 13.7	− 22
Major borrowers	11.4	10.5	19.1	0.2		− 8.0	− 15.5	− 22
Low-income Africa	1.4	2.8	2.6	1.9	1.7	0.7	0.8	

Source: World Bank *Development and Debt Service*. Abridged version of World Debt Tables, 1985–6 Edition. Washington DC 1986.

a very limited number of fairly small debtors undertook multilateral debt negotiations.

The existence of established procedures for dealing – particularly in the case of official debt through the *Paris Club* – with a few 'problem' debtors had a significance for the post-1982 deals, not sufficiently highlighted. *A sort of blueprint existed designed by a collective of creditors*, for dealing most appropriately – from the creditors' point of view – with a few 'problem' debtors, whose debt crises could to a large extent be attributed either to specific ill fortune affecting that country (e.g. drought, weak price of its exports) or mismanagement. These 'problem' debtors had little bargaining power, given the small size of their debts and economies; as much of their debt was official, their debt crises did not pose any threat to private banks' stability. Precedent and initiative – both important elements in negotiations, as bargaining theory rightly tells us – were heavily biased towards the interests of the creditors, at the time when the major and widespread debt crises erupted in 1982. The framework adopted for debt crises management and operated since 1982 has the following general features.

1   Crisis management of bank debt brought back to the *centre of the stage* official international organisations, as well as central banks of the major industrial governments. This was in contrast with the seventies when industrial countries' governments and international institutions had almost abandoned the field of international lending and borrowing to their private banks. It is a paradox that, while there was so little monitoring at the time the funds were being actually lent and spent, there has been so much monitoring and conditionality by official institutions after 1982, when new inflows of foreign capital became so scarce and net transfers negative!

The IMF played a key role in assembling 'rescue packages' which have simultaneously included an upper credit tranche (high conditionality) adjustment programme between the debtor country and the IMF, rescheduling of maturing debts and arrangements of new finance by all the creditor banks. The Fund's influence became crucial, particularly in 1982-mid 1985; adjustment financing provided by the IMF (which would bless the whole rescheduling package) became not only conditional upon adjustment following IMF 'advice' in the debtor country, but also upon the extension of new credit by the creditor banks. As time passed, not only the IMF, but increasingly the World Bank – through its Structural Adjustment and Sectoral Loans – has contributed financially to the 'rescheduling/new money packages'. From the debtor point of view, the involvement of the World Bank has had one advantage (its more long-term perspective on adjustment) but also a disadvantage, in the sense that the World Bank imposes additional elements of conditionality to those required by the Fund. Such 'cross conditionality' not only creates additional elements of ideological tension between debtor governments and international financial institutions (e.g., on the scope and pace of import liberalisation) but also makes negotiations far more complex and time consuming.

Though the role of international financial institutions in managing debt crises was broadly welcomed in debtor countries in the first stages (*c.* 1982–4), resistance to the conditionality imposed by the IMF and other institutions, as part of the 'financial packages', has increased particularly since 1985, even amongst those debtor governments willing to service their debts on a multilaterally agreed basis. A good example of this is Brazil. Since 1985, the new democratically elected government has been radical in rejecting an agreement with the IMF on its adjustment, whilst otherwise broadly complying with multilaterally agreed debt servicing procedures. These procedures have implied a negative net transfer of resources abroad from Brazil of around 4 per cent of GDP in the 1985–6 period. Thus, the position of the Brazilian authorities differs from that of the Peruvian government since 1985 which is radical both in its clear rejection of an agreement with the IMF on its economic adjustment and in its unilaterally imposed ceiling on debt servicing.

2 An important characteristic of post-1982 rescheduling deals has been 'involuntary lending' by creditor private banks, the level of which was not determined by banks' management but more or less imposed through pressure by the IMF, the industrial countries' central banks and to a certain extent by major creditor banks.

Since 1982 'involuntary lending' was for major Latin American countries with debt-servicing difficulties significantly less than interest and amortisation payments being made on the debt, leading to negative net transfer of financial resources from the debtor countries to creditor banks. 'Involuntary lending' was in the interest of the *collective of creditors*, because it avoided default, at least temporarily and possibly for always and the additional funds lent were significantly less than what the country was paying in debt service. Though the creditors had a 'collective' interest in new lending to avoid default, this was less clear at an *individual* level, as individual banks could have tried to 'free-ride' by refusing to lend new money or by the involvement of two types of banks: those whose loans to the major debtors formed a high proportion of their total assets, often exceeding their capital (their fundamental target was default avoidance of major debtors, and they were willing to increase their exposure for this purpose); and those banks whose loans were smaller in relation to their assets and capital had less incentive to increase lending for default avoidance and more preference to withdraw loans. To deal with the problems of 'free-riders' and different categories of creditor banks the IMF 'imposed' involuntary lending, whereby *all creditor banks were forced to increase* their exposure by a certain percentage.

Since 1982, the IMF (with the help of central banks from industrial countries) to a certain extent 'created' a market, by pressing all and each creditor bank to lend where they did not necessarily wish to do so. It could be argued that this involuntary market is in fact not a market at all in the sense conventionally adopted by economic theory, and that since late 1982 a proper market of international private lending to Latin America and Africa largely ceased to exist.

Involuntary lending merely prevented a greater fall of net new lending than would have occurred if markets had operated spontaneously since 1982. As can be seen in Table 3, net new lending to Latin America declined significantly (from US $30.5 bn in 1981 to US $ 3.6 bn in 1985, and even became negative during the first half of 1986), in spite of 'involuntary lending'. A similar, though less dramatic trend, occurred for bank lending to Africa. Though net new bank lending has become increasingly marginal, it should be stressed that a drastic reduction of existing bank exposure in Latin American countries has been avoided, a trend which would have further aggravated the problem.

The fact that a market for private international lending to Latin America and Africa has practically ceased to exist, and was replaced by administered decisions, in which governments (of both creditor and debtor countries) as well as official international institutions determine flows involving private agents implies that bargaining theory (as well as analysis of relative power positions of the actors involved) can throw useful light in explaining the types of deals reached.

3   A third feature of debt crisis management has been the formation of steering committees by the private banks for the purpose of negotiating with debtor governments. The private banks represented in these committees are those holding the largest debts of a particular country; they tend also to be the largest banks in the industrial countries. The steering committee performed a positive role in coordinating hundreds of banks and representing them in negotiations, thus facilitating the negotiations. They assured some 'new money' was granted to

Table 3: *New net flows from private banks to Latin America and Africa, 1980–4 (US $ billion)*

	1980	1981	1982	1983	1984	1985	1st half 1986
Latin America	27.3	30.5	12.1	7.8	5.7	1.3	−1.6
Africa	2.0	2.2	1.7	0.3	0.1	0.4	−0.1
Asia & Middle East	9.7	7.4	5.9	3.5	4.6	6.8	−2.1
Total non-OPEC LDCs	39.0	39.9	19.8	12.2	10.4	8.5	−3.8

Source: BIS *1986 Annual Report*, p. 95 for 1980–5. Coverage of information has been slightly enlarged for 1984. For 1986 (first half), BIS *The maturity distribution of international bank lending, first half 1986*. December 1986; the figures exclude valuation effects.

Latin American countries and that debt was rescheduled; as the 'new money' that the collective of banks are willing to contribute declines significantly, their function is increasingly reduced to ensure maximum debt service repayment from debtor governments.

The existence and operation of the steering committee has been clearly functional to the interests of the big banks, mainly because it has implied *cohesion amongst themselves on the negotiating front with the debtors*, and subordination of the smaller banks' actions and interests to their own. An interesting difference arises here from the thirties, when creditors were much less able than in the eighties to organise themselves to represent their interests collectively. Another significant difference is that – linked to the nature of the finance provided, via bonds – negotiations and the attempted organisation of creditors occurred in the thirties *after default* was declared, with important implications for the relative bargaining positions of debtors and creditors.[3]

4   The intimate cohesion amongst creditor banks – and their close links with the IMF and other international financial institutions – has been in sharp contrast to the way that debtors have accepted or been forced to conduct negotiations, on an individual case-by-case basis. Since 1982, the governments of industrial countries and the IMF have extolled the virtues and successes of the 'case-by-case' approach and rejected 'global plans' for dealing with the debt problem.

Although, since early 1984, Latin American debtor government representatives at the most senior level have jointly discussed the debt problem in a series of meetings (and have created the Cartagena Group of main Latin American debtors), they have not broken the pattern of the actual financial negotiations whereby creditors negotiate as a bloc while debtors negotiated individually. Though the joint meetings of Latin American governments has doubtlessly had some impact on obtaining slightly better financial terms for all debtors (e.g., elimination of rescheduling fee, reduction of spreads), these concessions obtained from the creditors have been marginal, particularly if viewed in relation to the magnitudes of the net transfers involved. Futhermore, the Latin American debtor governments have not presented, and even less negotiated jointly, their own clear 'blueprint' for debt crisis management, which would have *provided an alternative to the creditors' blueprint*. Though informed Latin American observers[4] note the increased commitment by the Cartagena Group debtors to more precise proposals of alternative debt crisis management, recent economic developments may have sharpened differences towards debt negotiations amongst Latin American governments; for example, the fall in the price of oil in 1986 worsened the situation of oil exporters such as Mexico while easing that of oil importers such as Brazil or Chile, leading to far higher growth rates in the latter than in the former. This structure of the negotiation gives creditors two advantages.

Their collective and closely coordinated stance confronts each country separately, by which the countries are forfeiting the potential gains of a collective common bargaining stance. Also, this procedure gives the creditors the advantage of intersecting negotiations. As Schelling[5] points out, 'the advantage goes to the party that can precisely point to an array of other negotiations in which its own position would be prejudiced if it made a concession in this one'. Steering committees have used the argument of 'precedent' successfully as a bargaining tactic, to avoid concessions for which individual debtors have been pressing on grounds that – if granted to that particular debtor, which could be feasible – they would be obliged to grant them to other debtors. It is interesting that, for example, M. Castillo, ex-governor of the Costa Rican Central Bank has reported that the creditor banks took a tougher position *vis-à-vis* his government after the debt crisis became widespread, due obviously to the fear of precedent.

5 Debtors have been committed – till now – to multilaterally agreed negotiated deals with the banks, their host governments and international financial institutions. Unilateral action (leading to default or extended moratoria) has not been officially adopted by any major debtor since 1982. Several major debtors have unilaterally declared *temporary* moratoria; two medium-sized debtors, *Peru and Nigeria, in 1985 unilaterally put a limit on debt service payments*, which in the Peruvian case implied very little debt service payments to private banks; many small debtors, e.g., Bolivia, as well as several African countries have had prolonged moratoria or arrears. Futhermore, it was widely reported that the Mexican government was very close to taking unilateral action on limiting interest payments in early and mid 1986, though eventually such action was not taken.

The large debtors' approach thus, till now, implied a request to their creditors for debt restructuring and new loans, rather than a *unilateral initiative*, either on an absolute debt default, a temporary one (moratoria) or a limit on debt service payment. This contrasts with the thirties, when negotiations *followed* outright default; then financial institutions did not extend new loans as debt crises broke out, as it was their customers' rather than their own assets which were at stake; public international financial institutions and cooperation were either non-existent or far weaker in the thirties than in the eighties. Default avoidance mechanisms were therefore much weaker then. In the eighties, the heavy involvement of the industrial countries' major private banks in the debt problem as well as the development of important international *public* financial institutions competent at 'debt crises management' has contributed to default avoidance, playing an extremely positive role in preserving the stability of the international financial system. The unwillingness of debtors to take unilateral actions seems however to have been an important factor in making the 'solutions negotiated' to deal with the debt crisis, one whose *costs were mainly borne by the debtors' economies.*

6   The preservation of the international financial system in its existing form and particularly the mode adopted for debt crises management has had very high costs *not only for debtor countries but also for non-financial actors in the developed world.* The decline in growth (or of output) in Latin American economies, linked to the large negative net transfer of financial resources from the continent, has adversely affected the exporters of goods to that continent. It would seem that the interests of agents, such as exporters to Latin America and Africa, and foreign investors in these areas, have not been sufficiently considered or represented in debt crises management. The magnitude of the impact of the developing countries' debt crises on industrial countries' exports and employment levels has not been sufficiently stressed. According to UNCTAD estimates[6] as a result of the contraction of exports from industrial market economies to developing ones (linked to widespread debt crises) between 1982 and 1984 there has been a cumulative loss of jobs in the industrial countries of about 8 million man/woman years; of these 7 million man/woman years were lost in Europe and close to one million man/woman years were lost in the United States and Canada. *Financial interests, institutions and criteria have been extremely dominant in the way that debt crises have been managed.* The main actors involved in the negotiations have been representatives of the major private banks and the central banks of industrial countries, of the IMF and BIS, and of representatives from the Finance Ministries and/or central banks of debtor countries. Broadly absent from the negotiations have been private agents concerned with growth (such as exporters

or investors in LDCs) and public international institutions concerned with development (such as the World Bank or UNICEF). Representatives of LDCs have also not included private or government institutions involved in the productive sectors of their economies.

There has been almost a continuous process of negotiation. The time-intensiveness of recurrent negotiations, as imposed by the 'needs' of debt crises management, has distracted time and energy from the *more long-term concerns of developing countries governments, those of growth and development.* The dominance of financial institutions and criteria in debt crises management also had a major impact on perceptions of debt crises and growth as purely *temporary* phenomena.

Around mid 1985, it became evident however that, whatever the evolution of international economic variables, the debt overhang would still continue as a major constraint for development of debtor nations and would drag down world economic growth. For the major debtors, negative net transfers has since 1982 become pervasive, as private lenders were unwilling to 'throw good money after bad', and as interest rates, though decreasing somewhat in nominal terms, remained very high in real terms, given the weakness of prices of their main export commodities. Indeed, weakness of commodity prices has emerged since 1985, together with negative net transfers of financial resources as the major factors, which make the current debt crisis management strategy inconsistent with sustained development in debtor countries. This swing in trends and perceptions was reflected in mid 1985, first in the more radical position taken by the Peruvian government, and later in the US Treasury Secretary Baker's initiative of September 1985, the so-called Baker Plan. Though clearly implying important changes in perceptions and attitudes of some debtors and of the main creditor government, surprisingly the impact of the Garcia and the Baker initiatives on the way the debt problem was handled for most Latin American nations was relatively marginal. Though expressing broad support for Garcia's stance, Latin American governments did not follow his unilateral initiative by similar actions on their part (even though their negotiating stance was implicitly strengthened by his actions). Though expressing support for Baker's plan, creditor banks have not followed such verbal support with new lending. (As figures in Table 3 indicate, net new bank lendings actually became slightly negative after the Baker Plan was launched; however, official multilateral lending has expanded somewhat after Secretary Baker launched his initiative.)

A final caveat seems relevant. In a world economy with very sharp fluctuations in key international variables and great uncertainty about their evolution, *the diagnosis of the debt problem and the design of appropriate solutions is linked to forecasts of a very uncertain future.* This implies the need for solutions that not only accommodate the interests of different agents involved but also do so satisfactorily under *different* scenarios. This leads to the need for establishing contingency clauses and compensatory mechanisms on the one hand, and general principles on the other (such as no negative financial transfers, minimum growth) rather than precise numerical performance targets that have characterised debt crises management and adjustment monitoring in recent years.

The recent (1986) agreement between Mexico and the IMF seems to point to the beginning of acceptance of these principles. The deal signed in mid 1986 between creditor banks, the IMF and the Mexican government embodies two important principles. Perhaps the most important one is that growth should be a crucial target of debt crises management; the deal with Mexico implies that, if. 1987 growth falls below a minimum of 3–4 per cent, then new credits are automatically triggered off; similarly, there are contingency clauses which trigger off funds for increased lending should the oil price collapse to very low levels (and decreased lending should the oil price surpass a certain ceiling).

CONCLUSIONS AND SUGGESTIONS FOR FUTURE ACTION

The debt crises of the 1980s have been handled very successfully, if evaluated from the point of view of the banks. No important international bank has gone bankrupt as a result of the Third World debt crises. Far more importantly, this has implied that there has been no major contraction of international lending capacity, no major disruption of the international capital flows which did occur after the defaults of the 1930s. Developing countries have derived important indirect benefits from this achievement because demand from the developed world has not collapsed, though it has been sluggish, and because the level of trade finance to them has been maintained. However, developing countries have not directly benefited from the resilience of the private international financial system, as the private banks have almost stopped lending to them for the last four years, and are unlikely to resume such lending in the medium-term. This is not only due to the drastically increased perception of risk in bank lending to less developed countries but also because of the attractiveness exerted by the alternative demand for credit provided by the US current account and budget deficit. The non-disruption of private international financial markets has however implied severe costs in the real economy. Most obviously, the debt burden and the need to service it has implied that there is a major foreign exchange constraint on development for debtor nations. As pointed out above in Latin America, GDP per capita in 1987 is well below 1980 levels, which is in sharp contrast with the post World War Two performance, when Latin American per capita GDP had been steadily rising. This cost has been reflected in lower investment (which in 1986 was about 25 per cent below 1980 levels for

Latin America) and in declines in real wages and employment levels, that have been extremely severe in some Latin American countries.[7]

The need to maintain large positive trade surpluses in Latin America, so as to generate sufficient foreign exchange to make the negative net transfer, has largely been achieved through a reduction of the region's imports, whose value in 1983–6 has remained on average around 40 per cent below the 1981 level! This reduction of Latin American imports (accompanied by a similar one from Africa) has had a depressive impact on an already sluggish world trade; it has clearly damaged exporters from industrial countries who have seen their sales to the developing world sharply reduced. *This has accentuated both the US trade deficit problem and the West European unemployment problem.*

Is this state of affairs inevitable? Must trade, production, employment be sacrificed to preserve the private financial system? There are many who have argued that there are alternative ways of handling the debt overhang, which while continuing to avoid major disruptions of the international private financial market would allow for more rapid development in the Third World resulting in higher levels of trade and direct investment towards them, which would benefit economic growth in the industrial world. Instead of administering a crisis, where everybody except the bank have lost, a far more 'positive sum' approach could be taken.

It would seem that such a positive sum approach is feasible and requires a package of measures, some of which are outlined below.

Enhanced role of government in financial flows

The problems raised for debtor economies by private international financial intermediation, particularly but not only as practised in the 1970s, combined with a general abhorrence of balance of payments lending to developing countries widespread among private bankers since 1982, seem to make inevitable in the late eighties an expansion in the role of governments and official institutions in international financial intermediation if major changes in net transfers to and from developing countries are to be achieved. Part of this expanded public role could be temporary, and operate while the private markets are not performing fully their role of channelling funds from areas of low productivity to those of high productivity. A desirable package of measures would clearly imply, as regards new flows, either a significant expansion of new official flows (through increases in lending by the World Bank, regional development banks, bilateral flows), or an expansion of government guarantees, insurance or lender of last resort facilities that would combine basically 'public purpose and private finance'. The attraction of the second approach is that it requires far less government expenditure; the risk is that, unless government guarantees offered are very explicit, the impact on additional private flows may be fairly marginal. Recent exhortations by the US government to banks to increase lending and the granting of partial guarantees (in the context of the Baker initiative) have had very little impact in encouraging private flows. Thus, if significant new flows are to be generated to developing countries, it is crucial that this is done directly through public intuitive and/or through explicit government guarantees.

If public guarantees are given to future private flows, and/or some tax concessions or subsidies are given to banks to help fund interest or debt relief (see below), at the same time industrial governments could take the opportunity to increase their supervision, regulation and control of private flows simultaneously as a quid pro quo for the support they are giving to their private banks. In this, as in other aspects, the problems caused by the debt crisis could contribute in the long term to generating an international financial system which was more appropriate to development and world trade as well as more stable.

Debt relief for low-income countries

There seems to be increased recognition of the need for some debt relief for low-income countries, particularly but not only in Sub-Saharan Africa, as their debt burden is virtually unpayable on any reasonable projection and the problems of the debt overhang merely complicate the decision on future development strategies, as well as on new flows. It may be useful for negotiations to take place on *special* arrangements and guidelines for low-income countries, which could include debt relief for poor countries with heavy debt burdens and which have been most seriously affected by a deterioration in the international environment. (It should be stressed that several industrial governments have clearly granted debt relief to low-income countries in the seventies so that the precedent clearly exists.)

Reduction or elimination of 'perverse transfers' for middle-income developing countries

For heavily indebted middle-income countries, it seems unlikely that multilaterally agreed debt relief can be achieved in the current climate of opinion, even though at least partial debt relief could be of great benefit, not only to their economies and peoples, but also to the world economy.

General guidelines for middle-income debtors, through which individual negotiations could be conducted, would be extremely valuable. Such guidelines could imply minimum uniform grace periods for principal payments and a reasonable ceiling on real interest rates. The difference between the 'market' interest rate and the ceiling rate should *not* be added to future debt, but the cost of the interest relief shared by the private creditor banks and their governments. Different calculations show that both US and UK banks could grant fairly significant interest relief to major debtors *without* a major impact on their profitability, and even more clearly, *without* any threat to their stability. An alternative general guideline for middle-income debtors would be to fix as a target a drastic reduction or elimination of net transfers from those countries. A problem of a uniform target would be that those countries who had borrowed less in the past would get the same treatment as those who borrowed large sums. However, the fixing of clear limits on net transfers would focus attention and negotiation on the crucial variable for developing countries, net transfers of financial resources. It would also allow for a certain amount of flexibility, in the sense that different mechanisms or combinations could be adopted in different creditor countries to achieve similar targets of net transfers. (This would be consistent with the fact that tax treatment of interest relief would be quite different in different *creditor countries* particularly within Western Europe.)

Though limits on net transfers or on interest payments are not particularly radical, it is unlikely in the present climate that they would be accepted by creditor governments and institutions, unless and until debtor governments exert collective and clearly targetted pressure for such a measure to be adopted. Indeed, some collective action (or at least threat) for a temporary unilateral adoption of such limits may be necessary for the adoption of significantly improved multilaterally negotiated agreements. Any such unilateral action by debtor governments would have to be cautious and conciliatory, so as to avoid, not only threat of retaliation on its own economy, but also posing a threat to world financial stability.

Linkage of financial package to enhanced development

It seems crucial that any financial package to alleviate the debt crisis significantly should have maximum developmental impact on the debtor economy. The establishment of a clear link between changes in net transfers of foreign exchange and development spending will make concessions from creditor governments and banks easier to negotiate and justify industrial countries; more crucially, it would also give some assurance that these concessions would genuinely lead to increased economic growth, future balance of payments viability, and increased welfare, particularly of poorer and more vulnerable groups.

The concrete mechanisms to link debt and/or interest relief to development expenditure have begun to be suggested, both in Latin America and in some industrial countries. Osvaldo Sunkel and Raul Prebisch[8] both suggested that part of interest servicing should be made in local currency of the debtor economy and devoted to investment in development projects, following rigorous and clearly established public criteria negotiated between governments of industrial and developing countries, and monitored by development agencies. The President of the Inter-American Development Bank is reported (*Financial Times*, September 1985) to have endorsed a similar proposal.

NOTES

1 For a more detailed discussion, see, for example, S. Griffith-Jones and O. Sunkel, *The Crises of Debt and Development* (Oxford University Press, 1986).
2 Inter-American Development Bank, *Economic and Social Progress in Latin America* (Washington DC, 1986).
3 See Eichengreen B. and Portes R., 'Debt and default in the 1930s: causes and consequences', CEPR discussion paper 85, No. 75 (London, 1985).
4 D. Tussie, 'The coordination of the Latin American debtors', in S. Griffith-Jones *Bargaining on debt and adjustment* (Wheatsheaf, 1987).
5 T. D. Schelling, *The Strategy of Conflict* (Oxford University Press, 1963), Chapter 2.
6 UNCTAD, *Trade and Development Report 1985*, (UN, New York), pp. 119–20.
7 For recent figures, see UN ECLAC, *Preliminary overview of the Latin American Economy*, 1986, Santiago de Chile, December 1986.
8 O. Sunkel, *America Latina y la crisis Economica Internacional, ocho Tesis y una Propuesta*, Grupo Editorial Latinoamericano. Buenos Aires, 1985, and R. Prebisch, 'Statement to the US House of Representatives in July 1985', reproduced in *CEPAL Review* No. 27, Santiago de Chile, December 1985.

8 A view from the North

Stephen Thomas

nobody really understands the international monetary system . . .
H. Johannes Witteveen – former Managing Director of the I.M.F.

The international debt crisis in common usage refers to the difficulties which developing states are experiencing in repaying loans to international banks. Few would seriously argue that this international debt crisis is not a crisis for the South, given the large real transfers which are currently being effected towards the North, and the low and falling incomes of the South. The annual net resource transfer from Latin America since 1982 has been equivalent to about 4 per cent of gross national product, which contrasts unfavourably with the German World War One reparations payments of 'only' $2\frac{1}{2}$ per cent of GNP.

Yet this paper argues that the international debt crisis is but one aspect of a much larger debt crisis being played out also in the North; the debt crisis is a truly *global* crisis, and many of its effects are still poorly understood. As such debt is a crisis *both* for the North *and* for the South. In the case of the North, it is a crisis not only as is commonly understood because the Northern banks are over-exposed to the developing countries, but also importantly because of domestic strains within the Northern financial system.

The above quotation from Witteveen emphasises just how little is really known about the workings of the international financial system. Yet the frequent meetings of political leaders, their finance ministers, and their committees of experts suggest, first, that all is not right with the system, and, secondly, that world economic prosperity is not neutral with respect to its structure. Rather, exchange and interest rate volatility may adversely affect trade and growth, while misaligned exchange values may lead to resource misallocations and encourage protectionist tendencies. *If security in North–South relations requires an economic environment which encourages worldwide economic growth and resource flows towards the South* as part of the development process, then a clear understanding of the failings of the international financial system is paramount. What has gone wrong, and how can we put matters right?

The so-called 'case-by-case' rescheduling approach to the debt crisis, involving intricate rescheduling operations and often heralded as a great success by Northern bankers and politicians, is really irrelevant to the underlying problems, even though it has important consequences for the individual countries and banks concerned. This approach is comprised of a sequence of partial, short-term responses to a problem which requires immediate long-term attention; a *global* financial crisis, which involves the developed *and* developing worlds. The recent decision by Citicorp (May, 1987), to publicly acknowledge the need to massively increase its loan loss reserves against its Third World debt is a belated step in the right direction.

THE INTERNATIONAL DEBT CRISIS

The development of the international debt crisis has been described innumerable times,[1] and will not be repeated in detail here. The basic idea, bereft of supporting statistics, is that the OPEC countries ran balance-of-payments' surpluses on a large scale after 1973; these were usually denominated in US dollars, as oil was priced in dollars, and placed on deposit at international banks. The latter on-lent these funds to developing and industrial countries to fund their deficits and finance projects. In 1979 the US Federal Reserve Board switched from controlling interest rates to setting money supply targets, and also pursued a vigorous drive against inflation. Interest rates rose dramatically, and output worldwide fell. We experienced an increase in so-called 'systematic' risk,[2] i.e. risk which is not specific to a particular project or country, but which is common to all actors in the economic system. US tax cuts and increased defence expenditures led to a large growth in the US budget deficit, and interest rates continued to rise. The dollar rose dramatically as well. Shrinking world markets together with sharply higher debt service squeezed the developing countries' ability to repay their borrowings, forcing numerous acts of rescheduling or restructuring since 1982.

There are some aspects of the above story which are particularly important for understanding the debt crisis.

The dollar as a 'vehicle' currency

A vehicle currency is one which is used as a medium of exchange for private transactions between countries, neither of which need use it for domestic transactions. It may be used for invoicing contracts and intervention by governments to sustain fixed exchange parities. Commodities such as oil are priced in dollars. Vehicle currencies arise since there are attractive economies of scale in dealing bilaterally with a single, important, currency. Banks involved in recycling the OPEC surplus often made loans in dollars, having received dollars on deposit in the first place from surplus countries. In addition, US-based banks also lent heavily in dollars to developing countries in the early 1980s, bringing international borrowing through these sources to over $1,000 billion by 1986. Allowing for increases in our capacity to produce, this is about *four times the level* associated with the collapse of 1931.[3] We shall argue later that one aspect of the international banking crisis which is as yet not well understood is its implications for interest rates and the dollar exchange rate, and that this causes particular problems since the debt is largely denominated in US dollars.

Floating rate loans

The credits which were extended to the developing countries were usually at a floating rate, i.e. they varied as market interest rates changed. Hence banks did not have to guess the future course of interest rates except as it affected the ability of a borrower to repay its loan. Any risk attached to a particular interest rate was borne by the lender, since the bank simply passed on any changes in the rate it had to pay for its deposits. The only constraint on its profitability seemed to be the amount of loans it could make. Further, since the loans were in dollars, the borrower also had to bear any exchange risk. Banks failed to realise that by insulating themselves from exchange and interest rate risk they were really only disguising the increased *credit* risk associated with the loans.

Biased risk perceptions

Stories abound of bankers rushing to lend at all costs to developing countries in the 1970s.[4] There was inadequate statistical information available to properly assess the possibilities for the successful performance of many of the projects and deficits funded, and in its place was an optimism that sovereign countries somehow would not default on their loans. Few would now claim that this was prudent lending. Why did it occur? Most of those involved in making lending decisions had no experience of a serious financial crisis. Psychologists tell us that there is a tendency to underestimate probabilities of events occurring if they occur infrequently and have not occurred for a substantial passage of time.[5] Hence the bankers seriously underestimated the possibility of a serious shock to the international economic system; this is called 'disaster myopia'. It leads decision-makers to allow the shock exposure of the banks to rise and their ability to withstand shocks to decline (e.g. by allowing loans concentrated in particular geographical or industrial sectors to rise to an unhealthy proportion of capital). Even when evidence abounds that their shock exposures are too high, there is a reluctance to acknowledge the new reality; this is a reflection of 'cognitive dissonance', with decision-makers not wishing to cast doubt on the wisdom of their past decisions. Much of this confidence came from reassurances from the central banks of the industrialised countries that lender of last resort facilities would be made available to the international banking community in the event of a crisis; this was enshrined in the 'Basle Concordat' of 1975.

THE NORTHERN DEBT CRISIS

On a wider scale the North is confronting its own debt crisis, and many of the features characterising the international debt crisis are relevant here. There has been a rapid growth of debt owed by individuals, corporations and governments over the last fifteen years; in the US debt has grown from $1.0 trillion in 1964 to $7.4 trillion in 1984, up from one and a half to over *twice* US annual output. Currently 10 per cent of US banks are experiencing severe difficulties with their loan portfolios; the major source of the problem is *not* the developing countries or the energy companies,[6] but rather individual households. Credit cards appear unsolicited in the post, and some individuals have accumulated over 500 such cards with little cross-checking and no central register of debt. American banks had to write off 0.86 per cent of their loans as uncollectable in the first half of 1986, up by 50 per cent from 1982. Personal bankruptcies were at record levels in 1986. Even the giant Citicorp and Manufacturers Hanover have been downgraded by the debt-rating agencies. In the UK building society and local authority rent arrears are running at record levels and millions of consumers are behind in payments for essentials such as fuel; everyday newspapers carry advertisements offering to 'reschedule' household debt. The number of properties taken into possession by mortgage lenders in Britain rose fourfold between 1980 and 1985. The Governor of the Bank of England recently urged building societies to set up a national reference agency to check on the credit worthiness of would-be home owners (May 1987); some UK banks are already considering the possibility of a central debt databank for cross-checking the credit-worthiness of customers. This would collate details of individual borrowings to a number of different institutions and then the information would be available to all contributors. Total household debt has increased from around 40 per cent of disposable income in 1979 to over 70 per cent now. This easy availability of credit has helped to create the 'nouveaux poor'.

How did this situation come about and what are its implications? There has clearly been a lowering of credit standards accompanying the financial deregulation revolution, with a myriad of new credit products offered to individuals and corporations, including negotiable certificates of deposits, options, futures, and money market funds. These new financial products offer bundles of financial characteristics which satisfy the wide diversity of financing requirements of the markets, and offer an (illusory) sense of low risk. The volatile interest rate environment of the past ten years or so, stimulated by the switch to quasi-monetarism in 1979, prompted the change to variable rate financing, with both borrower and lender preferring continuous recontracting to longer-term commitments. In addition, the rapid growth in so-called off-balance activities by banks suggests that the above debt figures are serious *underestimates*. By September 1986, America's seven largest banks had off-balance sheet commitments of $1.4 trillion compared with under $550 billion on-balance-sheet. Bank regulators in the US, UK and Japan have been urgently trying to adequately assess the risks involved in holding these assets, resulting in a new set of capital adequacy proposals from the BIS in December, 1987.

The US government too has contributed to the growth in debt by running record budget deficits in recent years; whereas US government debt grew by only 3 per cent per annum in the 1960s, it was rising by over 13 per cent per annum in 1979–84; the deficit rose to 5 per cent of GNP after 1982 compared to under 1 per cent on average pre-1966. US non-financial corporations took on nearly $200 billion net of debt in 1984, up from $50 billion in 1983; in parallel the role of the equity market has diminished with around $75 billion net of equity being retired. This reflected merger, acquisition and leveraged buy-out activity.[7]

What are the effects of growth in debt? The rapid growth in debt was accompanied by certain phenomena which aggravated economic and financial instability; interest and exchange rates became more volatile – average *real* dollar rates of interest rose from 2–3 per cent in the 1960s, to over 8 per cent in the early 1980s; the increased borrowing was often short-term, increasing the risk of illiquidity; the private sector was increasingly willing to finance investment at floating rates and to shorten the maturity of borrowing from long to medium term; the long-term bond market became increasingly dominated by the government.

The deposit institutions operate under an umbrella of insurance. Until recently in the US they have paid fixed rates for this facility independent of the quality of their loans. Hence they attract funds at rates which vary little and do not reflect the difference in credit quality among institutions. Banks now charge only about 25 basis points more to a triple-B floating-rate borrower than a triple-A one, though the bond market requires an extra point on yields from the lower quality credit. Until 1934 large corporate depositors in the US monitored the quality of banks' portfolios, and differential returns ensued. However, it is no longer only the small depositors who are protected; *everyone* was bailed out in the recent (1984) Continental Illinois collapse, even though there is a notional limit of $100,000 per depositor. Failure could not be tolerated because the bank had wide-ranging relationships with other institutions at home and abroad. Further, public confidence in financial institutions in general would have been severely shaken, with potentially serious knock-on effects. Indeed the ripple effects of a financial institution's failure can be many times more extensive than those which ensue following the collapse of a similar sized non-financial firm. It is clear, then, that this lender-of-last resort facility may well encourage reckless lending policies; it enhances the attractiveness of risk-taking by insured financial institutions. The banks in the US are indeed in such bad shape that the federal insurance agencies are effectively broke and in need of new funding, i.e. a further bail-out.

It would seem essential that, if financial institutions really desire as few regulations as possible within which to operate, then they must accept that they may well fail if they make loans which do not perform well. If ailing institutions are kept going when the return on their investments is inadequate, then scarce resources are being channelled into less productive uses.

BACK TO THE INTERNATIONAL DEBT CRISIS

The international debt crisis will be recognised, then, as one aspect of the global financial crisis outlined above; the developing countries were the recipients of large amounts of floating rate, medium-term finance which was intrinsically unsuited to the uses to which it was put. The syndicated credits of the offshore banking system were a financial innovation as outlined above, and appeared as a product which satisfied both borrowers and lenders by its 'flexibility'. However, lower credit standards, biased perceptions, and financial innovation came face-to-face with an increase in the risk in the system as the world went into a deep recession; the debt can no longer be serviced and the banks are locked into the problem.

In an accompanying paper Stephany Griffith-Jones[8] quotes an influential paper by Portes and Eichengreen[9] to the effect that financial shocks are of limited importance relative to real shocks in knocking the world economy off course; they are incorrect in so far as the *structure* of the financial system has the *potential* to rapidly exacerbate the slightest real shock, and hence is critical to the prolonged health of the world real economy. If financial institutions are 'stretched' such that their assets and liabilities are seriously mismatched, or they have grown rapidly relative to their capital and reserves, or they have politely concealed substantial bad debts, then even small real shocks could spread rapidly through the system via financial institutions becoming illiquid or insolvent. The above evidence is intended to suggest that this may well be the case already, with Third World debt but one aspect of a wider potential debt crisis.

THE INTERNATIONAL DEBT CRISIS AND THE DOLLAR

Perhaps the major threat to the world economy and in particular the developing countries in recent years has been the increasing tide of US protectionism. This follows the remarkable real rise in the value of the dollar from 1980 to 1985 which made US exports uncompetitive on world markets. Recent research suggests that this latter phenomenon may well be linked to the debt crisis itself.[10] Figure 1 shows the remarkable volume of foreign exchange deals done each day (around $400 billion), international debt (around $3000 billion in total), and the growth of world trade. More recent estimates (December 1987) put the volume of foreign exchange dealings at over $1 trillion per day. Clearly trade has grown slowly compared to overall foreign exchange dealings and the debt itself. In fact trade and investment account for only 2 to 3 per cent of foreign exchange transactions; the rest come from the shuffling of the debt portfolios of international banks. Banks by their very nature receive short-term deposits and make longer-term loans. Unfortunately if the quality of those loans deteriorates then depositors may demand higher interest rates in return for bearing, in their eyes, a higher risk that the bank may default. In other words, the banks are locked into these long-term loans of dubious quality and have to raise deposits to continue funding them. As depositors attempt to withdraw their supply of deposits to these banks, interest rates rise, and so does the dollar. Hence the rise in the dollar and the poor quality loans may be linked more closely than previously thought. There may well be a direct link between the debt crisis and protectionism, though as yet it is not widely appreciated. Of course, this is not to exclude more traditional influences on exchange rates, such as the US budget deficit.

There are two key differences from the 1930s; first, as indicated above, the scale of the debt is now far greater than before; secondly, in the 1930s, the loans were predominantly bonds rather than bank debt, and default had little impact on exchange rates or other financial institutions. On the other hand the 1980s crisis involves banks whose existence is essential to the smooth running of the industrialised economies, and whose assets are often heavily interlocked with those of other financial institutions. If the build-up in debt in the 1970s had largely been in the form of bonds, then defaults would be a relatively private

BILLIONS OF U.S. DOLLARS

Figure 1
Trade, debt and foreign exchange deals
Volume comparisons 1972 to 1985
This graph is reproduced with the kind permission of Professor I. F. Pearce

matter between borrower and lender, without the wider ramifications and ripples which can spread to the rest of the economy, which occurs when banks are in difficulty.

RECENT DEVELOPMENTS

It has been suggested that the international debt crisis is one aspect of a much larger debt crisis being played out worldwide, particularly in the North. This is characterised by a rapid growth of credit, both public, private and corporate, relative to output; cash flow problems arise for individuals, corporations and countries as credit standards weaken and product innovations appear to offer tailor-made and superior financial items, with an illusory low level of risk.

Somehow we must wipe out the developing countries' bad debts to stop fresh resources being pushed in the wrong direction, while maintaining a stable

Table 1: *Indicated prices for less developed country bank loans.*

	Bid	Offer
Argentina	59.50	60.50
Bolivia	9.00	11.00
Brazil	63.00	64.00
Chile	70.50	72.0
Ecuador	52.00	55.00
Mexico	58.25	59.00
Nigeria	31.00	32.00
Peru	15.00	17.00
Philippines	70.50	72.00
Poland	44.50	45.50
Venezuela	72.50	73.50
Zambia	18.00	22.00

Note: Prices of 18 May 1987.
percentage of loan face value.
Source: Salomon Brothers.

financial system, and more fundamentally we must restore integrity to the process linking savers and investors. The implicit Northern position that neither banks nor governments must lose is quite untenable and unrealistic; the loans are bad, so who will bear the loss? Fortunately the Citicorp decision of May 1987 to increase its loan loss provisions massively and take an operating loss is the first step in the right direction. It is interesting to note that its share price *rose* on the news as analysts felt that future earnings would increase as the bank could now concentrate on profitable future opportunities and not stay locked into these bad and unprofitable loans. Other banks have followed Citicorp's lead, and have also included large provisions against domestic US loans (e.g. First Interstate). It may well be that the laborious 'case-by-case' approach is not the only way to return the debtor countries to voluntary borrowing. In addition, poor quality loans are beginning to disappear off banks' books as they undertake swaps of equity in projects in exchange for the fixed nominal debts they hold (e.g. $1.7 bn of Chile's $19 bn external bank debt has been swapped into equity over the last two years). In addition a secondary market in bank loans has developed. Within an appropriate accounting framework banks are generally very keen to arrange and package loans and pass them on to other institutions, a part of the process known as 'securitisation'; capital does not have to be held against such deals as they are not 'on the books' and fee-income is generated in the process. The table above shows the large discounts being offered against developing country debt. Banks are now facing up to the necessary losses; the institutions buying the second-hand loans, mainly other banks and multi-national corporations, presumably are well aware of the risky properties of the products, and the prices are set accordingly. It may even be sensible soon for developing countries to attempt to buy back these loans in the second-hand market rather than pay the contracted interest payments. Bolivia was the first country known to be working on such a plan, which is funded by Western governments. Mexico intends to follow suit on a much larger scale (January 1988). Perhaps these are the first realistic steps towards a long-term solution of the debt crisis and they should be encouraged by the regulators, though the quantity of debt involved is as yet very small, with net secondary market transactions less than $12 bn by the end of 1987, compared with Latin American bank debt of well over $400 billion.

Financial deregulation and lender of last resort facilities have led to a *global* debt explosion; one aspect of this is international debt itself. It is not a problem for the North or the South alone; we *all* have a problem.

NOTES

1 e.g. see H. A. Holley, *Developing Country Debt*, Chatham House, Paper 35 (London: Routledge and Kegan Paul, 1987).

2 See G. W. McKenzie and S. H. Thomas, 'The economic implications of international banking', in the *House of Commons, Treasury and Civil Service Select Committee on International Monetary Arrangements*, Appendix to Vol. III, 1983, pp. 207–13.

3 See W. Hogan and I. F. Pearce, *The Incredible Eurodollar* (London: Allen & Unwin, 1984).

4 e.g. see A. Sampson, *The Money Lenders* (London: Hodder and Stoughton, 1981).

5 See 'Disaster myopia in international banking', in R. J. Herring and J. M. Guttentag, *Essays in International Finance* (Princeton: Princetown University Press, 1986).

6 But see Mark Singer, *Funny Money* (Picador, 1986), for a highly readable account of the borrowing activities of the Oklahoma oil industry.

7 See Henry Kaufman, *Interest Rates, the Markets and the New Financial World* (London: I. B. Tauris and Co. Ltd, 1986), for further discussion of the rapid growth of debt.

8 'Whose crisis is the debt crisis? A view from the South', by S. Griffith-Jones, this volume.

9 See B. E. Eichengreen and R. Portes, 'The anatomy of financial crisis', *CEPR Discussion Paper* (London, 1984).

10 See S. H. Thomas and M. R. Wickens, "Vehicle currencies, bank debt and the asset market approach to exchange rate determination: the US dollar 1980–85', *CEPR Discussion Paper* (London, 1987).

Part V: Intervention in the developing world

9   A Southern perspective

Matin Zuberi

From its inception, the contemporary international system of states has had the 'European core and non-European penumbra'.[1] The four Papal Bulls issued by Pope Alexander VI in 1493 drew an imaginary line from the north to south at 100 leagues west of the Azores and Cape Verde Islands, granting the land and sea beyond the line to the sphere of Spanish exploration and dominion.[2] The duty of subduing the 'barbarians' in the distant lands by force depended upon on four factors: the naturally servile nature of the 'barbarian' and the consequent need of a 'civilised' master; the 'barbarian's' habitual crimes against natural law; the plight of subjects of 'barbarian' rulers; and the duty of making possible the peaceful spread of the Gospel.[3]

European diplomatic practice conformed to this dual character of the international system. The treaties of Cateau-Cambresis signed in April 1559 marked a watershed in European diplomacy. According to a verbal agreement, a line was drawn along the meridian of the Azores and the tropic of Cancer, to the west and south of which resort to arms was permissible. This was the origin of the 'the "amity lines" which divided the zone of peace from the zone of war'.[4]

During the era of colonial expansion, a balance of power was maintained in Europe while the rest of the world experienced a succession of naval hegemonies – Spanish, Portuguese, Dutch and British. Consequently, the colonial peoples became the objects of European diplomacy. This was exemplified by the Congress of Berlin 1885, at which the European states drew up a map of Africa according to their diplomatic convenience – 'Here is Russia and here is France. That is my map of Africa', said Bismarck.[5] Across the Atlantic, the United States had proclaimed the Monroe Doctrine – a new kind of line in the history of the international system which continues to have contemporary relevance. 'Chronic wrongdoing, or an impotence which results in a general loosening of the ties of civilised society, may in America, as in elsewhere, ultimately require intervention

135

by some civilized nation' – the language of the Roosevelt Corollary to the Doctrine is 'a secularised adaptation of the lofty language of the canonists'.[6]

The amity lines have reappeared in the contemporary era. The post-war period, characterised by the cold war international system, has had as its most distinguishing feature, peace in Europe and conflict elsewhere. The developing world has been the arena of more than 150 instances of armed conflict and in more than three-fourths of these the states of the developed world were, in varying degrees, involved. These included classic wars of decolonisation, intervention soon after decolonisation and wars resulting from unnatural boundaries drawn in the colonial era. The fragile stability of the cold war international system has been based on an understanding that conflict 'over there' need not spill over the fault line running across Central Europe.

THE EMERGENCE OF THE COLD WAR

The United States emerged from the World War Two as the most powerful country, while the rest of the industrialised world was in ruins. Her industry was booming and she had a monopoly of nuclear weapons which lasted until 1949. The grandiose conception of US security encompassed a strategic sphere of influence within the Western hemisphere, domination of the Pacific and Atlantic oceans, an extensive system of outlying bases to enlarge her strategic frontiers and to project her power globally, and the maintenance of her nuclear monopoly. This conception of security required a favourable balance of power in Eurasia as well as control over the Eurasian rimlands and a global economic open door. It necessitated an overwhelming preponderance of economic and military power. Conceived as a truly global responsibility and an imperative of Manifest Destiny, this conception of security was expansive and encompassed various regions of the globe.

The hegemonic conflict with the Soviet Union was related to the need for unimpeded access to the natural resources of the post-colonial world through the insistence on compatible systems of government in these areas.[7] Alliance solidarity also pushed the United States towards greater involvement as European colonial empires began to crumble. As her European allies got entangled in supressing national liberation movements, US involvement was rationalised in terms of support to allies and prevention of social chaos leading to communist expansionism.

This grandiose conception of security, developed in the unique circumstances of the immediate post-war world, continues to mould US thinking. Consequently, it is the growing disjunction between US economic and military power in relation to the rest of the world and the US security perspective which is one of the major causes of the recent intensification of the cold war and intervention in the developing world.

The Soviet Union, on the other hand, having suffered terrible devastation during World War Two, took considerable time to make her presence felt on a global scale. Her economic and technological weaknesses reduced her to the role of a regional power; her preoccupation with regions contiguous to her frontiers further emphasised this role. With the world's largest land frontiers and rich reserves of raw materials, Soviet conceptions of security have emphasised autarchy. This in itself reduced the compulsions for the Soviet Union to extend her sway beyond her immediate zone of security broadly settled at the Yalta and Potsdam conferences.

The gradual emergence of the Soviet Union as a global power has resulted in a historically unique development – the presence of two over-lapping global military powers with great strategic mobility. Unlike the colonial powers which were territorially confined in their military reach, the United States and the Soviet Union are now 'pursuing conflicting global policies in a dynamic setting of Third World instability'.[8] Nevertheless, despite considerable improvement in the Soviet Union's capability to project power, it has, according to some Western experts, 'only a rudimentary potential' to do so in distant areas *particularly when opposed by an adversary*'.[9] Furthermore, the so-called Brezhnev Doctrine, with its emphasis on proletarian internationalism, can be viewed as a formulation justifying intervention in the affairs of socialist countries. The Soviet notion of sovereignty, however, takes on a different connotation in the context of socialist and non-socialist countries – 'between socialist states, there is no such thing as intervention'.[10]

In this respect, the Soviet military intervention in Afghanistan was a major departure in Soviet policy for two reasons. Ever since the Bolshevik Revolution the Soviet Union had maintained friendly ties with every successive regime in Afghanistan. Moreover, it had not used its armed forces in any country outside the Yalta system. However, one continuing characteristic of Soviet use of armed force is that it has been used only in areas contiguous to Soviet frontiers. This is true of Hungary in 1956, Czechoslovakia in 1968 and Afghanistan in 1979.

THE SUPERPOWERS AND THE DEVELOPING WORLD

The United States has a tendency to consider the post-colonial world as a 'grey area' which is prone to convulsive change directed by forces from abroad. Indigenous forces are considered as pawns on a global chess board and a reputation for toughness and a capacity to intervene militarily in their affairs is considered an essential ingredient of the status of a great power. As revolutionary transformations become problems in the management of violence, US deterrence dogma is inverted in its application; while, in relation to the military blocs, smaller threats are taken care of by deterring larger ones, in the 'grey areas' effective use of force in dealing with minor contingencies is expected to eliminate possibilities of larger threats.

Superpower competition in the developing world is unstructured because of the absence of military blocs and a consequent lack of clarity in the demarcation of interests. Therefore, tensions generated by boundary disputes and the multifarious problems of underdevelopment provide opportunities for intervention. These in turn have to be exploited in a manner that is consonant with the maintenance of superpower credibility and run the risk of producing the dilemma the US encountered in the Vietnam War.[11] A country's interests normally define the goals of its foreign policy. This leads on to a definition of commitments and capabilities to defend them. But the deterrence dogma reverses the priorities. Credibility itself defines interests and as credibility is a subjective phenomenon, interests and commitments become interdependent.

The Soviet Union tends to view societal changes in the developing world in the context of indigenous forces and their interplay with the global balance of power. Its initially optimistic assessment of developments in the post-colonial era has been somewhat tempered by experience.[12] The use of Cuban troops in Angola raised the question of the use of proxies by the Soviet Union; however, the United States and its allies have on many occasions joined forces while engaged in interventionary activity.[13] It is worth noting too that Soviet interventions in Africa have generally been consistent with the consensus of the Organization of African Unity.[14]

While intervention from any quarter in the affairs of the non-aligned countries must be condemned and resisted, there is much to be said for a more balanced distribution of military power at the global level; if properly manipulated it can provide freedom of manoeuvre to the potential victims. The non-aligned countries have urged the withdrawal of Soviet forces and would like an independent non-aligned Afghanistan free from any kind of intervention in its internal affairs. The Western powers, however, have used the Afghan crisis as an alibi for renewed military confrontation and have augmented their interventionary capabilities to an extraordinary extent. All the major decisions regarding the Rapid Deployment Force, currently renamed the Central Command, the placement of US missiles in Western Europe, the forging of military linkages with China, the indefinite postponement of talks on the Indian Ocean, and the shifts in the declaratory US strategic doctrine took place before Soviet intervention in Afghanistan.

The countries of the Gulf have become the focal point of Western military planning with the declared objective of ensuring an uninterrupted flow of oil supplies. Furthermore, as the flow of oil tankers passing through the Cape of Good Hope has increased considerably, South Africa has assumed greater importance in Western strategic calculations. It is also a major supplier of precious metals and Namibia is rich in uranium deposits. Moreover, the US, Western Europe and Japan have signed long-term agreements with African countries having uranium deposits. One objective of the US pressure on Japan to increase its military spending is to release the US Seventh Fleet forces for duty in the Indian Ocean. All this adds up to a gigantic linkage; hence the increasing emphasis on the possibilities of resource wars in the future.

Saudi Arabia is the main pillar of the oil order established by the United States in West Asia. Pakistan's close military ties with Saudi Arabia make it an essential element of Western strategy in the Gulf.[15] The trilogy of Saudi wealth, US military technology and Pakistani manpower represents a potent factor in this strategy. The small, but financially liquid countries of the Gulf are so closely intertwined with Western strategy that it is difficult for them even to comprehend the threats they face. They may subscribe to the vague generalities contained in voluminous declarations issued at the end of non-aligned conferences; but their economic, political and military linkages pull them in another direction. While their membership of the non-aligned movement is a welcome development, it is necessary to persuade them to safeguard their interests jointly with other members of the community.

Western strategic literature is replete with references to the vulnerability of oil supply lines, but at least some countries in the West have increased their dependence on oil flows from the Gulf since 1974. This indicates a deliberate decision not to diversify sources of supply in order to use dependence on Gulf oil as a leverage for political, economic and military control. A possible Soviet threat to the uninterrupted flow of oil was conjured up in support of this thesis. This threat emerged on the basis of a CIA estimate made in 1977 according to which the Soviet Union would become a net importer of oil by 1985. This estimate was challenged by experts and the CIA later revised its own projections. As for Soviet naval forces in the Indian Ocean, 'alarmist nonsense was propagated' in the late sixties when the Soviet navy started making its presence felt. Soviet naval forces have generally increased during crises like the Indo–Pakistan war of 1971 and the Arab–Israeli conflict of 1973 in relation to the increased US naval presence. As the US forces were withdrawn after these crises, Soviet forces also declined.[16]

The continuing fascination of US strategists with the possibility of interruption of oil supplies from the Gulf countries in the present state of abundance of available and potential energy sources is all the more curious because the US is well-endowed in this respect. Its coal resources are sufficient for 1500 years of consumption at current levels. It is a major producer of uranium and has the largest number of nuclear plants in operation. It has at least 250,000 tonnes of U238 stockpiled as a by-product of its weapons programme. This stockpile has the energy equivalent of about a trillion tonnes of coal, or more than 400 years of oil at the 1976 rate of consumption. The US uses about 35 per cent of the world's electricity. Moreover, 'States are the more independent if they have the ability to be without, and if they have leverage to use against others.'[17] This leverage is substantial. Arab oil producers have about 80 billion dollars invested in the US. In 1981, for example, OPEC had more than 354 trillion dollars invested in Western banks, of which the Saudi Arabian share was 160 billion dollars.[18] In Western Europe, where dependence on imported energy is much greater, one does not notice the same level of anxiety regarding the interruption of energy supplies. On the contrary, West European governments have deliberately diversified their sources of supply by turning to the Soviet Union for enriched uranium, oil and gas.[19]

Western commentators have also been anxious about what they call 'internal irresponsibility' on the part of the indigenous people who may decide to change the ruling elites of their countries leading to major shifts in the balance of power.[20] The Rapid Deployment Force was established to deal with all kinds of internal changes and external threats in the region. Diego Garcia is the lynchpin of the US military network in the Indian Ocean. A large armada of ships, helicopters and aircraft along with prepositioning of the necessary weapons and supplies is now ready for any eventuality. It is the most powerful front line force that the US has ever assembled. The RDF was allocated to the US central Command in the Indian Ocean, established on 1 January 1983. Its jurisdiction extends over nineteen non-aligned countries, stretching from Morocco to Pakistan. Its shadow falls over Kashmir as well. This area is larger than the continental United States. It is worth noting that Israel and Lebanon are excluded from its jurisdiction; they are within the purview of the European Command. The Pentagon document called 'Fiscal Years 1984–1988, Defence Guidance' lists the Gulf–Indian Ocean region as a major US strategic priority and calls for 'forcible entry' capabilities for US troops.[21] The non-aligned countries thus face the threat of massive and instant military intervention. Robert Komer, who directed the 'pacification' programme in Vietnam and was the architect of the RDF during the Carter Administration, maintains that the presence of US forces would deter any Soviet conventional attack in the region – 'to punch through a US brigade, the Soviets would have to shoot American soldiers, and they haven't done that since 1919.'[22]

The Reagan Administration has spent more than $15 million a year on Central Command, an amount roughly equal to the annual total US aid to the developing world. It has also strengthened Special Forces – the Green Berets of Vietnam notoriety – to carry out psychological warfare, assassinations, sabotage and counter-insurgency operations. The Unconventional Joint Task Force is charged with these responsibilities. There are thus increasing possibilities of military intervention and use of force, including nuclear weapons, against non-aligned countries. A diversity of punitive actions is being contemplated; all rungs of the ladder of violence are within the range of possibility.

RULES OF THE GAME

The United States has attempted to establish a linkage between detente with the Soviet Union and a suitably low profile in the developing world. Support for national liberation movements became the main issue. As the global distribution of power was for a long time favourable to the United States, it was interested in freezing the status quo. The Soviet Union favoured a transformation of the 'correlation of forces' and the developing world played a crucial role in Soviet conceptions of such a transformation.[23] Attempts to establish the so-called 'rules of the game' pertaining to the Third World have simply exacerbated Soviet–US tensions.[24] Neither the Soviet Union nor the United States command the obedience of the tides of history. The transformations in the developing world are bound to have significant impact on the global balance of power and no country, however powerful, is in a position to tamper with this process with impunity. Their future cannot be decided in a game played by some gentlemen players. They have every right to decide what kind of political systems and socio-economic structures they would like as well as the right to create their own version of chaos. Even if the superpowers could, by a stroke of luck and cunning, agree on some 'rules of the game', they would not be able to impose such rules on countries which want to be free to chart out their own destinies. The international environment is now incalculable and uncontrollable. Gone are the days when the US ambassador in London could propose to President Wilson the conclusion of an Anglo–American alliance on the plea that 'the world would take notice to whom it belongs, and be quiet'.

CONCLUSION: THE NON–ALIGNED STATES IN THE GLOBAL SECURITY ENVIRONMENT

The non-aligned countries are placed within a pluralistic world economy and a bipolar security regime. There has been a steady diffusion of power in many dimensions: from the United States to the Soviet Union resulting in essential equivalence, from the two giants to the other industrialised countries, especially

Western Europe and Japan, and even from the industrialised world as a whole to a small group of developing countries which have become producers of manufactured goods and commodities. The United States is still the dominant power but its capacity to govern the international system and the world economy has been considerably eroded. There is a growing disequilibrium between the governance of the international system and the underlying distribution of power within it.

The novelty of the present situation lies in the fact that, unlike the old imperial systems which were territorially confined and constrained by technology, there are now two overlapping global military powers which are pursuing conflicting global policies in the dynamic setting of change and turmoil in the peripheries: The era of risk-free intervention is over. The two global powers counter-balance each other and there will be a premium on pre-emption; each power may try to move in first, hoping that by staking out a claim it will be able to prevent the other from intervention; to arrive second would be to incur the cost of escalating the conflict. But a premium on pre-emption would lead to spiralling interventions. Moreover, fragile policies suffering from the disorientations of the development process may 'search for borrowed power' by involving the overlapping global military powers. Such crises in the setting of nuclear parity could easily get out of control with catastrophic consequences. Superpower intervention in the developing world, as a consequence, will remain as much of a threat in the 1990s, as it has in the past.

NOTES

1 Martin Wight, *Systems of States*, edited by Hedley Bull (Leicester: Leicester University Press, 1977), p. 152.
2 J. H. Perry, *The Age of Reconnaissance: Discovery, Exploration and Settlement, 1450–1650* (London, 1963), pp. 151–2.
3 Ibid., p. 313.
4 Wight, *Systems of States*, See G. Mattingly, 'International law and international diplomacy', in *The New Cambridge Modern History*, Vol. III (Cambridge University Press, 1968), pp. 159–4.
5 Quoted in A. J. P. Taylor, *Europe: Grandeur and Decline* (Harmondsworth: Pelican, 1967), p. 157. See also B. V. A. Rolling, *International Law in an Expanded World* (Amsterdam, 1960).
6 Wight, *Systems of States*, p. 120.
7 For a comparative analysis of the Roman, British and US imperial expansion, see George Liska, *Career of Empire: American and Imperial Expansion Over Land and Sea* (Baltimore: Johns Hopkins, 1978).
8 Zbignew Brezinski, 'Peace and power', *Survival*, December 1968, p. 391.
9 Dennis M. Gormley, 'The direction and pace of Soviet projection capabilities' in Jonathan Alford (ed.) *The Soviet Union: Security Policies and Constraints* (Aldershot: Gower, 1985), p. 146 (emphasis in the original).
10 Caroline Thomas, *New States, Sovereignty and Intervention* (Aldershot: Gower, 1985), p. 63.
11 'What has happened is that one of our promissory Asian notes has had to be met.' Robert W. Tucker, *Nation or Empire: The Debate Over American Foreign Policy* (Baltimore: Johns Hopkins, 1968), p. 110. See also Robert H. Johnson, 'Exaggerating America's stakes in Third World conflicts', *International Security*, Vol. 10, no. 3, Winter 1985–6, pp. 32–68.

12 See Bruce D. Potter, *The USSR in Third World Conflicts: Soviet Arms and Diplomacy in Local Wars: 1945–1980* (Cambridge University Press, 1984). Also Robert H. Donaldson (ed.), *The Soviet Union in the Third World: Successes and Failures* (Boulder, Colorado: Westview Press, 1981) and Mark M. Katz, *The Third World in Soviet Military Thought* (London and Sydney: Croom Helm; 1982).

13 Walter C. Clemens, Jr., 'The Superpowers and the Third World: aborted ideals and wasted assets', in Charles W. Kegley Jr. and Pat McGowan (eds.), *Foreign Policy USA/USSR* (Beverley Hills, 1982), pp. 116–35.

14 Hedley Bull, 'Intervention in the Third World', in Bull (ed.), *Intervention in World Politics* (Oxford: Clarendon Press, 1984), p. 143.

15 Sir John Hackett, 'Protecting oil supplies: the military requirements', in *Third World Conflict and International Security, Part 1*, Adelphi Papers, No. 166, Summer 1981, pp. 41–51.

16 G. Jukes, 'The USSR and the strategic balance', *World Review*, October 1981, pp. 27–8.

17 Kenneth Waltz, 'A strategy for rapid deployment force', *International Security*, Spring 1981, p. 51.

18 Martin Shubik and Paul Bracken, 'Strategic purpose and the international economy', *Orbis*, Fall 1983, pp. 567–89.

19 Miguel S. Wionczek, 'Energy and international security in the 1980s: reality of misconceptions', *Third World Quarterly*, October 1983, pp. 839–47.

20 James R. Schlesinger, 'The international implications of Third World conflict: an American perspective', in *Third World Conflict and International Security, Part 1*, Adelphi Papers, No. 166, Summer 1981, p. 12.

21 Richard Halloran, 'Pentagon draws up first strategy for fighting a long nuclear war', *The New York Times*, 30 May 1982, p. 1.

22 Robert Manning, 'Rapid deployment force or farce?', *South*, March 1983, pp. 10–13, and John Reed, 'Us Rapid Deployment Force – building a credible deterrent', *Defence*, September 1982, pp. 493–503.

23 H. Trofimenko, 'America Russia and the Third World', *Foreign Affairs*, 59, Summer 1981, pp. 1,021–40. See also Richard Falk, 'Intervention and national liberation' in Bull, *Intervention in World Politics*, pp. 119–33.

24 Alexander L. George (ed.), *Managing US–Soviet Rivalry: Problems of Crisis Prevention* (Boulder, Colorado, 1983) and Raymond L. Garthoff, *Detente and Confrontation: American–Soviet Relations from Nixon to Reagan*, (Washington D.C.: Brookings, 1985).

10 A Northern perspective

Phil Williams

INTRODUCTION

The principle of non-intervention and the practice of intervention reflect the basic tension in international politics between the idea of international society on the one hand and the reality of international anarchy on the other. Although those who emphasise the anarchic aspects of international politics tend to discount international law and international morality, they cannot ignore the fact that international relationships are not totally devoid of rules and regulations. Furthermore, there is widespread acknowledgement of the importance of sovereignty and the concomitant of non-intervention. In December 1965, for example, the United Nations General Assembly declared that 'no state has the right to intervene, directly or indirectly, for any reason whatever, in the internal or external affairs of any other state' and 'no state shall organise, assist, foment, incite or tolerate subversive, terrorist or armed activities directed towards the violent overthrow of another state, or interfere in civil strife in another state'.[1]

At the same time, the elements of anarchy cannot be disregarded. After all, great powers are, in a sense, laws unto themselves and act according to the dictates of national interest, the demands of national security, and the temptations of strategic advantage rather than according to legal prescriptions and proscriptions. In theory, there is a sovereign equality of states; in practice the international system is hierarchical and is one in which the strong, through a variety of means, attempt to dominate the weak. As Martin Wight pointed out, 'it is in the relations between great powers and weak powers that intervention most frequently occurs'.[2] Military intervention by the United States and the Soviet Union in the affairs of other states, therefore, can be understood as a function of both anarchy and hierarchy. As such, it has a long and even respectable history in what remains predominantly a Hobbesian international system. As Hans Morgenthau has noted,

Intervention is as ancient and well-established an instrument of foreign policy as are diplomatic pressure, negotiations and war. From the time of the ancient Greeks to this day, some states have found it advantageous to intervene in the affairs of other states on behalf of their own interests and against the latters' will. Other states in view of their interests, have opposed such interventions, and have intervened on behalf of theirs.[3]

The fact that even the superpowers develop formal and quasi-legal justifications for their interventions, however, suggests that they are not wholly insensitive to the widely accepted norms of behaviour nor to their own violations of these norms. Yet in presenting these justifications, each superpower is also implying that there are certain principles and values which are more important than the norm of non-intervention. Consequently, this paper examines the reasons why the superpowers intervene militarily in other states. It then looks at the arguments that are offered to justify such behaviour. The final part of the paper offers a brief discussion of the implications for North-South relations of what are essentially doctrines of intervention.

MILITARY INTERVENTIONS IN THE THIRD WORLD

Military interventions in the Third World by the superpowers have a variety of causes and purposes. Rather than looking at individual instances of intervention, however, it is more useful – at least at the outset – to consider the fundamental sources of interventionism as a regular feature of Soviet and American behaviour. In this connexion, three considerations stand out as particularly important: the bipolar structure of the international system; the self-images of the two superpowers which give their competition for power and influence a distinctly Manichean quality; and the persistence of geopolitical mind-sets. In addition to these factors relating to the superpowers there are also certain characteristics of both the state and interstate relations in the Third World which encourage superpower intervention.

Bipolarity impels the superpowers into an adversarial relationship. As Kenneth Waltz has pointed out, in a bipolar world, who is a danger to whom is never in doubt.[4] Much of the resulting competition between the superpowers has been channelled into the development and deployment of strategic capabilities. A bipolar structure, however, also encourages geopolitical competition and makes the superpowers sensitive not only to territorial gains made directly or indirectly by the adversary but also to changes in alignment resulting from internal change in Third World states. As Waltz has summed up: 'In a bipolar world there are no peripheries. With only two powers capable of acting on a world scale, anything that happens anywhere is potentially of concern to both of them. Bipolarity affects the geographic scope of both powers' concern.'[5] Indeed, the bipolar structure encourages policy-makers in both Moscow and Washington to impose an East-West framework on local and regional problems.

This sensitivity to possible changes of alignment – which reflects traditional concerns over the balance of power – is exacerbated by ideological consider-ations, which give the post-war international system its fundamentally heterogeneous character. The superpowers are engaged not only in a great power struggle but also in a competition for the hearts and minds of other nations. As Morgenthau noted, the contest is one between 'two secular religions'.[6] Each superpower regards itself as the repository of all virtue and sees the adversary not only as the repository of evil but as the main obstacle to the spread of virtue. This contributes significantly to a conception of their relationship as a zero sum conflict in which geopolitical gains for the other side are automatically translated into losses for oneself. This is also underlined by the fact that

the war between communism and democracy does not respect national boundaries. It finds enemies and allies in all countries, opposing the one and supporting the other regardless of the niceties of international law. Here is the dynamic force which has led the two superpowers to intervene all over the globe, sometimes surreptitiously, sometimes openly, sometimes with the accepted methods of diplomatic pressure and propaganda, sometimes with the frowned-upon instruments of covert subversion and open force.[7]

This competition was initially focussed on Europe, but, with the division of the Continent and the creation of the two blocs, the attention of the superpowers turned to the Third World where there was much greater fluidity. Although the allegiance of particular Third World states had no more than marginal impact on the central balance between the superpowers, it nevertheless took on consider-able symbolic importance and encouraged a concern with territorial gains and losses that was out of all proportion to the intrinsic significance of such shifts.

This concern with territorial aspects of the Soviet American competition is in some ways rather ironic. Klaus Knorr pointed out some years ago that, in a world which has understood Keynes, territorial conquest looks relatively unattractive as a means of increasing national power.[8] Furthermore, in a world of nuclear weapons, it appears unnecessary. The rise of nationalism has also meant that it becomes inordinately costly. The crucial point, however, is that the superpowers are not interested in direct conquest but in supporting friendly governments and, where possible at reasonable cost, over-throwing governments more sympathetic towards the adversary. This helps to explain the persistence of geopolitical mind-sets even in an era when territorial gains no longer have the attractions they did in the nineteenth century.

Other considerations also help to sustain geopolitical competition in the Third World. Superpower concern over ideological defections from one camp to the other have already been touched upon. These concerns are exacerbated by fears that such defections could have a 'falling domino' effect, and that either through example, or by direct means the defector will encourage others to do the same. Furthermore, Third World competition is something that is important in terms of what can crudely be described as prestige or status. The Soviet Union believes that in order to legitimise its position as leader of the international communist movement, it has to support 'wars of national liberation', while the United States, through much of the post-war period, has assumed that its commitments are interdependent and that if it displays weakness in one area it will be challenged elsewhere. These concerns encourage activist policies by both superpowers and ensure that the logic of bipolarity becomes institutionalised in the mind-sets of policy-makers in both Washington and Moscow.

Another consideration which accounts for the persistence of geopolitical assessments is that the Third World is a vital source of raw materials, especially for the West. It is essential for the prosperity of both the United States and its allies that they have continued access to these resources. This combines with fears about the global nature of Soviet ambitions to intensify American sensitivities about Soviet geopolitical gains. Not only are these gains seen as a challenge to American credibility, but also as something which, in the long term, might enable the Soviet Union to disrupt or interdict the raw material supplies that are essential to the functioning of the Western economies. Although the advanced industrialised states could cope with temporary interruptions rather better than is often assumed, if they were consistently denied access to key metals and minerals their economies would suffer significantly.

The importance of the Third World to the superpowers is further underlined by the fact that it offers bases and installations which help to sustain the strategic competition. In a sense, the Third World provides much of the infra-structure for superpower navies, and thereby helps to perpetuate a naval rivalry which stems not only from the widespread deployment of ballistic missile submarines but also from the desire to 'show the flag'. Once the bases are established, maintaining access to them becomes almost an end in itself, and the superpowers are made even more sensitive to any shift of alignment by the host nation.

The result of all this is that the superpowers have developed what might be termed extended national security zones, and are prepared to use force to uphold what they see as important security interests in many areas of the Third World. The problem with this is that it treats the Third World primarily as a battleground for Soviet American competition. Third World states themselves are seen less as actors in their own right than as participants in the 'great game' between the two superpowers. Furthermore, intervention is treated simply as something which, under certain circumstances, may be necessary to uphold or promote the security interests of either Washington or Moscow. Yet superpower intervention is not something that is completely negative. Although superpower rivalry often exacerbates tensions in the Third World, the superpowers make a significant contribution to international order. Their tacit understandings about each other's sphere of influence combined with a basic rule of prudence which might be termed the norm of asymmetric intervention, ensure that their competition is not wholly unconstrained. Furthermore, the tacit acceptance of this norm by both Washington and Moscow gives international politics a degree of order and predictability it would otherwise lack.

The implication of all this is that there are often considerable incentives for superpower interventions in the Third World. Furthermore, in an international system that is fundamentally anarchic, to expect the superpowers to engage in restraint that is not based predominantly on prudential calculations of self-interest is to engage in wishful thinking. In this connexion, the Third World has to be considered not only in terms of incentives for superpower intervention but also in terms of opportunities for such action. Because they provide so many opportunities in what is after all a Hobbesian international system, Third World states themselves must bear a great deal of responsibility for encouraging superpower intervention. Yet they are the victims of the same kinds of security dilemmas and systemic constraints and imperatives which confront Moscow and Washington. Although Third World states promote the norm of non-intervention and the principle of non-alignment, many of them nevertheless become aligned to one or other of the superpowers. They seek alignment and support either because they have to contend with local or regional challenges to their security, or because they believe that without such support they will be an easy target for the other superpower or other extra-regional powers. Furthermore, the ideological divisions between the superpowers are reflected within many societies, thereby encouraging both the faction in power and the factions trying to seize power to obtain outside support. The result is that, though the general principle of non-intervention is promoted zealously by Third World states, there are occasions when particular states or internal factions welcome intervention as a means of enhancing or maintaining their positions. Both the weakness of the state throughout the Third World, and the endemic insecurities of Third World states *vis-à-vis* one another lead to instabilities which the superpowers, because of their own competition, may feel unable to ignore.

The failure of Third World states to provide regional institutions or mechanisms for promoting stability and managing or resolving conflicts is also conducive to intervention by the Soviet Union or the United States. For example, if the Organisation of African Unity had been able to provide greater backing for the Alvor Accord of January 1975 which was designed to end the internal faction fight in Angola, external intervention by the superpowers and their proxies would have been much more difficult. As it was, the three major factions sought external support, while the external powers which became involved were able to justify and legitimise their own actions in terms of the interventions of others. The inability of regional organisations to provide mechanisms for crisis management or conflict resolution at the local level both permits and encourages intervention, either directly or indirectly, by one or other of the superpowers.

The imperatives, incentives, and opportunities for superpower interventions in the affairs of Third World states are generally played out in terms of four major scenarios. The first is that one or other of the superpowers attempts to impose ideological conformity and uphold the status quo by intervening to provide support for an existing government threatened by internal unrest, as the United States did in Vietnam and in Lebanon in 1958. A second contingency is superpower intervention to overthrow a government which is beginning to deviate from the ideological norm or is losing control of the society. Soviet interventions in Czechoslovakia and Afghanistan were of this nature, as was the United States intervention in the Dominican Republic. A third possibility is an intervention to overthrow a government which has already departed from the established ideological pattern. The American attempt to overthrow Castro through the Bay of Pigs invasion of 1961 falls into this category as does the more successful, although less direct attempt to overthrown Allende in Chile. A fourth kind of intervention may occur during civil wars when the superpowers intervene either directly or indirectly in order to bring their preferred faction to power. Angola is the classic example of this kind of intervention, with Soviet and Cuban support for the MPLA proving decisive.

These possibilities are not intended to be exhaustive. Indeed, the deployment of American Marines in Lebanon as part of the multinational peace-keeping force illustrates just how difficult it is to be definitive in any categorisation based on the purposes of intervention. The other difficulty, of course, is that interventions differ not only in their objectives but in their degree of overtness. The overthrow of Allende did not result from direct military action by the United States but from destabilisation of the Chilean economy inspired by the CIA and ITT. The final outcome, however, was one that the Nixon Administration was very anxious to obtain. Should this kind of indirect intervention be treated in the same way as the more overt military kind?

In order to consider this, it is useful to start with John Vincent's definition of intervention as 'that activity undertaken by a state, a group of states or an international organization which interferes coercively in the domestic affairs of another state'.[9] Although this definition is extremely helpful, it is open to both broad and restrictive interpretations. A restrictive interpretation suggests four main conditions which have to be met for intervention to take place. The first is that there has to be a stepping in or interference in another state beyond the normal level of penetration. Secondly, this interference must involve the use or the threat of military force in order to meet the requirement that coercion be involved. The third condition is that the action should break the prevailing pattern of international relations, and the fourth is that it must aim to influence the domestic affairs of another state. This final criterion is what distinguishes intervention from wars of conquest; after the domestic affairs of the state have been influenced in the desired direction the intervening power withdraws its forces.

The problem with this restrictive approach is that it sees coercive interference in strictly military terms, and excludes other forms of coercion, based on economic or political instruments of foreign policy. Under this restrictive interpretation, American action in Chile would be excluded, whereas under a broader interpretation of 'interfering coercively' it would clearly be included in any comprehensive analysis of interventionary behaviour by the Soviet Union and the United States. Indeed, Caroline Thomas has argued very persuasively that the essence of intervention is compulsion which limits the rights and powers of incumbent governments and is not desired or welcomed by them. The form of compulsion, or the agents through which it is achieved, are less significant than the fact of compulsion.[10]

The focus in this paper, however, is on the restrictive definition. Although there is something artificial about this, it does lead to a tighter focus on what are clear and blatant cases of military intervention. Furthermore, although other kinds of intervention are in certain respects more insidious, military intervention remains the most brutal form that intervention takes. Not only is it the most obvious violation of state sovereignty but it involves the use of violence by the strong against the weak. Moreover it is military intervention which most obviously reflects the realities of international anarchy while contravening the norms of international society. Because the superpowers, ostensibly at least, accept these norms they have to provide justifications for their transgressions. The prime importance of these justifications lies in the fact that they effectively qualify the conditions under which each superpower deems it necessary to respect state sovereignty and adhere to the norm of non-intervention.

JUSTIFYING MILITARY INTERVENTION

The justifications that have been offered for both Soviet and American military interventions in the affairs of other states are cast partly in terms of dealing with threats to national security – the sole justification that is necessary in an anarchic international system. Because of the ideological dimension of superpower rivalry, however, they have also been cast in ideological terms. The result is that both Moscow and Washington have professed a belief in certain over-riding values – whether it be freedom and democracy on the one side or the class struggle and national liberation on the other – which effectively qualify their respect for sovereignty. Indeed, upholding these values is sometimes presented as an imperative which, on occasion, demands military intervention.

This is evident, for example, in the justifications offered by Moscow for its intervention in Afghanistan in 1979. A careful examination of Soviet policy towards Afghanistan in the period which followed the revolutionary coup of 1978 suggests that direct military intervention by the Soviet Union in December 1979 was a last attempt to retrieve a deteriorating situation, which was deemed to be a threat to Soviet security – highlighting once again the notion of an extended national security zone. The main Soviet justification for its military action rested upon the need to respond to a 'real threat that Afghanistan would lose its independence and be turned into an imperialist bridgehead on our southern border . . . To have done otherwise would have meant to watch passively the origination on our southern border of a seat of serious danger to the security of the Soviet state'.[11] This rationale is important for the way in which it combines the imperative of national security with the notion of counter-intervention. The emphasis on the dangers in Afghanistan effectively acknowledges that in an anarchic international system the prime responsibility of the government is to its own national security. At the same time, the stress on the creation of an 'imperialist bridgehead' implies that Soviet action was a counter-intervention rather than an unprovoked intervention, thereby offering at least a genuflection towards the norm of non-intervention. The emphasis on the need to protect an endangered socialist regime as well as the fabrication that the Soviet Union was responding 'to the request of the government of friendly Afghanistan' reveal that Moscow was not insensitive to the fact that it was breaching a norm of international society.[12]

Indeed, Soviet doctrine and Soviet conceptions of international law place considerable emphasis on non-intervention. Although the Soviet concept of peaceful coexistence encompasses the non-intervention principle, however, this is not deemed to be inconsistent with proletarian internationalism and support for wars of national liberation. On the contrary, the two doctrines are held together by the Soviet concept of sovereignty: 'As well as that of state sovereignty, Soviet international law recognises a right to national sovereignty, a right of each nation to self-determination and independent development whether or not it has its own statehood'.[13] Consequently, intervention on behalf of nationalist movements is regarded as legitimate behaviour which contravenes respect for state sovereignty but is justified by its contribution to the attainment of national sovereignty.

Even during the period of superpower detente during the early 1970s Moscow made clear that the international class struggle had not ceased and that it would continue to support wars of national liberation. Soviet and Cuban intervention in Angola in 1975 and 1976 was justified in terms of this obligation, and a Soviet spokesman unequivocally rejected Henry Kissinger's complaints that such behaviour was incompatible with Soviet-American detente. As Brezhnev stated at the Twenty Fifth Congress of the Soviet Communist Party in February 1976:

Our party supports and will continue to support peoples fighting for their freedom. In so doing, the Soviet Union does not look for advantages, does not hunt for concessions, does not seek political domination or exact military bases. We act as we are bid by our revolutionary conscience, our communist convictions . . .[14]

Although there is considerable hypocrisy in a statement which denies any geopolitical motive for intervention, the Soviet emphasis on the ideological rationale for its intervention reveals once again the tendency to subordinate the principle of non-intervention to other values and principles.

American policy has been very similar and has evolved within a doctrine of counter-intervention which was echoed in Soviet statements justifying intervention in Afghanistan. The basic rationale was enunciated in the Truman Doctrine of 1947 which stated that 'it must be the policy of the United States to support free peoples who are resisting subjugation by armed minorities or by outside pressures'. Like Soviet justifications this is based on the idea of obligation. It is not that Washington wants to intervene in the domestic affairs of other states, but it has an obligation which cannot be shirked. The language of the Truman Doctrine – it 'must be the policy of the United States' – implies that there is a moral imperative for intervention when the values for which America stands, and which it believes must be upheld, are under challenge. At the same time, there is a certain ambivalence which means that the United States stops short of a frontal challenge on the concept of sovereignty. The fact that the states in which it intervenes are being subjected to internal disruption or outside pressure means that their sovereignty is already being violated by others. In intervening, therefore, the United States is taking action designed to restore sovereignty rather than undermining or challenging it. The Truman Doctrine is not a doctrine of intervention as such but one of counter-intervention.

If the Truman Doctrine could be given almost global application through its reference to 'free peoples', the United States has also developed more specific justifications for military intervention in its sphere of influence in Latin America. A continuing theme in American pronouncements on Latin America is that communism is alien to the region and that any communist advancement into the hemisphere effectively represents an act of intervention by an outside power – the Soviet Union, whether acting alone or through its Cuban proxy. Any American intervention to prevent communist gains, therefore, can be understood as self-defence in the extended national security zone. There is nothing new about this, and in many respects it can be understood simply as an extension of the Monroe Doctrine which was designed to keep all foreign powers out of Latin America. Furthermore, American military intervention south of its borders has a long tradition which pre-dates the Cold War and concerns over Marxism-Leninism. Even when the United States was isolationist, it still had what was effectively an extended national security zone in the Western hemisphere.

Since 1945, this national security zone has increasingly been defined in ideological terms, thereby linking it to the doctrine of counter-intervention enunciated in the Truman Doctrine. The ideological dimension took on even greater importance after Castro's victory in Cuba. It is hardly surprising, therefore, that the principle of hemispheric solidarity and anti-communism was invoked by the Organisation of American States in a declaration of January 1962 which stated that 'adherence by any member of the OAS to Marxism-Leninism is incompatible with the Inter-American system and the alignment of such a government with the communist bloc breaks the unity and solidarity of the hemisphere'. Such declarations were not only intended to isolate Cuba, but also to provide additional justification in the event that the United States felt it necessary to intervene in order to prevent further communist inroads into the hemisphere. Indeed, similar concerns over external intervention had been used to justify US interventions in Guatemala in 1954, Cuba in 1961, and would emerge once again when the United States intervened in the Dominican Republic in 1965.

The Dominican intervention of 1965 is particularly important because of the series of rationales that were presented to justify the American action. Initially the emphasis was on protecting American citizens whose lives were endangered by the growing disorder in the Dominican Republic. This was buttressed by the argument that military intervention was necessary to restore law and order in a situation where there was no responsible authority able to do this. Increasingly though the emphasis was placed on the danger from 'Communist conspirators' who had been trained in Cuba and who had taken over what had begun as a popular democratic revolution.[15] Following on from this, President Johnson elaborated a rationale which asserted the 'unilateral right of the United States to intervene militarily in any sovereign state of the hemisphere if, in the opinion of the US that state were in danger of falling to the communists'.[16] Although this became known as the 'Johnson Doctrine', essentially it was little more than a specific regional application of the principle that had been established by President Truman in 1947.

The Reagan Administration's justifications for its intervention in Grenada were remarkably similar in both content and evolution to those used by the Johnson Administration to justify the Dominican intervention. As in 1965 the initial emphasis was upon the threat to the lives and well-being of American students in Grenada. The 1965 theme of restoring order in a chaotic situation also had echoes in 1983. President Reagan claimed that the United States intervention was designed to restore 'democratic institutions' in the wake of a coup in which 'a brutal group of left wing thugs violently seized power'.[17] An additional element in 1983 was the stress laid on the fact that five Caribbean nations, members of the Organisation of Eastern Caribbean States, had requested the United States to participate in the attempt to restore order in Grenada. Within a few days, however, the emphasis had shifted, as it had in 1965, to preventing further communist gains, and President Reagan had claimed that Grenada 'was a Soviet–Cuban colony being readied as a major military bastion to export terror'.[18] Although these claims were greeted with some scepticism both in Congress and amongst America's European allies, the justification fitted a pattern that has been established throughout the post-war period.

Similar arguments were used by the Reagan Administration in an effort to justify its aid to the Contras in Nicaragua. Reagan's portrayal of the contras as freedom fighters and the Sandinista regime as not only a proxy of Cuba and the Soviet Union, but also as a threat to the security of its neighbours in Central America, can be understood not only in terms of mobilising support for aid in Congress, but also as an attempt to provide an advance justification for direct military intervention, should it prove necessary.

One of the most interesting aspects of the way in which both Washington and Moscow have justified military intervention in other states is the process of cross fertilisation which has occurred. It is claimed by some analysts, for example, that the Johnson Doctrine provided a model which the Soviet Union applied to Eastern Europe through the promulgation of the Brezhnev Doctrine in the aftermath of the invasion of Czechoslovakia in 1968. The doctrine, which applies to states belonging to the socialist commonwealth, asserts that members cannot unilaterally withdraw from the ideological community. Furthermore, deviation from the norms of the community by any state is sufficient cause for the other members of the community to use military force to alter the policies and government of the delinquent. Furthermore, 'any socioeconomic or political doctrine varying from that of the community is alien ... its espousal constitutes foreign subversion of, and aggression against, the community in response to which collective force may be used in self defence.'[19] Emphasis is also placed on the need to respond to requests for help from 'loyalist' leaders.

The precise formulation of the Brezhnev Doctrine owed much to similar American statements. As Franck and Weisband put it: 'virtually every concept of the Brezhnev Doctrine can be traced to an earlier arrogation of identical rights by the United States *vis-á-vis* Latin America.'[20] If the Soviet Union has emulated American justifications for intervention in its sphere of influence, the United States has emulated the Soviet Union by declaring its willingness to support counter-revolutionary struggles being waged against Marxist-Leninist governments. In his 1986 State of the Union Address President Reagan affirmed American support to freedom fighters who are challenging Communist regimes. As he put it 'America will support with moral and material assistance your right not just to fight and die for freedom, but to fight and win freedom – in Afghanistan, Angola, Cambodia and Nicaragua.'[21] Although this declared strategy, known as the Reagan Doctrine, has encountered considerable opposition from within the United States itself – and does not justify direct American intervention – it is a clear statement that the imposition on a Third World society of a Marxist government is not an irreversible process. There is still a gap, however, between the rhetoric and the means to implement the strategy. Nevertheless, the Reagan Doctrine reveals very clearly that the Third World is still regarded as a crucial arena for the playing out of Soviet-American rivalry. As such, it seems unlikely that the incentives for intervention in the future will be significantly less than in the past.

ASSESSMENT: MINIMISING INTERVENTIONISM

There are two broad approaches to minimising the likelihood and frequency of superpower interventions in the late 1980s and 1990s. One is by reducing the incentives for such intervention. Yet this is something which depends crucially on the superpowers themselves and on the form their competition takes during the years ahead. For those who want to promote both the principle and the practice of non-intervention, the prospects for reducing incentives are not good. After all, from the perspective of both superpowers military intervention in the affairs of Third World states is not a serious problem which in any way jeopardises international order – unless it is done by the adversary. When it is done by oneself then, as outlined above, it can readily be justified. Indeed, one's own interventions are seen not as violations of established norms but as solutions or responses to specific problems and challenges in particular geographic areas. So long as this attitude prevails then the prospects for reducing the incentives for Soviet or American interventions in the Third World are negligible. Indeed, in terms of reducing incentives, there is little that Third World states themselves can do to ensure that the non-intervention norm is observed more scrupulously.

Where Third World states may have greater effect, however, is in reducing the opportunities or occasions for superpower intervention. Yet there are two fundamental prerequisites for such an approach to have any chance of working. In the first place it requires strengthening the institutions of the state throughout much of the Third World and overcoming those divisions within society that provide standing invitations for external intervention. Secondly, it requires sustained efforts to establish effective regional mechanisms for both crisis management and conflict resolution in the Third World. These requirements are much easier to identify than to meet. The alternative to progress in these two areas, however, is to hope that the superpowers will cease to behave as great powers and will drop military intervention from their repertoire of foreign policy instruments. For Third World states to plan on such a development would not only be to abdicate responsibility for their own destiny, but would be to rely excessively on the norms of international society and to ignore the over-riding realities of international anarchy and hierarchy. As Thucydides, Hobbes, and Machiavelli would testify, to ignore these realities would be a mistake.

NOTES

1 Quoted in H. J. Morgenthau, 'To intervene or not to intervene' *Foreign Affairs*, Vol. 45, April 1967, pp. 425–36 at p. 425.
2 M. Wight, *Power Politics* (London: Pelican, 1979), p. 194.
3 Morgenthau, 'To intervene or not to intervene', p. 425.
4 K. Waltz, *Theory of International Politics* (Reading Mass.: Addison-Wesley, 1979), p. 170.
5 Ibid., p. 171.
6 Morgenthau, 'To intervene or not to intervene', p. 429.
7 Ibid.
8 K. Knorr, *On the Uses of Military Power in the Nuclear Age* (Princeton: Princeton University Press, 1966).
9 R. J. Vincent, *Nonintervention and International Order* (Princeton: Princeton University Press, 1974), p. 13. The subsequent analysis relies heavily on Vincent's discussion.
10 C. Thomas, *New States, Sovereignty and Intervention* (Aldershot: Gower, 1985) p. 20.
11 Brezhnev, quoted in R. Garthoff, *Detente and Confrontation* (Washington: Brookings Institution, 1985), p. 928.
12 Quoted in Ibid., p. 929.
13 Vincent, *Nonintervention and International Order*, p. 185.
14 Quoted in A. P. Schmid, *Soviet Military Intervention Since 1945* (Oxford: Transaction Books, 1985), p. 109.
15 Vincent, *Nonintervention and International Order*, pp. 202–4.
16 T. M. Franck and E. Weisband, *Word Politics* (New York: Oxford University Press, 1971).
17 See P. E. Tyler and D. Hoffman, 'US says aim is to restore order', *Washington Post*, 26 October 1983.
18 See A. Lewis, 'What was he hiding', *New York Times*, 31 October 1983, p. 19.
19 See Franck and Weisband, *Word Politics*, for a fuller elaboration of the Brezhnev Doctrine and its relationship to the Johnson Doctrine.
20 See Ibid.
21 Quoted in R. W. Copson and R. P. Cronin, 'The Reagan doctrine and its prospects', *Survival*, Vol. 29, No. 1, January–February 1987, p. 42.

Part IV: Political violence and the international system

11   A view from the South

George Joffé

Any discussion of the phenomenon of international terrorism, particularly in the context of the Middle East, is fraught with emotive semantic problems. The central role played by Israel in the apparently chronic crises that have plagued the post-war Middle East, together with the profound sense of guilt still widely felt in Europe and the United States over the genocide against Europe's Jewish communities during World War Two, makes it virtually impossible to sustain an objective dialogue on the issue of terrorism in the Middle East. The problem has been intensified by the success of the Islamic revolution in Iran in 1979, which made the West uncomfortably aware of what it perceives as the new menace of Islamic fundamentalism. Most recently, the simplistic cynicism of US policy on the issue of international terrorism has persuaded most people that there is little point in seeking to understand the twin issues of terrorism and Islamic fundamentalism in the region. Instead, the only response is to confront all violent manifestations of the Middle East's problems that spill over into the outside world with the armed force of the state – except when national interest appears to demand less blunt methods, as the Irangate scandal, which confronted the Reagan administration in 1986–7, showed.

Given the emotive connotations attached to both terrorism and to Islamic fundamentalism, it is useful to establish precisely what meaning should be attached to each term. In the case of terrorism this is particularly important since it is frequently assumed that the term is synonymous with violence and crime.[1] Fundamentalism suffers from the virtually automatic assumption that it is not more than a reassertion of traditionalist – and thus more primitive – moral values. To this is added the popular assumption that it is also inherently violent, an assumption which is manifestly untrue.

There is little doubt that there is a close relationship between violence and terrorism, although suggestions that these links arise solely (or even predominantly) from a philosophical preoccupation with the cathartic effects of violence do not seem to advance the argument very far.[2] In fact, it seems far more likely that the rationale for violence – apart from the outright destruction of symbols and institutions to which those involved in terrorism are opposed – is that it is the essential means to achieve desired ends. The act of violence itself, however, is not the crucial consideration; it is the potency of the threat of violence which is far more significant, since it is this threat which, ideally, is intended to achieve change.

Closely associated with the terrorist threat of violence is its designated target. It is in this context that terrorist activity is at its most unique, for its targets do not necessarily have to have any direct relation with the issues with which it is concerned. Indeed, it often seems to be the case that terrorist victims should, almost by definition, be innocent – partly, no doubt, to underline thereby the terrorists' determination to achieve their defined aims. If the victims are not merely innocent bystanders, then they are often only *indirectly* linked to the issues involved. Dissidents, for example, are not necessarily actively opposed to a particular government, but they do typify an implicit rejection of that government's legitimacy. Police and officials become terrorist targets as embodiments of the state which is the ultimate target of terrorist activity. Journalists and politicians serve the same purpose, while foreigners are taken to embody (by a peculiar reductionism) the policies of the state from which they come. Victims, in short, are objectified into categories defined as antagonistic to the terrorists' aims and thus become legitimate targets.

At the same time, the use of violence does not necessarily imply that terrorists are merely engaged in a particular form of military action. Terrorist activity lacks the essential component, inherent in military action, of an opponent which is intended to be and accepts that it is the *direct* target for violence. Furthermore, the complex corpus of limitations on military action through internationally recognised rules and principles are specifically rejected in terrorist practice, although they may be invoked as a means of defence. At the same time, there are frequently situations, particularly in the Middle East, where such a distinction becomes highly ambiguous and those condemned by their victims as terrorists can often claim, with considerable justification, that they are involved in guerrilla warfare or in a struggle for national liberation.

Indeed, it is precisely this ambiguity which reinforces the need for effective and objective analysis of the problem, at least in its Middle Eastern context. The point was nicely made recently by Colonel Qadhafi, when he told a journalist that, 'We support Hizbullah if it calls for martyrdom on Palestinian soil. But if Lebanon is the target, then this is terrorism' (*Guardian*; 12.3.87.). For the colonel, the struggle against Israel was a matter of national liberation and thus legitimate warfare. Actions inside Lebanon, however, would be an attack on the

Arab nation – a legitimate and legitimised political entity in his political credo – and thus terrorist in nature.

The issue of criminality seems far more open to dispute, for terrorism is essentially a political act, designed to achieve changes in the political sphere. It is not primarily intended to achieve personal benefit through acts defined by national law as criminal. Terrorist activity may well, indeed, usually *does* involve acts which are construed by national law as criminal, but, since it usually disputes the legitimacy of the institutions which define the law, it can justify itself by underlining the illegitimacy of the system of law involved. Terrorists can, in fact, extend the argument into a claim that terrorism is justified by the very fact that the illegitimacy of the legal system prevents essential change being achieved by other means and that the desirability of such change justifies the means being used. The same consideration applies to the ambiguity between terrorism and warfare, where actions defined as criminal acts by one side are justified as acts of national liberation by the other.

Terrorism is, therefore, the use of violence, or the threat of violence, to achieve specifically political ends against a target or victim who has no necessary correlation with the factor inciting terrorist activity originally and the primary means for achieving the desired end is fear. In the Middle Eastern context, this definition covers a wide range of activities which have been conventionally defined as terrorist. They have involved violent confrontations between ethnically and ideologically differentiated communities, between movements and states and between states and individuals. Nor are these activities only of recent date, for it could be argued that the precursor of them all was the Assassin movement, the *hashishiyyin*, a branch of Isma³ili Shi³ism, which thrived from the tenth to the fourteenth century.[3]

The Isma³ili movement adopted violence largely in a desperate attempt to survive and the techniques of the assassins were as much an admission of the movement's weakness in the overall historical context of the development of Islamic society. This quality, too, is a crucial factor in modern Middle Eastern terrorism – it is a weapon of the weak, or those who perceive themselves to be weak, in the face of what they consider to be overwhelming institutional strength.

THE ARAB–ISRAELI CONFLICT

It is this perception of weakness that also provides a starting point for Middle Eastern terrorism in the modern age. In fact, modern Middle Eastern terrorism really began in the 1930s and formed part of the wider struggle that was beginning then against colonial structures in the region. It also began over the issue which has continued to be central to Middle Eastern conflicts up to the present day – the issue of Zionism. In fact Arab objections to the Balfour declaration and its consequences were not merely over practical issues of access to land or control of the local economy. They were also specifically directed against the growth in influence of a Jewish political ideology that justified migration and a claim to the territory of Palestine, one that they increasingly saw as a direct threat to the survival of their own community and its access to the territory under dispute.

The Zionist movement justified its activities before the end of the Mandate in terms of a struggle for national survival and liberation. Since its inception in 1964 the PLO, with at least equal justification, has claimed it is engaged in a justified war of national liberation in which acts defined as terrorist by the West are a legitimate part of the struggle, particularly if they are directed against Israel. The Zionist movement laid exclusive claim to the territory of Cis- and Trans-Jordan on grounds of historical rights of occupation. The Palestinians, with a far more recent memory of territorial control can make an equally justifiable claim. Although the Arafat wing of the PLO may now have abandoned actions against Western institutions and individuals – although up to 1975 it saw such actions as a legitimate part of the struggle — extremist elements within the overall Palestinian movement continue to use this argument to justify attacks on apparently unconnected Western targets because of what they see as a Western predilection for Israel and discrimination against legitimate Palestinian demands.

The role of nationalism

The essential consideration is that, for all involved – Arab, Israeli or Palestinian Arab – the context of the struggle in which terrorism is encapsulated is a nationalist one. Furthermore, it is structured around a concept of territorial nationalism, in which a national community is entitled to unique control of a territory to which it lays historical claim and on which it creates its own state. Zionism, after all, was a highly successful nationalist ideology based on the assumption that a Jewish community existed that was unique and differentiated from all other communities by its culture and language. In accordance with European political tradition – at least since the Treaty of Westphalia[4] – such a community was entitled to a territory uniquely its own in which to live under the institutions of a state unique to the community itself. For Zionism, the historical record indicated clearly where that territory should be, for, central to any nationalist movement, is a myth of origin. The use of the term 'myth' in this context merely underlines the fact that the ultimate historical accuracy of the claims of origin made by any nationalist movement are not the intrinsically important factor; it is the perception that the claims of origin are true that legitimises the nationalist movement itself in the eyes of its members.[5] Furthermore, in the case of Israel, the legitimacy imposed by this nationalist myth on the state itself is also the ultimate justification for the unrestrained violence that Israel visits on those it perceives to threaten it – a violence that to many observers often seems to be 'terrorist' in a very similar way to actions taken against Israel by groups opposed to it.

Yet, if such arguments over nationalist legitimacy are held to be true for Zionism, it is difficult not to accord equal validity to Arab and Palestinian arguments in favour of their own nationalist communities. The only difference, perhaps, is a temporal displacement in awareness of the crucial role that nationalism and the concept of the nation-state play in modern international relations. Palestinians, indeed, most Arab communities, have not habitually expressed their sense of cultural identity through an ideology of territorial nationalism – at least until the colonial period. In large measure this was due to a pre-existing indigenous political culture in which nationalism, in its European interpretation, had a minor role to play.[6]

In fact, three different levels of political loyalty vied for attention and coexisted with degrees of intensity that varied in space and time. The overriding reality of the *umma*, the concept of the single Islamic community occupying a definable territory, was buttressed by the dominant role of Islam as an ideology and a culture and was further reinforced by the multiethnic political structure of the Ottoman empire. At the same time, a basic sentiment of patriotism, *wataniya* (derived from *wata*, homeland), was universally evident, although its importance varied in response to the vitality of Ottoman control in different locations. In Egypt, for example, it became a dominant factor during the nineteenth century, so that by Egyptian independence in 1922 under the Wafd Egyptian intellectuals were often far more concerned with their country's pharaonic credentials than with its Islamic inheritance. From the end of the nineteenth century, however, a third concept began to play an ever-increasing role – the idea of a common cultural and linguistic identity based on Arabic and known as *qaumiya*, which reflected a much earlier concept of the tribe (*qaum*) as a cultural unit.

The development of *qaumiya* was the result of two independent ideological trends. On the one hand, in the 1890s Christian and Muslim Arabs in Syria and Lebanon sought to define an Arab identity, separate from the wider Muslim *umma* and, although culturally linked to it, not dependent on religious legitimation through Islam. At the same time, a wave of religious revivalism spread through the Middle East from the 1860s onwards. Stimulated by Al-Afghani, the founder of the Salafiyyah movement, it was refined later by Mohamed Abduh, Rashid Rida and Shakib Arslan. All these thinkers were determined to revive Islam as the conscious ideological motivator of the Islamic world. However, at the same time, they found it increasingly difficult to avoid emphasising the dominant role of Arabic within that world and thus, indirectly, stimulated the concept of *qaumiya* as well as reviving that of the *umma*.[7]

However, as these indigenous political developments were taking place, the Middle East found itself increasingly under European colonial control – particularly after 1918. Colonialism had two major effects on indigenous political ideology. First, it imposed rigid territorial division and centralised administrative structures that had little to do with local practice. As a result, however, it also codified the paths along which the dialogue between colonised and coloniser, whether violent or pacific,[8] over the political futures of the states thus created would develop. Colonialism, in short, reinforced the dominance of *wataniya* in the modern form of territorial nationalism within the Middle East by enforcing a particular political vocabulary in which the inevitable dialogue would take place. At the same time, however, the colonial experience also stimulated the growth of a more generalised sentiment of *quamiya*, of secular cultural unity – Arab unity, in short, that was to reach its formal expression in the creation of the League of Arab States in 1945.[9] Its most intense expression has been manifest in the growth in influence of Nasserism and Ba²athism during the 1950s and 1960s.

Its most important area of activity at a popular level has been the adoption of the Palestinian issue and the confrontation with Israel as an Arab responsibility. Unfortunately, the individual states within the Arab world have not always shared this perception, a factor which has created an increasing sense of disillusionment and bitterness among the masses and Palestinians in particular. It has also stimulated a search for alternative means of prosecuting the struggle, one in which the failure of Arab states to act is reflected in a profound belief in Arab political and military weakness. In this context, at the popular level at least, a terrorist response is seen as legitimate; an expression of support for national liberation.

The problem of the state

The result has been that, quite apart from the destructive effect of virtually forty years of tensions and violence, Middle Eastern states have existed within a profound ideological contradiction. The moral imperatives of Arab unity, which require continuing confrontation with Israel and support for the demands of the impoverished, dispersed and increasingly embittered Palestinian community, often run directly counter to perceived national interest. (In the case of Egypt in the late 1970s, support for the Palestinian cause was moderated by the requirement of the pursuit of the national interest of the Egyptian state.) The

Palestinians, after all, have had the most direct and abrasive experience of the consequences of territorial nationalism and have, in consequence, developed an equally fierce sense of nationalism and right to the lost national territory. Furthermore, in the service of that nation it is difficult for them, like the mass of the population of the Arab world, to accept any limitation to political and military action designed to achieve its legitimate expression through a nation-state.

However, the relative failure of the Arab world to resolve the Palestinian problem forces the Palestinian community on to its own resources – limited when compared with those of the opposition – so that terrorism is an inevitable concomitant of the struggle and is directed both against Arab states and the West as well as against Israel. Indeed, a large part of Palestinian bitterness towards Arab states is a consequence of what is seen in Palestinian eyes as repeated betrayal of their interests by Arab leaders. Ironically, it is a betrayal that is heightened by Palestinian awareness that, even at a popular level, ideological support for their cause is not necessarily reflected in acceptance of Palestinian communities inside other Arab states. In that betrayal lies a further justification for the weak to use terrorism against their betrayers.

The ideological contradiction over the nature of political legitimacy in the Arab world, however, has more profound effects as well. Although states such as Syria, Iraq and Libya lay claim to an ideology of Arab unity, they suffer from profound disagreements over the specific nature of that ideology. Syria and Iraq are both Ba'athist states, but each differs over the actual structure of Ba'athist ideology – with Iraq emphasising its Arab nationalist nature and Syria its socialist content.[10] Libya, on the other hand, is the inheritor of Nasserism, which is still the underlying ideology of the Qadhafi regime, despite the idiosyncratic accretions of the *jamahiriyah*.[11] In reality, however, each state eventually accords primacy to its own national interest, although that may be clouded in ideological imperatives that become the justification for conflict amongst them. Thus Syria and Iraq, despite their public support for the Palestinian cause, have often been far more concerned over their internecine quarrels.

The problem is not confined solely to the issue of ideological contradiction, however. A far more serious problem is that the structure of the state in the Middle East is, in itself, inherently unstable and this instability – or metastability in many cases – reflects itself in foreign and domestic politics, particularly in connection with the issue of terrorism. Middle Eastern states are, in a word, inherently 'defective'.[12]

Modern nation states acquire stability as a consequence of their ability to support the egalitarian assumptions of their nationalist populations through access to or intrusion by the institutions of the so-called 'scientific state'.[13] Only if the institutions of the state – which are increasingly intrusive and dominant – are perceived as disinterested, in that they do not differentiate between individuals in the population, can they be accepted by the nation they control.

In the Middle East, this situation is remarkable by its absence. On the contrary, the institutions of the state are perceived to be (and usually are) repressive and discriminatory. Furthermore, this discrimination is often expressed in ethnic or kinship terms. Conversely, access to the benefits of the state depend on such links and control of the institutions of the state which reflect the personalised nature of power and its close linkage to ethnic identity. Such structures are inherently unstable since they stimulate competition to control the benefits offered by these institutions.

Terrorist states

The result is that, in the Middle East, the egalitarian assumptions inherent in the territorial nationalism that all states seek to foster as a means of guaranteeing their legitimacy are undermined by the inherently unegalitarian and personalised structure of the state. Not surprisingly, therefore, groups within the nation will attempt to capture control of different institutions within the state or even of the structure of the state itself and, conversely, the elite controlling the existing state structure will tend to use any means to legitimate and maintain its control. However, its very isolation within the population will persuade it of the need to coerce and intimidate its opponents, for it cannot effectively use the authority of the state, since most of the population perceive the state to be alien and oppressive. Terrorism by the state against those perceived to threaten its ruling elites, or by groups opposed to the elites, is the inevitable result.

The problem is intensified in those states in which there is already an inherent ideological contradiction, particularly states such as Libya, Iraq and Syria. The ideological imperatives, both in a national and a regional context, impel the elites within each state – which reflect ethnic interests within the state concerned (the Tikriti group in Iraq, the Alawites as opposed to Druse and others in Syria, and the Qadhadhfa in Libya) – to defend both their own positions and the ideologies they claim to represent. It is this that explains the endless purging of both Ba'ath party and the army in Iraq, even at the cost of endangering the country's military effectiveness in the Gulf war. Similarly, the arcane struggles and disagreements between Damascus and Baghdad over the past two decades are, in essence, frequently no more than attempts by the ruling elites, with their minority support amongst the population at large and their dependence of specific groups within it, to maximise their support bases.

At the same time, the absolutist nature of the ideological imperative justifies any method of combating the threat to the state or of extending the reach of influence of the ideology itself. Ba'athism is involved in the sacred duty of reconstructing the Arab nation; Colonel Qadhafi's Libya is the embodiment of a perfected political system, so the *Green Book* tells us. No wonder Libya's revolutionary committees feel little compunction over the ways in which they treat dissidents, both within and outside the country. Furthermore, individual groups within the state can claim the same justification for their actions on its behalf. In Syria, for example, the various secret service organisations enjoy an autonomy that frequently ensures foreign policy initiatives that seem to run counter to wider national interest.

The popular response

The fragmentation and personalisation of political authority in the Middle East, coupled with the Palestinian struggle for national recognition and a territorial base, have, therefore, been responsible for much of the violence and terrorism that has characterised the region for the past forty years. There have, however, been two other ideological tendencies which, although not synonymous with terrorism, have both been connected with the phenomenon and have also, on occasion, catalysed terrorist activity. The first of these reflects a profound ideological dispute which has riven the Palestinian movement since the late 1960s and which has significantly contributed to its division and weaknesses.[14] It derives in a large measure from the feeling of alienation within the Arab world that has developed amongst Palestinians since the 1950s, with their awareness of the resentment felt by other Arab groups at their presence as refugees.

It is articulated by the Palestinians themselves when they refer to themselves as Uthman's shirt.

We are only Uthman's shirt. After the Caliph Uthman was murdered, leaders would say, 'I do this in the name of Uthman', when they wanted people to believe them. But they only used his name. They waved his bloody shirt. Today we Palestinians are Uthman's shirt . . .[15]

In other words, the Palestinians see themselves as being merely a symbol of Arab frustrations, while their own very real problems are not taken seriously by an Arab world that claims the Palestinian problem as its own, but, in reality, treats the Palestinian diaspora with contempt and dislike.

The response has been twofold – either the Palestinian problem is one of national recovery or it is one of revolution. In other words, either, as the Palestinian National Charter makes clear in Article 29, the Palestinian people has the fundamental right to liberate and recover its national territory – a directly nationalist aim and the original primary objective of the PLO and Al-Fath – or, as the Popular Democratic Front for the Liberation of Palestine (PDFLP) argued in 1967, in opposing UN Resolution 242, the struggle over Palestine is to lay the basis for a popular democratic revolution against reactionary regimes in the region – a specifically revolutionary aim involving a class struggle both within and outside the border of Palestine.[16] The importance of this aspect of the Palestinian issue has led W. W. Kazziha in his book *Palestine and the Arab Dilemma* to postulate an unresolved ideological and political contradiction between Arab regimes and the Palestinian resistance movement which will inevitably bring them into conflict.[17] In fact, the contradiction is also one specific example of the wider problem of the legitimacy of state structures in the Middle East, for the failure of Arab states to lay successful claim to legitimacy in the eyes of their populations is, in itself, a further justification for a popular regional class struggle.

This dispute over the real purpose of the Palestinian struggle has inevitably been expressed through violence, as well as in debate. It has justified the PLO usurping the sovereignty of some Arab states (Jordan before September 1970 and, thereafter, Lebanon); it has led to direct attacks on governments by factions within the movement; and it has led to violent clashes within the Palestinian movement itself. Since a mass class struggle has failed to appear, the proponents of regional revolution as the means by which the Palestinian problem can be resolved have, on occasion, fallen back on political violence and terrorism. Equally, the dispute over the movement's aims within the Palestinian community has led to terrorism practised by one faction against another. The most striking case is that of Sabri Al-Banna (Abu Nidal) who has rejected all questions of compromise and has attempted to assassinate all Palestinian leaders who are prepared to compromise on the issue.[18] Furthermore, the factionalism and splits within the movement occasioned by the debate has also resulted in the use of terrorist tactics against Israel and the West precisely because the movement has been so profoundly weakened by them.

However, quite apart from the nationalist and revolutionary strands within the movement, there is also an Islamic ideology that justifies the struggle. In a fascinating analysis, Nels Johnson has shown that the simple fact of the Islamic environment in which the Palestinian movement was formed, has allowed many of its secular characteristics – struggle against Israel, anti-imperialism and so on – to acquire specifically religious connotations which reinforce the inherent justice of the struggle itself. The development of the struggle has changed its role from the Islamic justification offered by Sheikh Qassim during the Arab Revolt, when the struggle was one of *jihad*[19] and Islam the popular idiom, to the post-war period, when Islam can provide the vocabulary of struggle for both Christian and Muslim Palestinians. Equally, in such a situation, Islam can also justify acts that appear terrorist to the victim, but are legitimate acts of liberation to the perpetrator, just as was the case with the Isma'ili Assassins six centuries before. This coincidence of Islam and political radicalism also links the Palestinian struggle directly into the most recent ideological turmoil that has engulfed the Middle East – Islamic fundamentalism.

The failure of the Arab world to resolve the Palestinian issue began to lead, during the 1970s, to a deep sense of revulsion amongst large segments of the Arab population with the secular concepts of territorial nationalism (*wataniya*) and cultural nationalism (*qaumiya*) as enshrined in the defective Middle Eastern nation-state and the ideology of Arab nationalism. The consequent rejection of both these ideologies as vehicles for the reconstruction of the Arab world led, in turn, to a revival of interest in Islam as a unifying ideology (the *umma*) and as an alternative ideology of struggle. Indeed, insofar as Islam was the essential cultural environment and had already been one of the sources of inspiration for the initial indigenous response to European colonialism (the other being the limitation of the European political archetype, the nation state), it had in reality always formed part of the Middle Eastern ideological armoury. Now, however, it was to take a far more prominent role. The immediate catalyst was the 1967 war and, in its aftermath, radical and fundamentalist critics turned on the nationalists and on each other.

Fundamentalists argued that the Arabs had lost the war not because they were busy worshipping – as the radical caricature would have it – but because they had lost their faith and bearings: Disconnected from a deeply held system of beliefs, the Arabs proved easy prey to Israeli power. The argument made by thoughtful fundamentalists was similar to the one made by the radical critics: The latter, too, had argued that society needs a system of beliefs, an ideology, to guide it. The fundamentalists' contention was that Islam offered that system of belief, that it could do what no imported doctrine could hope to do – mobilise the believers, instill discipline, and inspire people to make sacrifices and, if necessary, to die.[20]

Islam, however, was not merely to be an ideology of struggle. As Muslim intellectuals in the *salafiyyah* movement – Afghani, Abduh, Rida and Arslan – had demonstrated, Islam was also capable of providing a basis for the organisation of the state. In this respect, Islam was perhaps unique amongst the world's great religions, in that, from the lifetime of the Prophet Mohammed on, one of its primary functions, in addition to mediating between God and man, was to define the conditions under which human society could and should organise itself. It had a corpus of law to regulate such an organisation – the *sharia* (a body of tradition) to inform the political system in the *hadith* (the traditional sayings of the Prophet) and *sunna* (the general practice of the Muslim community). In addition there was a political structure sanctioned by the *qur'an* – literally the divine word of Allah – to organise the community in the early caliphate.

Furthermore, provided that the essential principles were observed – that the ruler would ensure social order for the proper practice of Islam and that the community, in return, would accept his rule – the system was highly flexible and adaptable to novel conditions.

FUNDAMENTALISM VERSUS REFORM AND REVIVAL

These two ideas – of Islam as an appropriate ideology of struggle and of Islam as the sole legitimisation of social and political order – have come during the 1970s to embody a large element of Muslim and Arab aspirations. Indeed, in the wake of the failure of nationalism to realise those aspirations, the revival of Islam was quite predictable. It is an attempt which seeks to adapt and reform Islamic principles to cope with the problems of the modern world and it is a revival of indigenous political and cultural values which are designed to combat the alien values perceived to have originated from Western neo-colonial influence. Although some aspects of the revival are undoubtedly obscurantist, many others seek an active adaption to Middle Eastern and Muslim reality. Even though certain elements in the revivalist movement reject the legacy of colonialism and the Arab nationalism of the early years of independence in the post-war world, many others seek to find ways of adapting to circumstances as they actually are. However, the connection of the Islamic revival with terrorism is incidental and, compared with its significance in restructuring Middle Eastern society, essentially peripheral.

It is important in Western perceptions, however, because an inevitable component of the revival is confrontation with and rejection of Western values insofar as they have penetrated Middle Eastern society. Given the close interpenetration of the Middle East and the West, particularly in the economic sphere, this confrontation has inevitably extended into the international arena as well. The link with terrorism develops because Islamic revivalism has expressed this confrontation with particular force in areas where the collapse of political structures has fragmented those segments of the population which act as the vehicle of expression. This fragmented and alienated opposition then makes use of the best weapon available to it, given its political and military weakness – terrorism, through hijacks, kidnappings or bombings.

The fragmentation of political authority and ideological legitimisation and its replacement by Islamic revivalism has been expressed through a series of movements throughout the Islamic world, some of which have now acquired notoriety in the West. Several of them long pre-date the current period of revivalism, but some of the best known have sprung to prominence as a result of the Islamic revolution in Iran. The result has been that Western perceptions of the revivalist phenomenon have tended to assume that Iran has been the sole source of 'Islamic fundamentalism' and of the terrorism connected with it. It is an analysis which is incorrect and which obscures the reality, both of Iran and of the Islamic revival, for at least two separate strands can be identified – Shi³a and Sunni groups – which further sub-divide into rejectionist and reformist groups.

Sunni Revivalism

The Sunni revivalist movement really stems from the original *salafiyyists* of the late nineteenth century who had a major influence on twentieth-century nationalist movements, particularly in North Africa, Egypt and the Levant. Its best-known representative is the *Ikhwan Muslimin* movement (Muslim Brotherhood), but there is also the more extremist *Hizb al-Tahrir al-Islamiyya* (Islamic Liberation Party) and the various rejectionist factions associated with the Ikhwan – *Jihad, Takfir wa Hijra*, to mention the two best known examples in Egypt, or the *Mujahidin* and the *Jam³iyyat al-Shabiba al-Islamiyya* (the Society of Islamic Youth) in Morocco. There is also, however, a wide range of reformist movements, some of which are actually formed into political movements and others which are really no more than associations – the *Harakat al-Ittijah al-Islami* (Tendence Islamique) in Tunisia, Sheikh Kishk in Egypt or the so-called 'Islamic Marxists' in Egypt and Turkey.

Shi³a Revivalism

One of the great ironies of the radicalism now accorded to the Shi³a tradition is that traditionally Shi³a Islam has been the religion of the dispossessed in Islam. It has, equally traditionally, been used to maintain political passivism at the popular level, in that its tradition promises, not only a heavenly reward, but also a millenarianism which offers the hope of eventual earthly rectification of material injustice. Shi³a Islam rose from the early dynastic struggles of Islam and represented those who lost when Ali, the Prophet's son-in-law and cousin – and, to the Shi³a, the rightful inheritor of the Prophet's authority – was murdered.

The Shi³a preserved their vision of the true Islamic polity, however, by creating the concept of the Imamate – a chain of authority passing through the generations, despite assassinations and repression, to preserve the true legitimacy. Eventually, the line was broken when the last Imam vanished – different sects disagree about the precise chronology and the persons involved. However, the occulted Imam will eventually return to lead the Shi³a community to justice and revenge. It is evident that Shi³a Islam provides the perfect vehicle for political passivity, but with the promise of intense revivalism, once the vanished Imam returns.[21]

Although Sunni Islam has a similar tradition in the belief in Mahdism it lacks the same doctrinal coherence. Furthermore, Shi²a Islam also provides for a much more coherent chain of authority through the gradation of the culama – those recognised as proficient in religious matters and competent to comment on Islamic law, doctrine and principles – into a hierarchy. Such a structure, the *marja²iyyat* does not exist in Sunni Islam, so that it is far more difficult to articulate authoritative political statements with the backing of religious opinion. The marja²iyyat structure is not the equivalent of a Christian clergy, with all its overtones of authority and coercion, for individuals can still choose within the generally defined structure with *maraj* (religious leader) to follow. It is, however, far more cohesive then its Sunni equivalent.[22] It also provides a far better base for politicisation than does its Sunni counterpart.

Given these structures, it is possible to understand why Shi²a Islam was so successful in over-throwing the Shah in 1979. Ayatollah Khomeini, during his years of exile in Iraq, at Najaf after 1963, was able to create a powerful movement inside the Iranian population which not only condemned the Shah's regime for secularism and pro-Westernism, but also offered an alternative structure through the marja²iyyat *and* a leader who could easily be conflated into the occulted Imam. In fact, that connection has never been made explicit and many among the Ayatollahs reject it – Qomi and Shariat-Madari in Iran; Khu²i in Iraq. Nonetheless, the Khomeini faction in Tehran have been successful in creating a vast wave of propaganda to justify the assumption that Khomeini is, virtually, the occulted Imam returned. It is a sentiment that has been powerfully reinforced by the Gulf War and Iran's apparent success.

CONCLUSION

Terrorism in the Middle East is not an inarticulate act of protest, a celebration of the cathartic effect of violence nor merely a criminal response. It is, in reality, an attempt by groups that are inherently weak to assert demands which they see as legitimate and irresistible. These demands arise in large measure from competing nationalist visions and from the infirmities of the Middle Eastern state. The stimulation for them is primarily the Arab–Israeli conflict, a cause which has been intensified by the generalised hostility to the West encouraged by the Islamic revivalism that has characterised the area for the past decade.

It is notable that little attention has been paid here to the roles of outside powers, particularly the USSR. There has undoubtedly been considerable Soviet input into the struggles of the Middle East. However, it is difficult to see Soviet interest as in any way central to the development of the terrorist phenomenon there. The reality is that Middle Eastern terrorism has purely indigenous roots and responds to local realities. The outside world impinges insofar as it may be a source for material support (the USSR and other Socialist states) or is seen as an integral part of the problem through its support for Israel or for corrupt and reactionary regimes (the USA and Western Europe).

If this be true, then it is most unlikely that outside powers can radically alter the situation in the Middle East unless they address the real problems of the region – disparities of wealth and political inequalities. However, the primary problem that the West must address, if it is to achieve any reduction in terrorism, is that of the Palestinians. It is the West's failure to do anything constructive in this respect that has provided the most powerful spur to terrorism in the 1980s. Secondly, Western nations and states will have to learn to live with the uncomfortable facts of Islamic revivalism. Even if the Islamic state is confined to Iran, the implications of revivalism have already begun to affect government policies in a range of countries. Europe and America, however, have always found the notion of cultural equality difficult to tolerate.

Yet, even when all this has been achieved, there will still remain a terrorist residuum. It will take many years for the tradition of using terrorism as a legitimate political weapon – in the absence of any other means of articulating reasonable demands – to die away. There will still be many contradictions within the Middle East which will have to find their own resolution and that, in itself, may well let terrorism persist. For the outside world, the only sensible response is to take those technical measures it can to prevent terrorism from spilling over its frontiers, while seeking to understand and release the tensions of the Middle East that stimulate such violence. That, however, will require a massive change in policy in Washington – unlikely under present circumstances – and abandoning of cynical, self-indulgent and simplistic policies of military action that merely reinforce the problems they were supposed, ostensibly, to resolve.

NOTES

1 P. Wilkinson, *Terrorism and the Liberal State* (London: Macmillan, 1986), p. 55.
2 Ibid., p. 100.
3 B. Lewis, *The Assassins*, (Al Saqi, 1985), p. 11.
4 See E. G. H. Joffé, 'The International Court of Justice and the Western Sahara dispute' in R. Lawless and Monahan (eds.), *War and Refugees: The Western Sahara Conflict* (London and New York: Pinter, 1987).
5 See E. G. H. Joffé 'Frontiers in North Africa' in G. Blake, and R. Schofield, (eds.) *Boundaries and State Territory in the Middle East and North Africa* (Wisbech: Menas Press, 1987).
6 See J. Piscatori, *Islam in a World of Nation-States* (Harmondsworth: Penguin, 1986). Mr Piscatori's arguments should be treated with caution, however.
7 S. G. Haim, *Arab Nationalism an Anthology* (Cambridge University Press, 1962), 46ff. H. Eneyat, *Modern Islamic Political Thought* (London: Macmillan, 1982), p. 2.
8 I am using the term as defined as A. Memmi, *The Coloniser and the Colonised* (Souvenir Press, 1974).
9 See R. W. MacDonald, *The League of Arab States: A Study in the Dynamics of Regional Management* (Princeton: Princeton University Press, 1965).

10 N. Van Dam, *The Struggle for Power in Syria* (London and Sydney: Croom Helm, 1979), p. 84.
11 G. Wright, *Libya: A Modern History* (London and Sydney: Croom Helm, 1982), p. 158.
12 A. Smith, *Theories of Nationalism* (Duckworth, 1983), p. 235.
13 M. Heiberg, 'Insiders/outsiders: Basque Nationalism', *Arch. europ. sociol.*, Vol. VI, 1975, p. 186–93.
14 A. Smith, *Theories of Nationalism*, p. 195–202.
15 N. Johnson, *Islam and the Politics of Meaning in Palestinian Nationalism* (Kegan Paul International, 1982), p. 60.
16 L. Gaspar, *Histoire de la Palestine* (Maspero, 1978), p. 229, 241.
17 W. W. Kazziha, *Palestine in the Arab Dilemma* (London and Sydney: Croom Helm, 1971), p. 36.
18 P. Smith, *Theories of Nationalism*, p. 197.
19 N. Johnson, *Islam and the Politics of Meaning*, p. 99.
20 F. Ajami, *The Arab Predicament* (Cambridge University Press, 1981), p. 52.
21 F. Ajami, *The Vanished Imam* (Cornell University Press, 1986), p. 22–3.
22 C. Mallet, 'Aux origines de la guerre Iran–Irak: l'axe Najaf-Tehran', *Les Cahiers de L'Orient* (1986), *3*, p. 130.

12 A view from the North

Paul Wilkinson

PROBLEMS OF DEFINITION AND TYPOLOGY

One major complexity which has bedevilled debate and scholarly analysis concerning terrorism, has been the problem of definition. In recent years, however, a surprisingly broad consensus has emerged in the academic usage of the term in liberal democratic societies.[1] There is general recognition that terrorism is a specific method of struggle rather than a synonym for political violence or insurgency. Brian Jenkins has aptly described it as a kind of weapons-system. It can and has been employed by an infinite variety of actors in the international system, including governments, political factions, criminal gangs and even religious movements and cults. It is by no means the monopoly or exclusive weapon of any particular ideology, political philosophy or religion. It is also generally accepted in the specialist literature that what distinguishes terrorism from other forms of violence is the deliberate and systematic use of coercive intimidation. The terrorist is one who tries to terrify people into doing what he or she wants. For the politically motivated terrorist the object is generally to create a climate of fear among a wider target group than the immediate victims of the violence. Campaigns of terror violence can be used to publicise the terrorists' cause, as a kind of propaganda of the deed, as well as to coerce the wider target group to accede to the terrorists' aims. Thus there are at least five major participants in the process of terror; the perpetrators of the violence, the immediate victims, the wider target group or society which the terrorists seek to intimidate, the 'neutral' bystanders within the society experiencing the terrorism, and international opinion, in so far as it is aware of these events.

In any case the problems of establishing a degree of common understanding of the concept of terrorism have been vastly exaggerated. Indeed, I suspect that some have tried to deny that any common usage exists as a device for obstructing cooperation in policies to combat terrorism. Those who still genuinely believe that definition is a fundamental obstacle to the investigation of terrorist phenomena have clearly failed to study the growing academic literature, the proceedings of international scholarly conferences, and the modest but significant advances in international law and cooperation in this field. In a recent paper Gurr and Ross draw attention to Alex Schmid's thorough international review[2] of the definitional problem:

After an exhaustive analysis of over 100 expert definitions Schmid concludes that there is no 'true or correct definition . . .' Nevertheless, he develops a consensus definition consisting of five parts which we accept for our purposes. First, terrorism is a method of combat in which random or symbolic victims are targets of violence. Second, through previous use of violence or the credible threat of violence, other members of that group or class are put in a state of chronic fear. Third, the victimization of the target is considered extranormal by most observers, which fourth, creates an audience beyond the target of terror. Fifth, the purpose of terrorism is either to immobilize the target of terror in order to produce disorientation and/or compliance, or to mobilize secondary targets of demands (e.g. government) or targets of attention (e.g. public opinion). This definition encompasses terrorism by governments, by oppositions, and by international movements.[3]

The phenomena of terrorist violence can be identified in many different cultures and historical periods. It is nonsense to pretend that terrorism is a purely Western invention and therefore of no relevance in the study of Third World politics and international relations. The use of terror as a weapon can be traced in earliest recorded history. For example it was used by the Jewish Zealots in their struggles against the authority of the Roman Empire. The Shiʾite Assassin sect employed the weapon in the Middle Ages in a struggle to overthrow the Sunni Moslem order which ruled the Arab world. The Thugs were members of a confederacy of gangs of professional assassins which haunted parts of India for over 300 years. And today, the countries experiencing the most rapid growth in domestic and international terrorism are in Latin America, the Middle East and South Asia. But the most important point to note is that modern terrorism is an inherently international phenomenon. One of the negative manifestations in the development of global interdependence in the contemporary international system is that terrorist violence spills across frontiers and has become a major problem for the entire international community. Every year over half the nation-states in the world experience some form of international terrorist violence. Even the smallest and poorest of the newly independent Third World states now has to be aware that its civil aviation, its diplomats and embassies, its political leaders and its key business and symbolic targets, are all vulnerable to terrorism in some degree.

One obvious additional complication in operationalising this broad definition is that in many conflicts the use of terror violence is interwoven with a wider repertoire of unconventional warfare. In Central America, for example, terrorism is typically used in conjunction with rural guerrilla and economic and political warfare in all-out bids to topple governments. But in Western Europe and North America terrorism is usually seen in its 'pure' form, i.e. is unaccompanied by any wider insurgency. Terrorism is most easily identifiable precisely when it is being used in isolation by a weak and desperate minority surrounded by a 'peaceful' society rather than the fog of war. A common feature of such terror campaigns is that innocent civilians, including foreign citizens who know nothing of the terrorists' political quarrel, are either killed or injured or held hostage. Typical tactics of the modern terrorist are explosive and incendiary bombings, shooting attacks and assassinations, hostage taking and kidnapping, and hijackings. Terrorism as we have defined it is clearly a very broad concept. The role of taxonomies and typologies of terrorism is to sub-divide the field into categories which are more manageable for research and analysis.[4] One basic distinction is between state and factional terror. There is of course a very considerable historical and social scientific literature on aspects of state terror.[5] In view of the sheer scale of crimes against humanity and of mass terror that have been and are being committed by modern tyrannies, there should be no doubt that this is a far more severe and intractable problem for humanity than the containment and reduction of factional terror. Nevertheless historically state terror has often been an antecedent and to varying degrees a contributory cause of campaigns of factional terrorism. Once regimes assume that their ends justify any means they tend to get locked into a spiral of terror and counter-terror against their adversaries.

It is also very important to distinguish between international and internal terrorism. Internal terrorism is systematic violence which is largely confined to a single nation-state, or specific localities within a state. International terrorism in its most obvious manifestation is a terrorist attack carried out across international frontiers, or against a foreign target in the terrorist's state of origin. Yet in reality international dimensions often take a more indirect form; a terrorist group may seek foreign cash, weapons, political support or other resources. Or its members and leaders may occasionally find safe havens abroad or establish *ad hoc* cooperation with friendly foreign states and terrorist groups. Historically it is very hard to find a pure case of internal terrorism. Even the obsessively regionalised campaigns of the Provisional IRA in Northern Ireland and ETA-militar in the Basque region of Spain constantly spill over their respective international frontiers and raise international problems of bilateral cooperation and extradition.

It is useful to employ a basic typology of international terror perpetrators, based on their main declared aims and motives:

(1) *Nationalist terrorists.* These are groups seeking political self-determination. They may wage a combined struggle in the territory they seek to liberate and from bases abroad. Or, as in the cases of the Armenians and Croatians, for example, they may be forced by police action to campaign entirely in exile.

(2) *Ideological terrorists.* These groups profess to want to change the whole nature of the existing political, social and economic system, either to an extreme Left or extreme Right model. These groups have proved less durable than the well-established nationalist groups, and they are very prone to internal splits. Until comparatively recently they have been almost exclusively internal in character. However, since late 1986, the extreme left terrorist groups operating in Western Europe have been largely suppressed as a result of firm internal measures by governments. In the Third World extreme left ideological terrorist groups, such as M-19 in Colombia and Shining Path in Peru, are still a major challenge to the regimes.

(3) *Religious fanatics.* Certain religious groups employ international terrorism to undermine and ultimately overthrow what they regard as a corrupt and evil prevailing religious order. The best-known and perhaps most feared contemporary example is the Islamic Jihad group of fundamentalist Shi'ites who have been inspired by the Iranian revolution, and now challenge many of the moderate Arab regimes.

(4) *Single issue fanatics.* These groups are obsessed with the desire to change a specific policy or practice within the target society, rather than with the aim of political revolution. Examples would be anti-nuclear, anti-abortion and 'animal rights' extremists. There are some indications of international cooperation between these groupings.

(5) *State-sponsored international terrorism.* This is used as a tool of domestic policy (e.g. Gadaffi's hit-squads sent abroad to murder dissidents) and as a tool of foreign policy (e.g. Soviet assistance to Palestinian extremists in the late 1970s and early 1980s in order to disrupt the Soviet Union's adversaries in the Middle East and generally to help serve Soviet policy goals). State sponsors may use their own directly recruited and controlled terror squads, or may choose to work through proxies and client movements. They almost invariably work covertly in such support, so that they are liable to plausibly deny any involvement.[6]

Before leaving the subject of definition and typology, it is important to dispose of two surprisingly widespread misconceptions about the use of the concept of terrorism. First, it is sometimes objected that the word terrorism should be abandoned because it has an evaluative aspect. Of course it is true that in deciding to apply the word 'terrorism' to describe a particular campaign or act of violence the historian or social scientist is making a judgement solely about the means used, but it is a designation that nevertheless most terrorists seek to resist. Few wish to see themselves as terrorists. But this does not mean we can happily jettison the term terrorism from our discourse. Those who believe one can devise a totally value-free language for the study of politics and society are philosophically naive or disingenuous. Does any serious scholar suggest we abandon terms such as 'dictatorship', 'imperialism' and 'democracy'?

A second widespread misunderstanding arises from the confusion of means and ends. It is true that whatever criteria we may choose for assessing the legitimacy of a terrorist group to speak for the minority it claims to represent, the claim of the terrorists to speak for even a bare majority of their 'own people' are generally spurious. It is only in democratic societies that terrorist groups have the alternative of forming political parties and fighting elections. Even when given the chance, few take it, and if they do their election results are often derisory. (The ideological and religious fanatics do not even care about such tests of legitimacy because they already believe that their belief-systems are superior to all others and that these beliefs give them a transcendental justification for imposing their will by violence.) But even in those few clear cases where we may be persuaded that a terrorist group is motivated by a legitimate grievance or sense of injustice and can claim a degree of popular legitimacy among its professed constituency, does this mean we must refrain from designating any of their acts as terroristic in nature? Surely not, because terrorism is not a philosophy or a movement; it is a method of struggle. There have been a number of historical cases where terrorism has been used on behalf of causes most Western liberals would regard as just.

In any worthwhile analysis of a specific terrorist campaign it is, of course, essential to take account of the unique political, historical and cultural context, and the ideology and aims of the groups involved. Context is all in the analysis of any form of political violence. One needs to interpret the role and effectiveness of terrorism in the overall development of each conflict in which it appears. Is it being used as an auxiliary weapon in a wider strategy of revolutionary warfare? Or is it being used in isolation in a pre-insurgency mode? What degree of popular support, if any, do the perpetrators of terrorism enjoy? How severe and prolonged is the violence? Is it merely spasmodic and small in scale and destruction caused? Or is it growing in intensity, frequency, and lethality to the point where it threatens to trigger a full-scale civil or international war?

UNDERLYING CAUSES OF THE BURGEONING OF MODERN INTERNATIONAL TERRORISM IN THE LATE 1960s

One can identify certain conducive conditions which explain the considerable growth in international terrorism statistics.[7] First, there is the general strategic situation which favours unconventional war as a whole. The balance of terror and the fact that all major states wish to avoid an escalation of violence that could lead to a possible nuclear conflict are important factors. Most states today are even afraid of becoming involved in protracted and vastly expensive conventional conflicts which might escalate. Unconventional war thus becomes relatively more attractive. In terms of cost-effectiveness, it is the best means of achieving political-diplomatic objectives by coercion.

The balance of terror is also an important factor in the creation of a climate of thought about the use of violence. The balance of terror provides a paradigm of a mode of deterrence, and it is possible that revolutionary movements see terror and the holding of hostages as the most appropriate weapons to use in micro-conflicts. There is also the fact that, since the end of the colonial independence struggles, national borders have become firmly established. It is now very difficult for any minority movement to achieve a renegotiation of frontiers in its favour through some general diplomatic conference.[8] Hence the desperation, the argument from weakness mentioned earlier. Another factor is relative deprivation psychology – the feelings of political injustice felt by particular groups. Research has shown that feelings of political injustice – deprivation of political rights or exclusion from power or influence within a community – are especially likely to lead to violent rebellion.[9]

Weaknesses within the international community in general, and within particular nation states in responding to terrorism also contributed to the rise in terrorism. This was particularly true up until 1972. Since then, certain Western states have begun to take a firmer line; and there has been a widespread growth of elite units of special forces designed for hostage rescue, a development inspired by the success of the Entebbe and Mogadishu rescues. But, since the TWA hijack to Beirut in 1985, and the disastrous loss of life in a hijack to Malta in the same year, it has become clear that such rescue forces are not a panacea and do not necessarily restrain potential hijackers of the more fanatical type. The shift of revolutionary theory in the Third World away from the rural guerrilla concept toward the idea of urban struggle[10] is an important feature of contemporary terrorism. European revolutionaries in the nineteenth and early twentieth centuries have been through a similar process. The hunger for publicity tends to drive the revolutionary to the cities. As one Front de Liberation National (FLN) leader put it, 'It was more effective propaganda to shoot a couple of French businessmen in the middle of Algiers than to shoot a hundred or so soldiers in a lonely gully.' Other factors precipitating the move to cities are technological opportunity and the vulnerability of industrial societies and cities to terrorist techniques. One should also stress the contagion. Information flow effects of terrorism over a long span of time can cause a kind of bandwagon reaction.[11] There is also the growth of proterrorist ideologies and sub-cultures in Western cities right in the hearts of the countries that had the highest numbers of terrorist attacks in the last decade. Maverick states have also been active in funding and giving sanctuary to terrorists.

But of course all the factors mentioned so far are of a general nature. They characterise the international system of the late 1950s and 1960s. How does one explain the significance of 1968 as the starting-point for the upsurge in modern international terrorism? All specialists in the study of terrorism would agree that there were two international developments which had a key role in triggering this outbreak.

First and foremost there was the overwhelming defeat of military forces of the Arab states in their June 1967 war with Israel. Terrorism was by no means new to the Middle East, but there is no doubt that, as a result of this setback and the Israeli occupation of the West Bank, Gaza and the Sinai peninsula, and the Israeli takeover of the whole of Jerusalem, Palestinian militants concluded that the routes for defeating Israel by conventional military force, or regaining their homeland by diplomatic negotiation were blocked to them. The Arab states were too divided and Israel was too blocked to them. The Arab states were too divided and Israel was too militarily powerful. They concluded that they would gain more by a campaign of ruthless political violence striking at Israel and its supporters internationally in a war of terrorist attrition. Hence from 1968 to 1972 there followed a tremendous upsurge of hijack attempts, bombings, and other terrorist attacks against Israeli targets both in Israel and abroad, and against airline facilities, and personnel of the United States and other Western powers seen in Palestinian eyes to be guilty of supporting and collaborating with Israel. This shift to terrorism was intensified after the further disastrous defeat of the Fedayeen at the hands of Hussein's forces in Jordan in Autumn 1970. Between 1967 and 1974, about 15 per cent of all international terrorist incidents were carried out by Palestinian groups, many of them spilling over into Western Europe.

The impact of Palestinian terrorism should not be assessed purely in quantitative terms. Reports of their actions and the huge international publicity they achieved, undoubtedly had the effect of interesting other militant groups in other parts of the world in exploiting the techniques of international terror. And we should not neglect the direct influence of the PFLP and Fatah and the other

Palestinian organisations through their work of training foreign terrorists in various camps in the Middle East and in the constant Palestinian contacts with other terrorist groups around the world.

The second historical development was the resurgence of the extreme neo-Marxist and Trotskyist left among the student populations of all the industrial countries. Their common rallying points were bitter opposition to US policy in the Vietnam War, and to American policy in the Third World generally, which they designated neo-imperialism. Although the majority of the student left abandoned political violence following the street demonstrations and battles with the police in 1968–9, there was in each case a small hardcore of ideological extremists who decided that what was really needed was a more professional and long-term campaign of urban violence against the 'system'. These groups decided to form an 'underground' which engaged in a sustained campaign of terrorism. The main groups that sprang from this movement included the Baader-Meinhof Gang in the Federal Republic of Germany, the Red Brigades in Italy, and the Japanese Red Army. With their shared neo-Marxist ideology and self perceptions as part of a broader international revolutionary movement, they maintained international links with movements abroad, including the Palestinians. There is considerable evidence that they learned from each other.

So far we have been identifying the broader underlying causes of the burgeoning of modern terrorism in the late 1960s and early 1970s world-wide. But how do we explain the rapid growth and spread of urban terrorist activity in the Third World, especially since the late 1970s?

First, and perhaps most important of all, is the pervasive influence of regime terror among the military dictatorships of the Third World. Very few Third World states have the benefits of genuine parliamentary democracy, an independent judiciary, and the protection of human rights under the rule of law. In states where the population is routinely controlled by repressive terror it is hardly surprising to find that opposition movements feel impelled and fully justified in using extreme violence in their struggle to overthrow the regime. Sadly it is often the case that, when such movements do occasionally succeed in seizing power, they continue to use a reign of terror to eliminate opponents and sustain and strengthen their grip on the people. Sometimes, as in the case of the Khomeini's fundamentalist Islamic regime in Iran, the repressive terror of the new rulers soon outstrips in brutality even the worst excesses of the previous regime. Nevertheless, it is a key empirical observation that state terror tends to breed and stimulate oppositional terror, and is often the key factor in instigating a fresh spiral of destructive and lethal violence.[13]

Secondly, there are the profound and often bitter divisions between ethnic and religious groups within the boundaries of the Third World states. Some of these divisions were often temporarily suppressed during the period of colonial rule, but in the struggles and negotiation for independence these latent divisions soon surfaced again. Dramatic examples of this occurred in India where large-scale communal conflict between Hindus and Muslims broke out before and during the transition to independence, in the struggles between Arabs and Jews in Palestine before and after the ending of the Mandate, and in Cyprus where Greek and Turkish Cypriots became locked in conflict over the future of the island. The fact is that almost every former colony inherited at least one major challenge to the legitimacy and authority of its new government from a major ethnic/religious group which claims its rights of self-determination were betrayed in the period of decolonisation and the emergence of the newly independent state. In some cases, such as India and Pakistan there have been more than a half-a-dozen factions engaged in a nationalist struggle for independence against the new government. In many of these cases the leaders of the separatist movements have turned increasingly to the tactics of urban terrorism as either a major or auxiliary weapon in their campaigns. Hence, a major reason for the spread of terrorism in these areas is the inherent conflicts between rival ethnic and religious groups. It is important to note that 'nation-building' efforts by regimes in multi-ethnic societies are extraordinarily difficult and laborious and inevitably lag far behind the processes of state-building.[14]

Moreover, the problems of creating a multi-ethnic unity and allegiance to underpin the new state are greatly exacerbated by endemic economic weakness. Those groups which fail to win a position of dominance or influence in the new state inevitably tend to be at a severe disadvantage in competition for jobs, housing, investment and other resources. In many cases they will suffer from the cumulative effects of discrimination and acute deprivation. Examples of this would be the Indian populations of Latin American countries such as Brazil, Peru, and Bolivia, the Shi'ites of Lebanon, and the Pathans of Pakistan. It is noteworthy that there are active terrorist movements within all these ethnic groups. But perceived discrimination on purely cultural, religious, and political levels can be an equally powerful catalyst for ethnic group terrorism in the Third World. For example, the militant Sikhs of the Punjab and the Tamil extremists of Sri Lanka show that defence of religious and language rights can also be perceived as potent causes for terrorist campaigns.

Another major factor has been the rapid urbanisation of regions such as the Middle East, South Asia and Latin America. In some Latin American countries well over half the population are city dwellers. In countries like Brazil and Venezuela, it would be naive romanticism for the revolutionary to pin his hopes on the success of a Guevara-style rural-based foci. Indeed it is partly disillusion with purely rural-based strategies in Venezuela, Colombia and elsewhere that has driven many revolutionaries to develop the use of urban terrorist tactics. Also readily available in the cities are the practical assistance and skills – ideological, technological and organisational – that are essential to a revolutionary terrorist campaign. The growing importance of the city in the Third World as a centre of economic and political power also provides an abundance of key targets for the terrorists, in addition to all important access to the news-hungry world media.

Terrorism is an increasingly attractive weapon for disaffected nationalist and religious factions in the Third World for a number of reasons. It is low-cost, low-risk and potentially high-yield method of winning key short-term objectives, such as massive publicity in the world media, the release of movement members from gaols, the payment of large ransoms, and even, in some circumstances, the extortion of more significant concessions, such as changes in government policy and the supply of arms. The perception of radical Shi'ite groups that terrorism 'works' in this sense was clearly confirmed very strongly by the way in which their 'brothers' June 1985 TWA hijacking and hostage-taking forced Israel into the immediate release of 700 Lebanese from prisons in Israel. It is highly probable that the Israeli authorities planned to release the majority of those prisoners under their own volition in any case. But the important point is that the terrorists saw it differently. They believe it was *only* because of the hijacking and hostage-taking that the prisoners were given their freedom. There is no doubt that this helped to inspire other groups to emulate these tactics and this explains the sudden rash of kidnappings of Westerners in Beirut in the period 1985 to early 1987. These factors in combination would inevitably have led to an upsurge in Third World terrorism. But this terrorism has been all the more serious because of the political, economic and military weaknesses of the national governments with the responsibility for upholding law and order and preserving national security. In the extreme case of Lebanon the whole fabric of the state has been wrecked. The Lebanese 'government' cannot exercise any authority because they do not have sufficient military power to preserve internal sovereignty. The writ of the Lebanese President, Mr Gemayel, only extends to the door of his palace. In other cases, such as the conflicts in Sri Lanka and El Salvador, the government has the necessary will and political authority to suppress violent rebellion, but it is dependent on a powerful neighbouring state for the military resources to conduct an effective counter-insurgency. It is precisely because so many Third World states lack the necessary resources to provide adequate internal and external security against the challenges of unconventional warfare, such as guerrilla warfare and terrorism, that they are so vulnerable to take-over by insurgent groups. The insurgent has certainly been somewhat encouraged by the roll-call of regimes which have been toppled in these ways in recent years – Cuba, Vietnam, Nicaragua, Angola, Mozambique, Ethiopia, Kampuchea and Iran are all notable instances. The Third World thus provides potentially lucrative pickings not only for the armed indigenous rebel group, but equally for the interventionist predator power looking for opportunities to expand their influence and export revolution by means of proxies and clients.[15]

It is well known that Third World regions generally lack strong and well coordinated regional international organisations comparable to the EC which might be capable of concerting a more effective international response to terrorism in these areas. And even bilateral cooperation in this field between neighbouring Third World states is extremely limited and fragile. In most cases it is limited to cooperation on border security, as is the case with Malayasia and Thailand, and Turkey and Iraq. However, political differences are generally an immense obstacle to more comprehensive cooperation, both in the case of intra-Third World relations and relations between individual states and the industrialised states. Significant exceptions are the British–Indian anti-terrorist cooperation promoted by Mr Rajiv Gandhi and Mrs Thatcher, and the Federal Republic of Germany–Somalia links cemented by two governments following the GSG-9 hostage-rescue at Mogadishu in 1977. However, in general terms the average Third World state has no specific bilateral agreements or cooperation links of this kind to fall back on when a terrorist crisis occurs.

It is a paradox that these grave weaknesses in the capability and effectiveness of Third World international cooperation against terrorism continue at a time when the *rhetoric* of Third World governments increasingly recognises the gravity of terrorism as an international problem. The overwhelming majority now see that *their* civil aviation, *their* diplomats, and *their* cities are at risk from this type of violence. They are therefore ready to condemn international terrorism and to lend at least *tacit* support to the growing regime of international law established to combat this scourge (e.g. the Hague, Tokyo, and Montreal conventions on the protection of civil aviation, and the US convention on the protection of diplomats). Since 1985 the UN General Assembly has passed near-unanimous resolutions condemning terrorism and calling on the international community to suppress it. And in December 1987 the USSR and Third World countries joined the US and other Western countries to defeat a UN General Assembly proposal by Syria to call for a UN conference to define the difference between terrorism and acts carried out by 'legitimate' national liberation movements. It is significant that Syria was deserted in the debate by the USSR and its Arab allies. The General Assembly instead passed a resolution condemning all forms of international terrorism. Of course it is true that passing resolutions costs nothing and that no means have been found of enforcing UN policy on such matters. Even so these resolutions do indicate a major shift in the international *climate of opinion* towards a general condemnation of terrorism.

There is no simple solution or formula that can be applied by governments and the international community which will eradicate or even significantly reduce this problem. In the short term, a combination of legal, diplomatic, political, social, and security measures is needed to try to address the most severe symptoms of conflict and to alleviate their effects on the rights of the innocent and the fragile legal orders that are at risk from escalating violence.

However, in the long term we are only likely to see a significant reduction in terrorism if there are effective measures to resolve some of the major political conflicts which provoke and spawn terror violence by both states and sub-national actors.

The belligerents in such conflicts are usually too deeply involved and entrenched in 'immovable' positions to initiate and successfully conduct such diplomacy. The superpowers and their major allies are generally unacceptable as mediators to a greater or lesser degree by at least one party in the conflict, as their motives are immediately suspect. What is desperately needed is a strengthening of the only international political institutions with the necessary legitimacy, credibility and expertise to provide mediation, and to help negotiate cease-fires and peace agreements. I refer, of course, to the much maligned and neglected United Nations Security Council and Secretariat. Negotiations on the ending of hostilities in Afghanistan show that the UN can still play an invaluable role in such delicate diplomatic tasks. In the case of the Gulf War fresh efforts need to be made to revise the Security Council's efforts to persuade both parties to agree to a cease fire. It is highly significant – and encouraging – that both the Soviet Union and the US were willing to support SC Resolution 598 calling for a mandatory cease fire. This suggests that the superpowers do recognise the unique potential of the UN as an impartial vehicle for conflict resolution and peace-making. The international community must take urgent steps to revitalise this UN role, and to apply and support UN efforts towards the resolution of other intractable conflicts. International terrorism is a dramatic and cruel symptom of the increasingly anarchical character of the international system. The only rational way to counteract these dangerous and potentially enormously destructive conflicts, with their capacity to escalate into full-scale war, is to strengthen the international diplomatic institutions of conflict resolution and the international rule of law.

There still remain two huge obstacles to effective global cooperation in this field. Many states still persist in confusing political ends and means, and insist on regarding the use of terrorism for certain 'just' causes as legitimate and excusable. Thus, all Arab states view acts of terrorism by Palestinian militant groups as part of a just war of national liberation. Most African states view such acts when carried out in the name of the ANC in South Africa as legitimate national liberation struggle. Many other states are all too willing to adopt a similar double-standard, providing the terrorist acts concerned are happening a long way from home and do not threaten their own citizens.

The only effective way of exposing and combating this double-standard is to change *attitudes* and to educate publics and political leaders about the true nature of terrorism; by showing its callous indifference to the human rights of the innocent, its capacity to threaten national security, and by explaining the danger terrorism poses to peace by serving as a catalyst for civil and international war, as has been the case in Lebanon and Southern Africa.

Even more dangerous than this double-standard as an encouragement to terrorism is the role of the active state sponsor.[16] There are at least a dozen states in the contemporary international system which actively employ terrorism as a tool of foreign and domestic policy with the aims of hunting down and eliminating exiled dissidents, exporting revolution and weakening and subverting regimes. This state sponsorship enormously enhances the resources of terrorism. It provides a much wider range of high calibre weaponry and explosives. It can furnish the enormous benefits of the facilities of the diplomatic network of agents, missions, intelligence, documentation, organisation and logistics. Above all it can provide the inestimable advantages of ample financial resources, training, and safe haven. And, because state sponsors are particularly active in the Third World in promoting the use of terrorism for their own political, strategic and ideological ends, it is particularly useful to examine the role of one of these sponsors in closer detail before moving on to consider problems of international community response to this challenge.

THE ROLE OF THE STATE SPONSOR OF INTERNATIONAL TERRORISM: THE CASE OF IRAN UNDER THE KHOMEINI

The use of terrorism by the Iranian fundamentalist revolutionary regime is hardly surprising when one considers that this was the major weapon they have used for entrenching their own power and suppressing internal opposition.[17] The regime has used terror, torture and brutal repression as routine methods of domestic control. They have used it almost instinctively as a weapon of foreign policy. The regime's first use of international terrorism was the dramatic seizure of the entire American diplomatic mission in Tehran in November 1979. It soon became apparent from this and other actions that the Iranian regime completely rejected the norms and principles of normal diplomatic relations and international law. Far from being embarrassed or sensitive about its diplomatic isolation, the Khomeini regime has proudly defied the American superpower and other major powers.

The fanatical religious motivation of the Iranian regime terrorism makes it particularly intractable and hard to counter. The Ayatollah and his followers teach that those who oppose them are resisting the will of God and His prophets. These opponents are therefore seen as not only infidel but evil, because they are accused of trying to spread corruption on earth. In the eyes of the Khomeini any of the faithful who kill these evil opponents will have carried out the orders of the Iranian Islamic Revolutionary Court of Iran, and hence cannot be viewed as a terrorist by any foreign state. Moreover, if any of the *fedayeen* should die in the course of waging this *jihad*, they are promised a place in Paradise. Thus the religio-political ideology of the regime provides both a Divinely ordained injunction to commit acts of violence against the 'enemy' and a comprehensive justification for such acts. The Tehran regime prefers to use client groups abroad, such as Hizbollah, to carry out the majority of its desired terrorist actions. But, on occasions, particularly in attacks on Iranian dissidents abroad, they have used their own directly recruited and controlled agents.

The strategic aims of Iranian sponsored terrorism include the elimination of foreign-based Iranian opposition groups, the export of fundamentalist revolution to all Moslem states, the weakening and deterrence of Iraq and Iraq's allies in the Gulf War, and the establishment of an Iranian Islamic Republic in Lebanon. (It is very clear from recent events that the Iranian's regime's ability to control and influence Shi'ite extremist groups in Lebanon has been greatly underestimated. In Lebanon, the pro-Iranian grouping, *Islamic Jihad* has employed many other cover names, including *Revolutionary Justice Organisation*, *Right Against Wrong*, and the *Dawa Party*.) But the Iranian regime has also relied extensively on the Iranian Revolutionary Guard, formed in the early phases of the Iranian revolution. In summer 1982 a contingent of Revolutionary Guards was sent to the Bekaa Valley, and it has now established a permanent base. The Syrian regime, which has the upper hand militarily in most of the Lebanon and East Beirut, has had to accept the establishment of a *de facto* Iranian Revolutionary Guard base in the Bekaa and a virtual pro-Iranian Shi'ite Republic within the borders of Lebanon.

But Iran's state-sponsored terrorism has ramifications far beyond the internal struggle in Lebanon. In the course of the Gulf War with Iraq, Iranian-backed terrorism has been used to try to deter moderate Gulf states such as Saudi Arabia, Kuwait and Bahrain from supporting Iraq and assisting it economically. Part of this strategy is also aimed at destabilising and ultimately overthrowing what Tehran considers to be reactionary pro-Western regimes in the Gulf area with a view to replacing them with Islamic revolutionary leaderships. To this end Tehran organises the recruitment of disaffected Shi'a from the Gulf states, provides them with training in techniques of sabotage and terrorism, and gives them weapons and other logistic support. Examples of this activity were the series of sabotage attacks on Kuwaiti oil facilities and other key targets from June 1986. Iran also employs terrorism as an instrument of foreign policy in its much wider ideological and political conflict with the Western world. The 1979–81 abduction of the US diplomats in Tehran was an early instance of this, as was the 'Embassy War' with France, which occurred when French officials sought to question a suspected Iranian terrorist who took refuge in the Iranian Embassy in Paris. The Khomeini regime's blatant disregard for international law and. conventions goes far beyond its attack on the norms governing the treatment of diplomats. It has also taken the form of premeditated armed attacks against unarmed neutral merchant shipping in the Gulf. Such attacks can best be described as maritime terrorism which threatens the neutrals' rights and the freedom of navigation in the Gulf. Iran of course wants to continue to enjoy rights of access for its own shipping, but it is using maritime terrorism and intimidation to try to control its use by others. Such actions inevitably bring a danger of widening and escalating the conflict.

PROBLEMS OF COUNTERING STATE SPONSORSHIP AND OTHER SUPPORT MECHANISMS OF TERRORISM IN THE THIRD WORLD

There are seven essential prerequisites for mounting terrorism. There must be some main *aim or motivation* among the perpetrators, even if it ultimately amounts to little more than an intense hatred of their perceived enemies or a desire for violent revenge against some alleged injustice. There must be *leaders* to instigate and direct the struggle. In any sustained and significant campaign, there will also need to be some degree of *organisation*, some *training* in the special skills of terrorism, and *cash* which helps to buy *weapons and ammunition* and other essential needs. Finally it is clearly vital for the terrorists that they should have *access to the target* country and the precise target/s selected within that country. Of course, we know of numerous groups which possess considerable resources over and above those listed above. Some succeed in building up large numbers of supporters/sympathisers among the general population. Many obtain the substantial advantages of sponsorship by one or more states. In certain circumstances, terrorists can attain sanctuaries or safe bases beyond the reach of security forces or opposing factions; for example, in the remote terrain of the interior. But these are bonuses for the terrorists. We know that the majority of terrorists operating in the contemporary international system do not have these advantages. Let us identify the mechanisms of indirect and direct sponsorships of international terrorism as a form of surrogate warfare.

In the course of the Arab–Israel conflict on the issue of the Palestinians, many states have intervened by giving indirect sponsorship and help to factions of the

PLO. The major funds of the PLO groupings are derived from the contributions of the rich Arab oil states. And there is abundant evidence of the very substantial militiary support given to Al Fatah and the other main PLO formations since the mid 1970s. The Soviets were happy to use Yassir Arafat and his movement as a stalking horse to try to quietly expand Russian influence in the Middle East. Documents captured in the 1982 war in Lebanon confirm also the substantial Soviet and East European stake in training of PLO members.[18] This undoubtedly helped Moscow to capitalise on the conflicts and to build closer links with the rejectionist front states, such as Syria. But in 1982, it became clear that indirect sponsorship also has heavy costs; they could not *control* the behaviour of their clients. Yet they did not wish to risk a full-scale intervention war on behalf of Arafat's group in the siege of Beirut. After 1982, the situation was vastly complicated by the split of the PLO and the bitter struggles between the Musa and Arafat factions in Lebanon. The Soviets, like the Syrians, have found that state sponsorship is a costly and unreliable weapon which may backfire badly. They too have had their diplomats targetted by terrorists in Beirut, Tehran and elsewhere.

In 1984 a loose alliance of 'rejectionist' terrorist groups – that is groups totally rejecting diplomatic negotiation or compromise as a means to resolving the Palestinian issue – emerged with strong encouragement and indirect state sponsorship from the Syrian, Libyan and Iranian regimes. This new grouping included such groups as the Abu Musa faction, based in Syria and Syrian-controlled areas of Lebanon and the Abu-Nidal group, which has offices in Beirut and Tripoli. These groups have undoubtedly gained considerable benefits from the assistance of the secret services and diplomatic networks of President Assad and Colonel Gadaffi. Intelligence gathered during 1985 and 1986 by the United States and Israel and by various West European governments has disclosed a pattern of continuing flagrant Syrian, Libyan and Iranian abuses of 'diplomatic' facilities. The so-called Libyan Peoples' Bureaux, and Syrian embassies, together with Syrian and Libyan agents, have helped plan and assist terrorist attacks on Israeli and American targets in Western Europe and the Middle East. It cannot therefore have come as a complete surprise when Libyan 'finger-prints' were found in the bases of the December 1985 attacks on El Al ticket counters at Rome and Vienna. The evidence of Syrian involvement which emerged in the Hindawi trial in London was unusually detailed and damning. Damascus has normally been more successful at disguising its very extensive role in sponsoring international terrorism. But at his trial in London in October 1986, on charges of trying to plant a bomb on an El Al jet at Heathrow, Nezar Hindawi gave a detailed account of Syrian complicity in the crime. He claimed he was briefed by Syrian intelligence on how to set the bomb on the plane, that he was paid 12,000 US dollars by Syria to undertake the attack at Heathrow, and that he was constantly in touch with the Syrian Embassy in London. And, since the Hindawi trial, further damning evidence has come out on Syrian involvement in terrorism through a trial in the Federal Republic of Germany, and from investigations in Turkey. Normally it is exceedingly difficult to establish beyond doubt the identity of a state sponsor indirectly implicated in this type of international terrorist attack. A major aim of the state sponsor is to remain covert, at the very least to be able to plausibly deny any involvement. The use of Tunisian passports by terrorists, documents clearly supplied by the Libyan regime, and the interception of incriminating messages relayed by Libyan Peoples' Bureaux and Tripoli, provided convincing evidence of the Gadaffi regime's continuing role as a 'fairy godmother' to the groups. The uncovering of Hindawi's Syrian connection was a tremendous coup by British intelligence. They were alerted by a key message sent by the Syrian Embassy to Damascus, a message intercepted and decoded at Government Communications Head-quarters (GCHQ). It was MI5 surveillance which established the pattern of close liaison between Hindawi and Syrian diplomats in London before and after the attempt to plant a bomb on the El Al jet at Heathrow. Our secret intelligence capabilities are the most vital element of national and Western security. Those who seek to cripple it or who advocate a form of unilateral intelligence disarmament are either extremely foolish or malevolent.

It should be noted that state sponsorship of international terrorism takes many forms. Help and encouragement, even the provision of false documents and weapons, does not necessarily mean that the state sponsor has total control over choice of target and method of attack. Many of the militant and experienced Palestinian groups, for example, are quite capable of running such operations autonomously, and providing their own logistics, if need arises. A further complication is that some of these groups have a number of state sponsors helping them simultaneously in various ways, and are able to establish safe havens and operational bases in several different countries.

Some state sponsors have tried to avoid the uncertainties and problems of indirect sponsorship by resorting to direct state-controlled international terrorism using their own hit-squads to assassinate opponents or disrupt or undermine adversaries. The Libyan and Iranian regimes, for example, blatantly flout international norms and laws by such behaviour.

CONCLUSIONS

Most scholars are deeply suspicious of claims by politicians, officials and armchair strategists that they have found the 'solution' to terrorism. Some analysts apparently believe that, if only we could alight on the appropriate formula for a diplomatic settlement or political reform, the underlying grievance or demand of the terrorist movement would be met, and violence would melt away. This idea appeals to those utopian souls who believe there is a perfect rational solution to every human problem and that people will behave rationally enough to apply it if only you point them in the right direction. But let us take the intractable Arab–Israeli conflict; is it to be seriously believed that, if Arafat and Hussein were to agree on a settlement with the Israeli government tomorrow concerning the establishment of an autonomous Palestinian enclave in the West Bank and Gaza, this would bring an end to Palestinian terrorism? The anti-Arafat 'rejectionist' groups would undoubtedly view any such agreement as a betrayal, and would intensify their terrorist campaigns in order to stop or sabotage any such settlement.

Others argue that the appropriate solution to terrorism is the use of overwhelming military force to eradicate the terrorists and their bases and to punish and deter states that support the terrorists. General Ariel Sharon and his colleagues in the Begin government in Israel undoubtedly believed in the efficacy of absolute military force against terrorism in their invasion of Lebanon in 1982. What actually happened was that the Israeli people became deeply divided over the justifiability of the war and the Israeli Defence Forces suffered heavy losses in a long terrorist war of attrition far worse than the terrorism before June 1982 which they were supposed to be eradicating. In addition Lebanon slipped still further into chaos and division into warring factions, many of which are bitterly opposed to Israel. The invasion did not stop Palestinian terrorism and it did not make the northern border of Israel secure. Israel has again reverted to reprisal bombings of alleged terrorist bases in Lebanon. While it is true that these raids provide an outlet for Israeli outrage and anger against terrorist attacks, it would be foolish to claim, after years of Israeli use of this tactic, that such methods have 'worked' in reducing or eradicating terrorism.

This does not mean that political and military methods have no place in an effective strategy against terrorism. The important point is that they should be part of a more carefully considered long-term multipronged approach, using many other key elements, such as well chosen and effective legal, police and intelligence measures, and the skilful use of the mass media. Political reforms and initiatives can make a useful contribution to isolating the terrorist extremists and enhancing public support for the government. Selective use of specialist military units skilled in specific roles, such as hostage rescue, bomb-disposal and physical protection of key points can be an invaluable aid to the civil power. But the key point to be emphasised is that there are many pathways out of terrorism for individual states and the international community. They all take time and they are mostly extremely complex. We need to learn to use *all* the pathways, rather than place all our bets on one quick-fix solution which will probably turn out to be illusory, and may prove counter-productive.[19]

Among the least glamorous and most neglected of these pathways are those involving the countering of the life-support systems on which terrorists depend. Effective measures attacking all the key elements in the support mechanisms – aims and ideas, leadership, organisation, training, cash, weapons and explosives, and access to target – could make an extremely valuable contribution. It is true that, if they are to really be effective in undermining terrorism, they need to be applied by as many countries as possible. It is worrying to observe that, although we have a number of multilateral and bilateral mechanisms for anti-terrorism cooperation among Western governments, little or no effort has thus far been put into this particular set of tasks among governments in the Third World.

NOTES

1 There is an impressive array of evidence for the 'common ground' among scholars in Alex P. Schmid, *Political Terrorism: A Research Guide to Concepts, Theories, Data Bases and Literature* (Amsterdam: North Holland Publishing Company, 1983), pp. 5–159. For early discussions of the definitional problem see Paul Wilkinson 'Three questions on terrorism', *Government and Opposition*, Vol. 8, No. 3, Summer 1973, pp. 290–312, and at greater length the same author's *Political Terrorism* (London: Macmillan, 1974).

2 Schmid, *Political Terrorism*, pp. 5–159.

3 Jeffrey Ian Ross and Ted Tobert Gurr, 'Why terrorism subsides: a comparative study of trends and groups in terrorism in Canada and the United States', unpublished paper presented at the American Political Science Association Conference, Chicago, September 1987, p. 3.

4 For fuller discussions of typology see Alex P. Schmid, *Political Terrorism*; Wilkinson, *Terrorism and the Liberal State*, 2nd Edition (London: Macmillan, 1986), pp. 23–33; and Eugene V. Walter, *Terror and Resistance, A Study of Political Violence* (Oxford University Press, 1969), pp. 3–27.

5 For example, Hannah Arendt, *The Origins of Totalitarianism*, 3rd Edition (London: Allen & Unwin, 1967): Le Strauss, *On Tyranny* (Glencoe, Illinois: Free Press, 1963); Barrington Moore Jr., *Terror and Progress – USSR* (Cambridge, Mass.: Harvard University Press, 1966); and Robert Conquest, *The Great Terror: Stalin's Purge of the Thirties* (London: Macmillan, 1968).

6 The nature and modus operandi of the state sponsored international terrorism is discussed in the writer's *Terrorism and the Liberal State*, 2nd edition, 1986, Chapter 16. For a historical study of the Soviet role see Galia Golan, *The Soviet Union and the PLO*, Adelphi Paper No. 131, International Institute for Strategic Studies, 1976.

7 For analysis of trends in the growth of international terrorism see Paul Wilkinson, 'Trends in international terrorism . . .' in Lawrence Freedman, C. Hill, A. Roberts, J. Vincent and P. Wilkinson *et al.*, *Terrorism and International Order* (London: RIIA and Routledge & Kegan Paul, 1986), pp. 37–55.

8 See Yonah Alexander and Robert A. Friedlander (eds.), *Self-Determination: National, Regional and Global Dimensions* (Boulder, Colorado: Westview Press, 1980).

9 Felix Gross, *The Seizure of Political Power* (New York: Philosophical Library, 1958), pp. 388–90 and 'Political violence and terror in 19th and 20th century Russia and Eastern Europe', in Vol. 8 of *A Report to the National Commission on the Causes and Prevention of Violence*, James F. Kirkham, Sheldon G. Levy and William J. Crotty (eds.) (Washington DC: US Government Printing Office, 1969), pp. 421–76.

10 See excellent discussion of this shift in Gérard Chaliand, *Terrorismes et guérillas* (Paris: Flamarrion, 1985), pp. 109–142.

11 This phenomenon is discussed in Amy Sands Redlic, 'The Transnational Flow of Information as a Cause of Terrorism', in *Terrorism: Theory and Practice* (Boulder, Colorado: Westview Press, 1979), pp. 73–98.

12 For statistics on the role of Fedayeen groups see Robert Friedlander, *Terrorism: documents of International and Local Control*, Vol. 3 (New York: Oceana Publications, 1981), pp. 39–98.

13 For an analysis of this process of terror see E. V. Walter, *Terror and Resistance* (New York: Oxford University Press, 1969).

14 These problems are examined with great insight in Elie Kedourie (ed.), 'Introduction', in *Nationalism in Asia and Africa* (New York: New American Library, 1970), pp. 1–152; and in Anthony D. Smith, *State and Nation in the Third World* (Brighton: Wheatsheaf Books, 1983).

15 See Bard O'Neill, William R. Heaton and Donald J. Alberts (eds.), *Insurgency in the Modern World* (Boulder, Colorado: Westview Press, 1980), pp. 1–44 and 269–82; and Geoffrey Fairbairn, *Revolutionary Guerrilla Warfare; the Countryside Version* (Harmondsworth: Penguin Books, 1974).

16 For a discussion of state-sponsorship and its implications see Paul Wilkinson, 'State-sponsored international terrorism: the problems of response', *World Today*, Vol. 40, No. 7, June 1984, pp. 292–8.

17 For a detailed analysis see Amir Taheri, *Holy Terror* (London: Hutchison, 1986); Cyrus Elahi, 'Political violence and war: an overview of the Iranian Revolution', in H. H. Han (ed.), *Terrorism, Political Violence and World Order* (Lanham, MD: University Press of America, 1983), pp. 303–12; and Seperh Sabih, 'Aspects of terrorism in Iran', *The Annals of the American Academy of Political and Social Science*, 463, September 1982, pp. 84–94.

18 See Roberta Goren, *The Soviet Union and Terrorism* (London: Allen & Unwin, 1984); Jillian Becker, *The PLO: The Rise and Fall of the Palestinian Liberal Organization* (London: Weidenfeld & Nicolson, 1984); and Emil Sahliyeh, *The PLO After the Lebanon War* (Boulder, Colorado: Westview Press, 1985).

19 For a full examination of this multi-pronged approach to international response see Paul Wilkinson, *Terrorism and the Liberal State* (London: Macmillan Press, revised edn, 1986).

Conclusion

Paikiasothy Saravanamuttu

It is apparent from the arguments presented in this volume that the conventional stereotyping of the North as realists and the South as idealists is inadequate. Elements of both paradigms can be discerned on either side of the debate. They are expressed in the paradox that emerges as its salient feature. Hence, the immutable realist acceptance of competing interests among sovereign states and the consequent absence of a central authority to arbitrate in disputes between them, exists alongside an acknowledgement, consistent with idealist beliefs, that in an increasingly interdependent world this conception of international relations is ultimately self-defeating. International relations *can* and *must* be made more orderly as well as more just. Accordingly, the prospects for constructive debate lie in the ability of the participants to devise a new pragmatism for international relations in an interdependent world which emphasises prudential considerations in the prosecution of interest.

To a large extent, the Northern perspectives presented here display, if not a *basic* satisfaction with the current state of affairs, an unwillingness, couched as an inability, to take the *initiative* for major change. As John Simpson points out in his chapter on the International Political System, this stems from the political realist vision of the international system which contains a number of factors that are appealing to the North. Especially important, in this respect, is the belief that the intrinsic nature of international relations cannot be changed – a belief which also underpins Graham Bird's assessment of global negotiations on the international economic order and the prospects for South–South economic cooperation in his chapter on the International Economic System. Phil Williams too, in his chapter on Intervention, cites Thucydides, Machiavelli and Hobbes to warn that it would be a 'mistake' to ignore the conventional wisdom of political realism. Accordingly, this belief legitimises the dominant position of the North in the international system by equating it with a natural state of affairs. Moreover, it allows the North to allocate to itself the major role in determining the principles of conduct in international relations and the means to modify them in practice, to their own advantage, through appeals to the imperative of international order and the complexities of interdependence. That partiality in this activity could be injurious to order and interdependence is reconciled by the belief that the North alone is responsible enough to be their custodian.

Two main consequences arise from this position. The first is that the sovereign equality of states, the organising principle of contemporary international relations, is in effect undermined by the power hierarchy among states. This in turn creates a problem of legitimacy and credibility which has serious repercussions for international order. Aswini Ray's chapter on the international political system, with its emphasis on 'structural hierarchies' and 'distorted development', stresses this point and warns at the outset that 'the continuity of any system is a necessary, but not sufficient evidence of its stability and much less its moral legitimacy'. The second consequence following from this, given the North's concern with order, is that it is willing to concede the *need* for change, albeit of an extremely limited and reformist nature, as necessary for the maintenance of order. Improvements in crisis management techniques, financial instruments to alleviate the international debt problem and efforts to treat political violence as the isolated phenomenon of terrorism are examples of this. Indeed, John Simpson acknowledges the realist intellectual antecedents of the research project of which this volume is a part –

it is infused with the ideas of political realism, not least in its focus upon the development of techniques for preventing international crises developing at the North–South interface. The . . . vision is of an unchanging and unchangeable Machiavellian and Hobbesian world existing 'out there'. All that can be done is to minimise its potential for death and destruction, rather than engineer any radical change . . .

It is precisely this formulation, however, with its limited problem-solving approach and concern with technique that exemplifies the nub of contention inherent in the North's position when viewed from the perspective of the South. In all the areas of tension cited above, the South is treated as the *problem* or the *problem* is shifted into a *Southern location*. Aswini Ray, as well as Matin Zuberi in his chapter on intervention, put forward this argument with reference to the effect of the cold war, nuclear stalemate and deterrence on proxy wars in the developing world. In both instances, the interests of the South are in the main demoted in the resolution of conflict and as a consequence the South has to bear the principal burden of adjustment. The notion of a *partnership* in the *management* of international order that Paikiasothy Saravanamuttu advocates in his chapter on bases and alliances – *restructuring*, however urgent, being effectively ruled out – is absent. This reinforces Southern perceptions of inferiority and discrimination and precludes constructive debate in the interests of all.

All the Southern perspectives, whilst acknowledging the Northern emphasis on order, point to its self-defeating character if their demands for greater equality and justice are not heeded. They underpin this point by constant reference to colonialism, the principle of sovereign statehood and the structural hierarchy of the international economic system. These appeals are consistent with a notion of political realism; they remind the North that it created the order in the first place and also constitute an admission of Southern limitations in the realisation of change. More importantly, they also augment the *legitimacy* of Southern views on the nature and direction of change. Viewed in this context, the Southern notion of realism, by recognising constraints and the indispensability of partnership, is less Hobbesian in orientation than its predominant Northern counterpart with its stress on the inevitability of conflicting interests and the resort to self-help. Marc Williams illustrates this when he argues in his chapter on the international economic system that the demand for a new international order is 'neither new nor a radical break from past practice'. He goes on to conclude that the South has questioned

the legitimacy of the prevailing order but this dissatisfaction is based (for the most part) not on a rejection of the mode of production which sustains the order but rather on the liberal principles which enshrine a particular form of capitalist organisation. They demand redistributionist measures which ameliorate some of the negative tendencies of the unrestricted play of market forces.

From the North's standpoint, however, Southern limitations obviate the conditions for partnership, and in any event are not all attributable to the North or as insurmountable as they are made out to be. Graham Bird ends his chapter with a reminder that 'developing countries exert significant control over their own destinies through the domestic economic policies which they pursue'. He warns that

governments which persistently defend over-valued exchange rates or, through an understandable desire to increase government expenditure designed to improve living standards, create large fiscal deficits, are likely to encounter payments problems which adversely impinge on economic development irrespective of the nature of the international economy within which they find themselves.

Therefore the South's failure to implement changes deemed to be within its competence, particularly in the economic sphere, can be interpreted to be indicative of its ineligibility for partnership. Reinforcing this perception is the persistent evocation of colonialism and preoccupation with a sense of grievance which is seen as inconsistent with the spirit of such an enterprise. Christopher Coker in his chapter on alliances and bases asks with reference to the non-aligned movement, 'Does not reflecting on one's own weakness only compound it? Not only does the Third World insist on recalling its colonial past, it recollects recollecting it. This may act as a form of political exorcism, but a painful and obsessive one.'

Accordingly, Southern intransigence and grievance can be interpreted as the measure of Southern immaturity and as a negative component in the debate, thus confirming the North's belief in its pre-eminent responsibility for international order. Recognition of limitations and the incessant demand for major change, it is argued, are not in themselves sufficient for constructive debate. This also requires an awareness of possibilities, however small, and the willingness to pursue them. Moreover, compromise is a necessary ingredient and the sacrifices it entails are inherent in the very activity of international politics.

There is no denying that in one reading, the preceding chapters can be used in support of the argument that the South/North security debate is deadlocked and even irretrievable. Indeed, the evidence of the power politics paradigm on both sides of the debate, with its narrow interpretation of interests, lends credence to such pessimism. To the extent that there is a consensus, it is on the inevitability of conflict. Both John Simpson and Aswini Ray in their analyses of the post-war international political context recognise this as an integral part of the intellectual dominance of the North in the security debate. Ray castigates the 'parasitical elite' of the South who have acquired the values of their former colonial masters and control over institutions of executive power conceived and constructed by them. He maintains that as the 'Holy Cow' of national security is fattened to encompass more areas of human concerns that the management of the global system will involve control over the 'minds of men' on a larger scale. The thrust of his argument suggests that this will result in the proliferation of the political realist mind-set. Simpson reiterates the point about the intellectual dominance of the North, represented in the tacit, if not overt acceptance of political realism by the Southern political elite. For him, this is what sustains the impasse, but, 'at the same time, this lack of acceptable alternative visions of the nature of the international political system makes possible a North/South dialogue on security issues. A consensus exists on how the international system functions, even if there is no acceptance of the consequences of that functioning.'

Nevertheless, despite the apparent stalemate arising from differences in emphasis over the consequences of the international political system there are grounds for cautious optimism as far as a constructive South/North security debate in the 1990s is concerned. Although a tension will always persist between the competing interpretations of security, and the disjunction between aspiration and performance on both sides will be maintained, the attachment to political pragmatism evinced on both sides of the debate underscores the importance of prudential considerations in the prosecution of interests. This has been an underlying theme in the preceding chapters and it holds out the hope that a consensus could develop on the logic and consequences of international order appropriate to genuine interdependence. This entails an understanding of the actors in international relations that breaks out of the 'power politics' school's obsession with states as homogeneous units in constant and conflictual interaction and addresses the domestic source of insecurity. Furthermore, this also entails critical analysis of the relationship between the internal/external dimensions of security as a crucial determinant of international relations in an interdependent world. Insufficient investigation of the security problem along these lines, attests to the strength of entrenched prejudices in the academic discipline of international relations and the degree to which they have been duplicated in practice by politicians and diplomats. Indeed the overwhelming perception of stalemate that attends this security debate is in large measure attributable to it. The failure to comprehend the internal dynamics of the societies that make up the categories of South and North and their impact on international relations leads to gross miscalculations of the nature of socioeconomic development and nation-building on the one hand, and frustration in the insistence upon radical change, on the other. The contributions in this volume will help to clarify the broad areas of conflict and consensus in the South/North security debate and stimulate efforts to mitigate the former and build upon the latter in the direction outlined above. Above all else, it is important that the debate be revitalised and sustained rather than be allowed to fester on the agenda of international politics as another issue, albeit a vital one, that induces a variety of responses ranging from cynicism to inertia and apathy.

Index